THE ILLUS D

Frankenstein

MOVIE GUIDE

Grateful acknowledgement is made to the following studios, distributors and collections whose stills and posters illustrate this book in the spirit of publicity:

ABC-TV, The Forrest J Ackerman Imagi-Movie Archives (2495 Glendower Avenue, Hollywood, CA 90027-1110; indicated by [FJA] throughout this guide), Allied Artists, Alpha, American International Pictures, Amicus Productions, Astor Pictures, Avco Embassy, Azteca Films, *Ronald V. Borst* (Hollywood Movie Posters, 6727 $^{5}/_{8}$ Hollywood Blvd, [Inside Artisan's Patio], Hollywood, CA 90028; indicated by [RVB] throughout this guide), British Film Institute, Brooksfilm, Cannon Films, CBS-TV, Chriswar, Cinerama, Columbia Pictures, Deutsche Bioscop, Edison Film Company, Embassy Pictures, Emerson Film Enterprises, EMI Films, Empire Pictures, Entertainment Releasing, Eureka Film International, Exclusive, Fantasy Films, Focus Film Distributors, Fulvia, Futurama Entertainment, Gaumont-British, Guild Film Distribution Ltd., Hammer Films, Hollywood Producers & Distributors, Independent-International Pictures, ITC, Majestic Pictures, Metro-Goldwyn-Mayer, Mutual Productions, NBC-TV, New Star Entertainment, New World Pictures, Noteworthy Films, Orion, Pagu, Panther, Paramount, Pinnacle, Republic Pictures, Screen Gems, Selmur, Severn Arts, Taft Entertainment, Thames Television, Tillie Productions, Trans-Lux, Tucker Production Company, Turner Pictures Inc, Twentieth Century-Fox, UFA, Unistar Pictures, United Artists, Universal City Studios, Vestron, Virgin Vision, Warner Bros and Wildstreet.

Very special thanks to *It's Alive! The Classic Cinema Saga of Frankenstein*, *Cinefantastique* and *Famous Monsters of Filmland* for many of the quotes used throughout this guide.

Top right: *Bride of Frankenstein.*
Centre right: *Son of Frankenstein.*
Bottom right: *Dracula vs. Frankenstein. (FJA).*

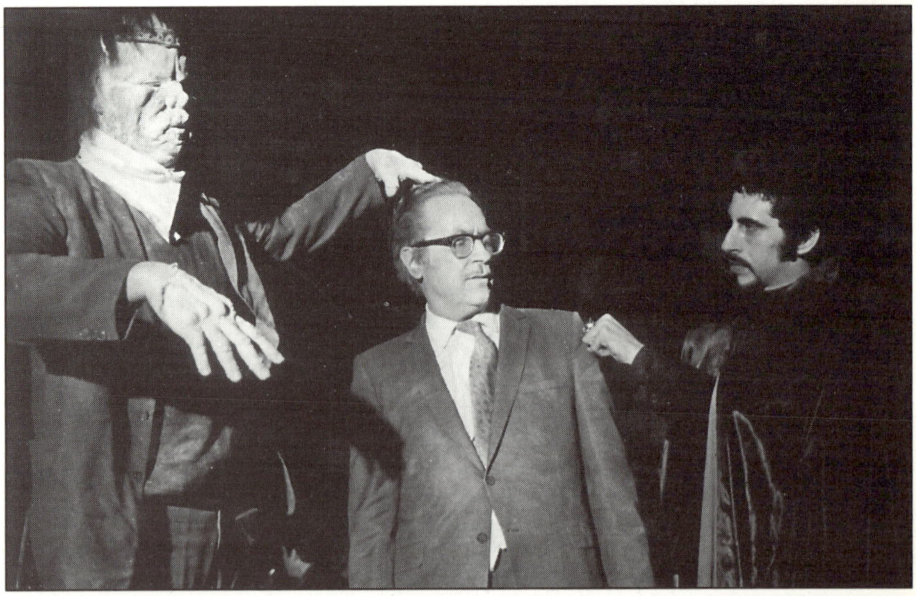

THE ILLUSTRATED Frankenstein MOVIE GUIDE

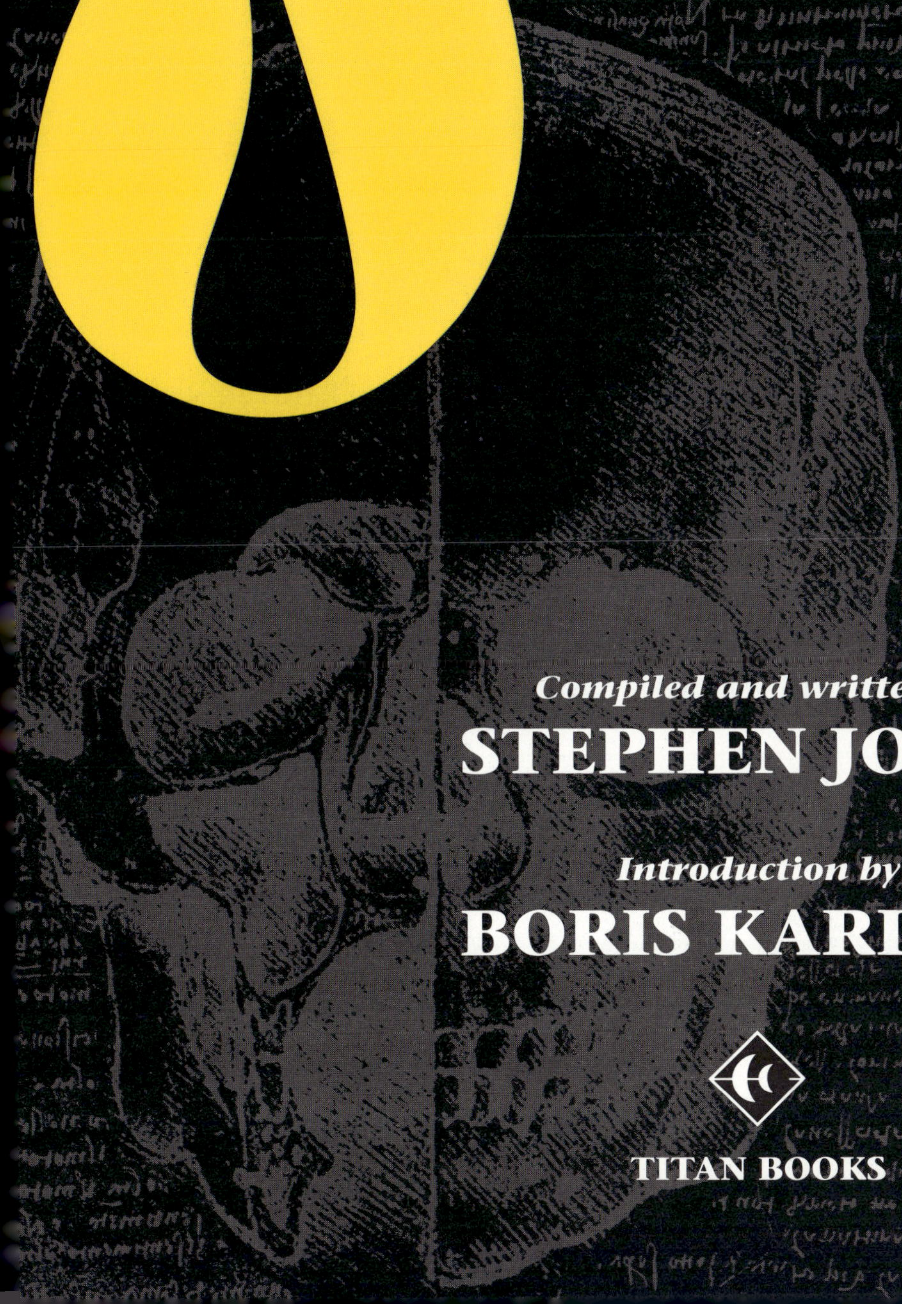

Compiled and written by

STEPHEN JONES

Introduction by

BORIS KARLOFF

TITAN BOOKS

THE ILLUSTRATED FRANKENSTEIN MOVIE GUIDE
ISBN 1 85286 524 5

Published by
Titan Books
42-44 Dolben Street
London SE1 0UP

First Titan edition September 1994
10 9 8 7 6 5 4 3 2 1

British Library Cataloguing-in-Publication Data. A catalogue record for this book is available from the British Library.

Designed by Chris Teather
Production by Bob Kelly

Any book as detailed as this needs friends, and I would like to thank Randy and Sara Broecker, Kim Newman, Stefan Jaworzyn, Forrest J Ackerman, Jo Fletcher, Nicolas Barbano, Marcelle Perks, Frank Eisgruber, Jay Broecker, Marcel Burel, Mike Wathen, Alan Jones, Steve Roe, Sue and Lou Irmo, Brian Aldiss, Dennis Etchison, Mandy J. Slater, Doug Bradley, Anthony Timpone, Mark Burman and Brian Mooney for all their help and support in compiling what I hope you will discover is a useful and entertaining reference work. Special thanks to my editor, David Barraclough, for his always invaluable help and support; Chris Teather for getting all the pictures in the right place as usual; Katy Wild (who has never appeared in *The Evil of Frankenstein*) for signing the cheques on time; Gregory William Mank and Donald F. Glut, who had already done much of the spade work, and to Sara Karloff for allowing me to reprint her father's article.

Printed and bound in Great Britain by Stephens and George Ltd, Merthyr Industrial Estate, Dowlais, Merthyr Tydfil.

Right and opposite top: *Frankenstein (1931).*
Opposite centre: *Frankenstein Meets the Wolf Man. (FJA).*
Opposite bottom: *Behind-the-scenes, Meet Frankenstein.*

This one has to be for Forry, who created the spark

Contents

Author's Notes

The Illustrated Movie Guide series is designed to be of use to both the casual viewer and the hardened movie buff. Films are arranged alphabetically by the whole title and reviewed under their most common usage title, with spelling and punctuation taken directly from the screen wherever possible. These are cross-referenced in the index with the original or British and American alternative titles. The year given is usually the copyright date taken from the print, with the actual release date of the version reviewed (if significantly different) listed in parenthesis. Wherever such information is available, I have included the names of the director and major stars (with alternative spellings or real names in parenthesis), production company and/or distributor, and whether the film was made in colour or black and white. Any disparity in the spelling of character names is also reflected in the text. The information in this book supersedes all previous editions and printings in this series.

Within these pages you will discover the many creations of Dr Frankenstein and his numerous offspring, others who have attempted to delve into those regions Man Was Never Meant to Know, plus associational themes like brain transplants, reviving the dead, and the creation of such synthetic life as golems, homunculi and clones. However, mechanical robots, cyborgs and more general mad doctors will be covered in subsequent volumes.

I should also point out that a number of the films reviewed in this volume obviously contain adult material and may therefore not be suitable for viewers of all ages. It should also be noted that readers may encounter some difficulty tracking down every movie listed herein.

Obviously, no book about Frankenstein movies can be definitive, although this volume should be more complete than most, and I would be grateful to receive any updates or corrections c/o the publisher. Credit will be given in all future editions.

Below: *Cut scene from Bride of Frankenstein.*

RATINGS

A brief explanation of the ratings system is probably needed. As with any at-a-glance recommendation, this unapologetically reflects my own biased opinions of whether a film is worth viewing or not. As a criterion, if I were to base all the films listed in this book on, for example, Orson Welles' *Citizen Kane*, then most of them would hardly rate more than one lightning bolt. Therefore, as a general rule, I've tried to take into account whether these films would appeal to the horror fan and the Frankenstein *aficionado* in particular. After all, as is so often the case with genre movies, a really *bad* example can still be worth watching...

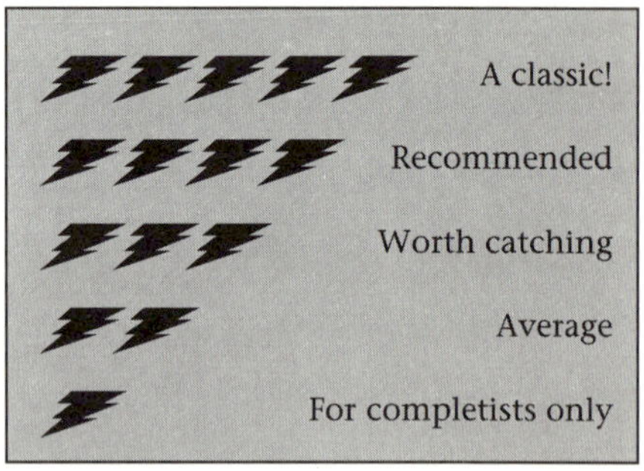

Please note that the above ratings should be used as a guide only. Obviously, it has not been possible to see every film listed in this book, therefore some of the ratings are based on provisional material or contemporary reviews. Any reassessment will be noted in subsequent editions.

Stephen Jones
London, 1994

Introduction

Boris Karloff

I dislike the word 'horror' yet it is a word that has been tagged to me all my life. It is a misnomer...for it means revulsion. The films I have made were made for entertainment, maybe with the object of making the audience's hair stand on end, but never to revolt people. Perhaps terror would be a much better word to describe these films, but alas, it is too late now to change the adjective. My films even prompted the British censor to introduce a certificate in the early thirties known as 'H'...for horror.

Early in 1931, when the first Frankenstein film was released, the Universal publicity department coined the phrase 'A Horror Picture' and from that day on the 'horror film' was here to stay. This genre of film entertainment obviously fulfils a desire in people to experience something which is beyond the range of everyday human emotion. This conclusion can be drawn from two facts.

Below: *Frankenstein (1931).*

First, from the tremendous success financially and otherwise of the early Frankenstein films and subsequent pictures of a similar type. Secondly, because of an incident on the set of *Grip of the Strangler* (1958; USA: *The Haunted Strangler*), a British 'horror' film which I have just finished making at Walton Studios. We were about to shoot a sequence in which a man is flogged. Suddenly the set was crowded by studio workmen and office girls all eager to have a look! There is a violent streak in all of us: and if it can be exploded in the cinema instead of in some anti-social manner in real life, so much the better.

Perhaps the best possible audience for a 'horror' film is a child audience. The vivid imagination with which a child is gifted is far more receptive to the ingredients in these pictures than the adult imagination which merely finds them artificial. Because they have vivid imaginations we must not underestimate children...they know far more than we think they do.

When I played Frankenstein's Monster I received sack loads of fan mail...mostly from young girls. These children had seen right through the make-up and had been deeply moved by sympathy for the poor brute.

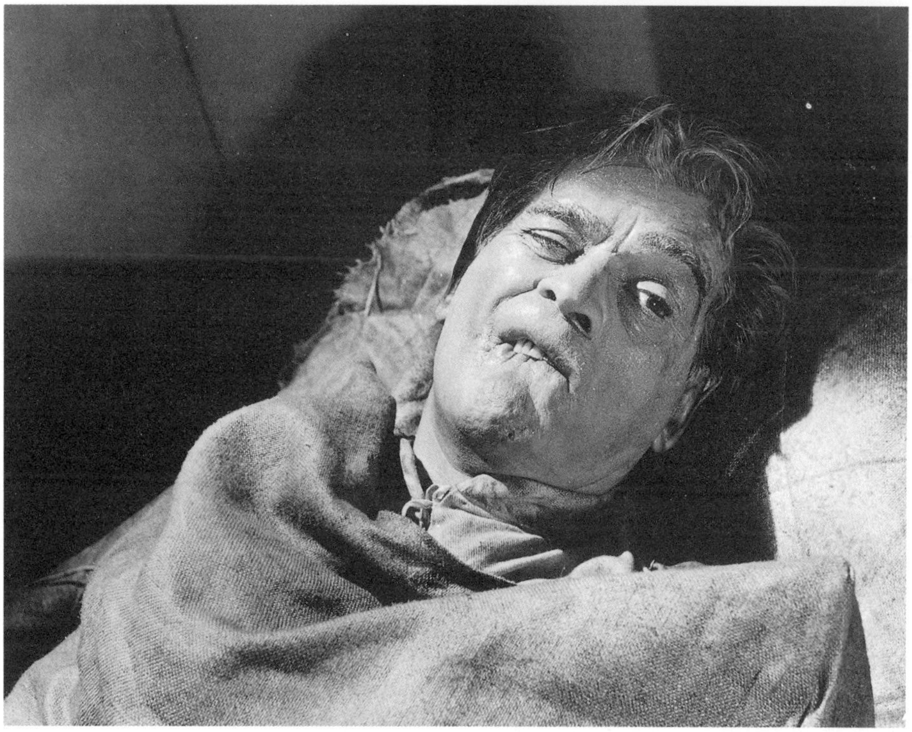

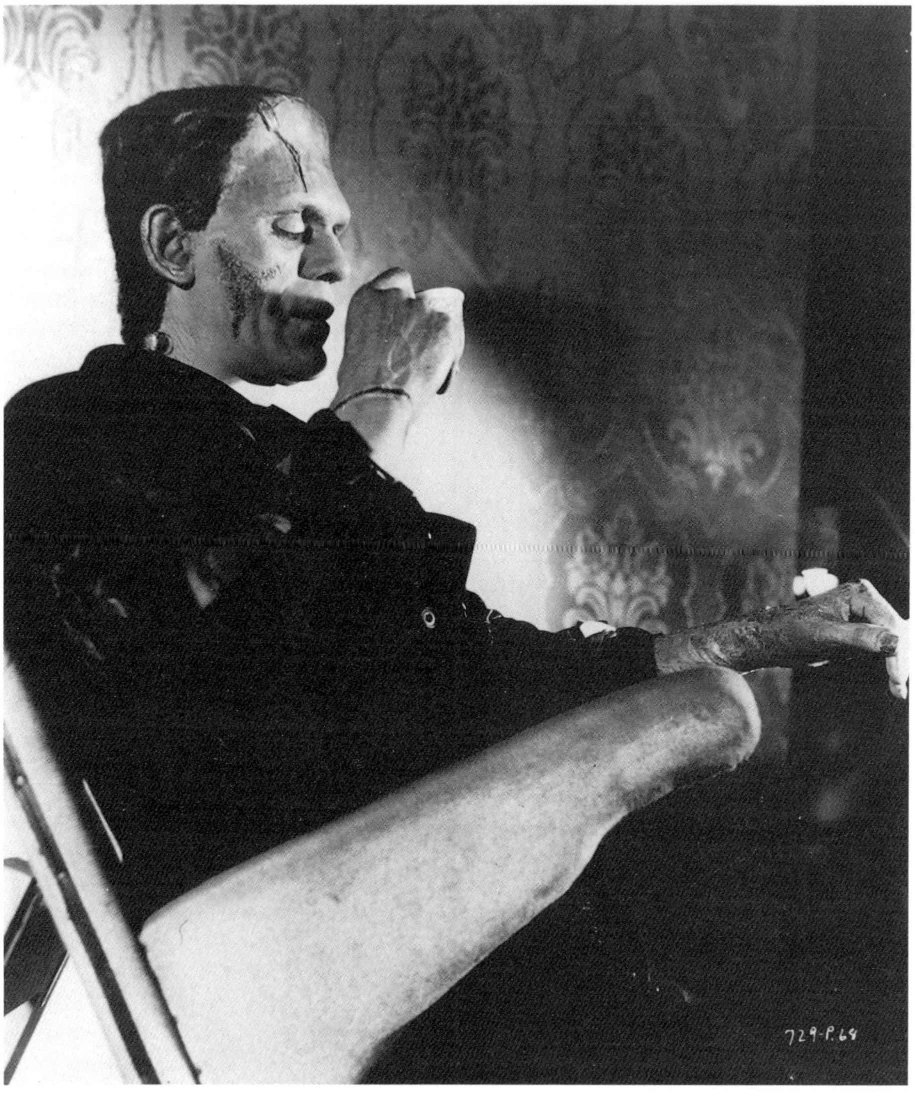

Top: *Grip of the Strangler.*
Above: *Frankenstein (1931).*
Left: *Behind-the-scenes, Bride of Frankenstein. (FJA).*
Opposite: *Frankenstein 1970.*

Children choose what they want to see in an entertainment. This was brought home to me during the record run of Barrie's *Peter Pan* at the Imperial Theatre in New York. I played Captain Hook and, being interested in the children's reaction to the play, I invited a horde of them to

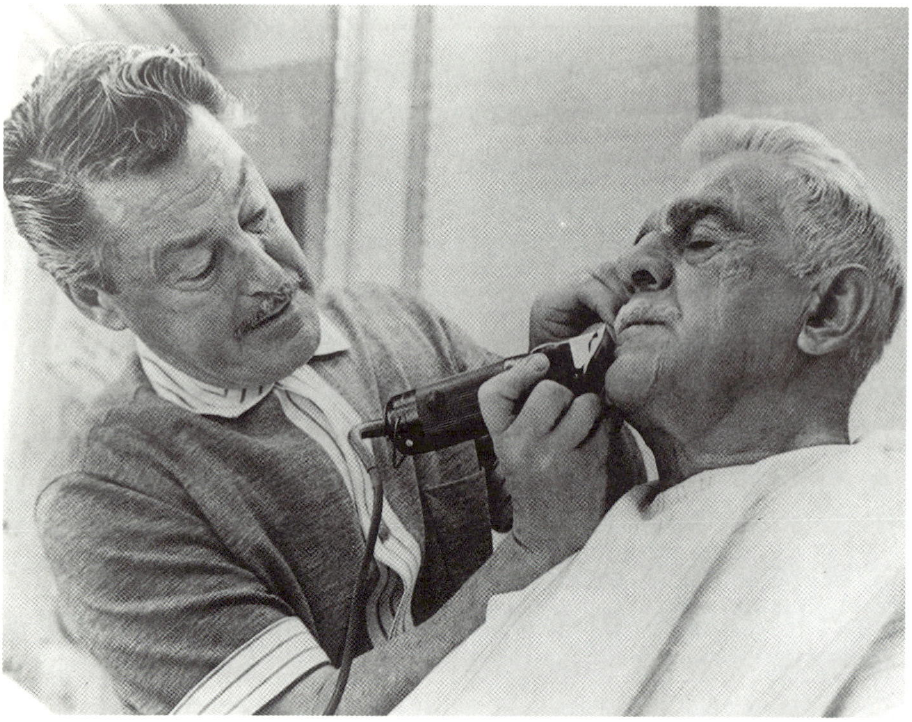

come along to the theatre. *Peter Pan*, as everybody knows, is a mixture of romanticism and adventure. The somewhat frightening exploits of Captain Hook are off-set by the whimsy of Tinker Bell. The frightening element would possibly, one would think, stay in a child's mind far longer than the fairy element. After the final curtain I took them backstage and introduced them to the cast. Almost all the children would first want to meet Wendy and Tinker Bell and then they would want to put on the Captain's hook.

Above: *Behind-the-scenes, Frankenstein 1970.*

Their first reaction when they looked at themselves in the mirror was to grunt and scowl and make the same type of lurching gestures as does Frankenstein's Monster.

The fascination of the 'horror' film is perhaps because it is make-believe. Most people like to pretend that there is something just behind the door. It transports the audience to another world. A world of fantasy and of imagination. A world inhabited by the characters of Hans Andersen and the Brothers Grimm. The 'horror' film is concocted more or less from the folk tales of every country. When I am asked if these films are harmful to children, my answer is always the same: Do Grimm's fairy tales do any harm to children? I have never heard of fairy tale books being used in evidence in a juvenile delinquency case!

Naturally, good taste plays a very important part in the telling of a 'horror' story on film. Some have taste, others regrettably have not. As there are no rules laid down to give an indication of good taste it is up to the film's makers.

You are walking a very narrow tightrope when you make such a film. It is building the illusion of the impossible and giving it the semblance of reality that is of prime importance. The moment the film becomes stupid the audience will laugh and the illusion is lost...never to be regained. The story must be intelligent and coherent as well as being unusual and bizarre...in fact just like a fairy tale or a good folk story. The 'horror' has to be for the sake of the story and not, as a few recent films have done, have a story outline just for the sake of injecting as many shocks as possible.

The central character is most important in a 'horror' picture because he is more complex. You must understand his point of view although you know he is mistaken. You must have sympathy for him although you know he is terribly wrong. An example of a good central character of this type was Columbia's Mad Doctor in the famous series. Although you were pleased to see him destroyed you were sorry that it had happened.

The special technique of 'horror' film-making is to stimulate the imagination. This is usually done by showing bits and pieces which gradually build up a picture in people's imagination. For instance, in the Frankenstein films one saw the doctor with fuming liquids, bubbling test tubes, lights flashing and electrical circuits buzzing. These various images cut together heightened the tension. At the correct moment the Monster would appear and (I hope) the audience would jump. It is important in any visual entertainment to allow the audience to use its imagination — never underline the action. If sympathy is wanted for the character, he himself must reject sympathy.

Although I am devoted to the part of the Monster in the Frankenstein films (if I lived to be a thousand I would always be associated with them) I pulled out after making the third in the series. After the first three I could see that the possibilities were exhausted for both Dr Frankenstein and his Monster. In fact, the poor brute was becoming a comic prop for the third act. I always felt that the first three in the series were tasteful and well produced, unlike the trend of too many films today which seem intent on degrading an audience rather than purging their emotions with a kind of terror that is cathartic in its effect.

I remember the advent of the 'horror' picture. I had kicked around Hollywood for ten years playing extra and various small parts in films. When the Depression came in America I even took up lorry driving. When things became a little more stable I landed a role in a play called *The Criminal Code*...as a convict. I had ugly cropped hair and a gruesome make-up. I played the same role in the film. One of the studio executives no doubt thought, "Here's an ugly looking customer let's try him for the part of the Monster." I was given a test and got the part, although the make-up was not at that time created. Jack Pierce, the chief make-up artist at Universal, and I, worked three hours almost every evening for three weeks creating the make-up. Finally James Whale, who directed *Frankenstein* (1931), saw the test and was overjoyed. Jack Pierce's words still echo in my mind: "This is going to be a big thing." How right he was. I felt that the role was a challenge. I had to portray a sub-human of little intelligence and without speech, still getting over the sympathetic qualities of the role. When the Monster did speak (in the second film) I knew that this was eventually going to destroy the character. It did for

Left: *Son of Frankenstein.*

(FJA).

me, anyway.

I believe the British censor cut a scene from *Bride of Frankenstein* (1935) because of what he thought in his own mind were necrophile tendencies. I must say now that I have never knowingly been in a scene that was objectionable to good taste. Some of my films have been stupid and silly, because they did not have good stories; but they have never been distasteful. I am opposed to censorship in any form. Censorship always seems to me to be a mistrust of people's intelligence. I believe that good taste takes care of licence. It is also worth remembering that one does not have to go and see a film.

I have been asked many times: What is the best 'horror' film you have made? I would say, without a doubt, the original *Frankenstein*.

I always try to see a film in which I have appeared when it goes on release, so that all the technical details are not too fresh in my mind. I am afraid that 'horror' films do not excite me much. Possibly because I have made so many; but for millions of filmgoers, they relieve the hum-drum life of the average individual better than any other kind of story, and that after all is what entertainment should always do.

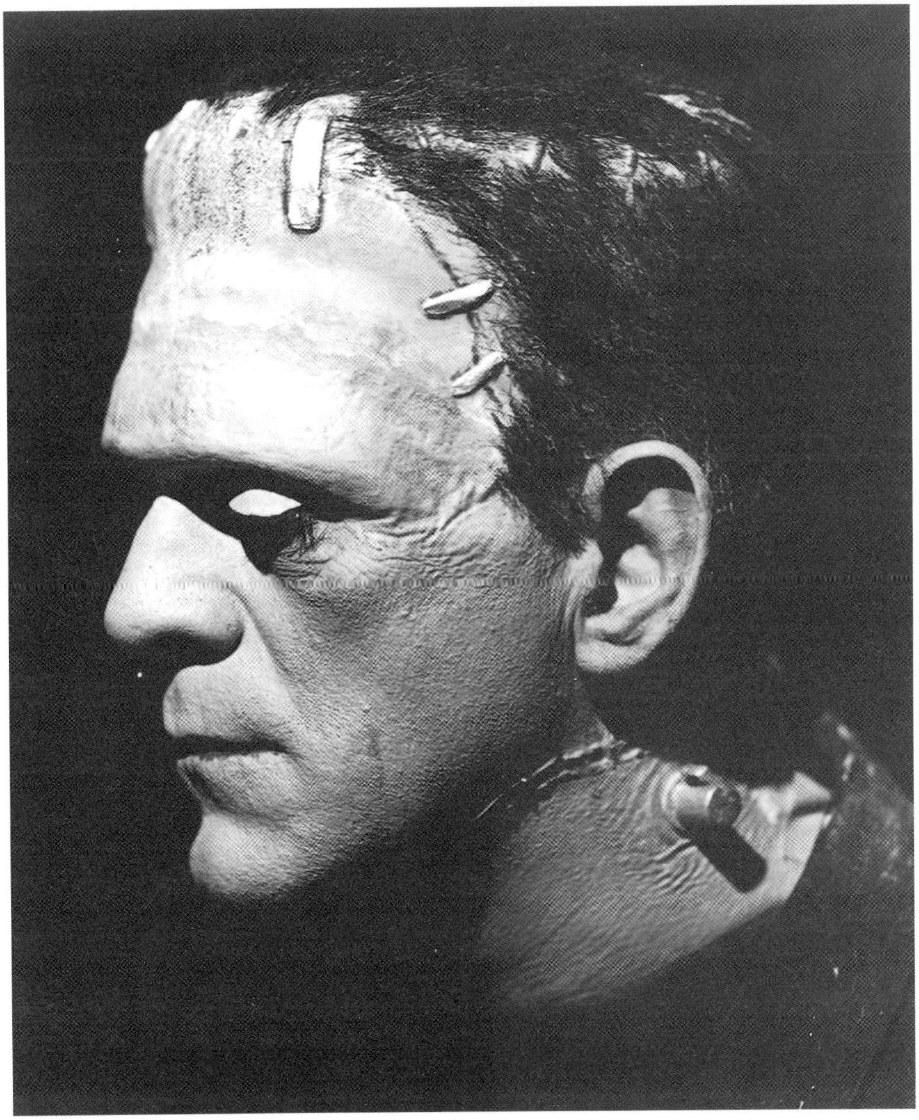

Right: *The stars of The Walking Dead.*
Below right: *House of Frankenstein.*
Below: *Bride of Frankenstein. (FJA).*

Boris Karloff, London, 1957

the

Frankenstein and his monstrous creation were originally conceived in the imagination of eighteen year-old Mary Wollstonecraft Shelley née Godwin (1797-1851) during a stormy evening in June on the shores of Lake Geneva.

Mary Godwin was born in London, the only child of novelist and political philosopher William Godwin and the early female emancipator Mary Wollstonecraft, who died ten days after the birth of her daughter. In 1814, while still a teenager, she eloped to Europe with the English poet Percy Bysshe Shelley, finally marrying him in December 1816 — the same year she wrote the original version of her classic novel, **Frankenstein; or, The Modern Prometheus**.

While spending the summer of 1816 in Switzerland, Mary, Percy and her half-sister Claire Clairmont discovered they were neighbours of Lord Byron and his physician, Dr John Polidori. Byron suggested that, to pass the time, they each try their hand at writing a ghost story. Mary was later urged by her husband to develop her manuscript into a book-length work and the result was published anonymously a year and a half later.

In her introduction to the 1831 edition of **Frankenstein**, the author recalled how the story first came to her in a vision: 'When I placed my head on my pillow I did not sleep, nor could I be said to think. My imagination, unbidden, possessed and guided me, gifting the successive images that arose in my mind with a vividness far beyond the usual bounds of reverie. I saw — with shut eyes, but acute mental vision — I saw the pale student of unhallowed arts kneeling beside the thing he had put together. I saw the hideous phantasm of a man stretched out, and then, on the work-

Silents

ing of some powerful engine, show signs of life, and stir with an uneasy, half vital motion. Frightful must it be; for supremely frightful would be the effect of any human endeavour to mock the stupendous mechanism of the Creator of the world...'

The novel was a huge success, and by 1823 at least five different adaptations were being staged in London, with **Presumption! Or, The Fate of Frankenstein** *the most popular. The author herself attended a performance of the play and enjoyed it, despite the liberties already being taken with her original story.*

(RVB).

The story was first brought to the screen in 1910 as a short entitled **Frankenstein**, *produced by the Thomas Edison Film Company and starring Augustus Phillips as Dr Frankenstein and Charles Stanton Ogle as his misshapen Monster birthed from a vat of chemicals (in a scene which stands as a remarkable precursor to the animatronic special effects designed to dazzle today's audiences).*

Five years later, the distinguished British actor Percy Darrell Standing portrayed the 'brute man' in **Life Without Soul**, *the first full-length movie version of Mary Shelley's story, which featured William Cohill as his creator. In 1920, Italian producer Luciano Albertini starred in his own version of the story,* **Il Mostro di Frankenstein**.

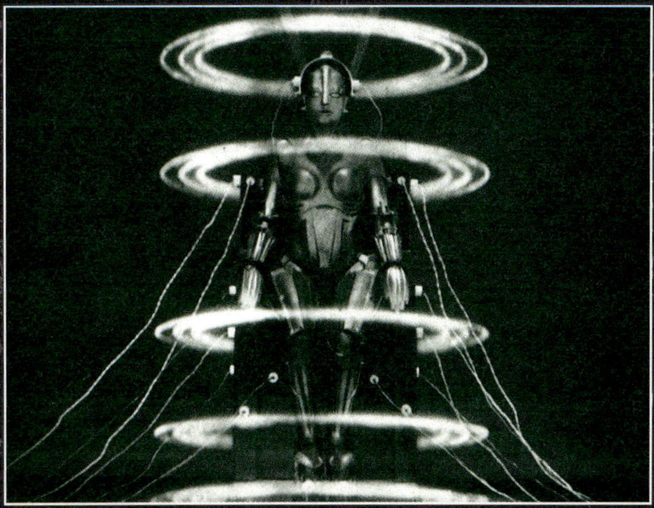

Metropolis.

But it would be another eleven years before two Englishmen working in Hollywood brought their own distinctive talents to the first sound adaptation of the novel, making Mrs Percy B. Shelley's nightmarish creation the most famous monster of them all...

ALRAUNE

Germany, 1918. Dir: Eugen Illes. With: Hilde Wolter, Gustav Adolf Semler, Friedrich Kuehne, Max Auzinger, Ernst Rennspies. Neutrat Film/Luna. B&W.

First film version of the 1913 story by Hanns Heinz Ewers, subtitled *Die Henker-stochter, Genannt die Rote Hanne*. Mad scientist Ten Brinken artificially inseminates a prostitute with the semen of a hanged man. The result is a soulless woman, Alraune (Wolter), who eventually turns against her creator. Apparently now a lost film.

Remake: ALRAUNE (qv; 1918)

ALRAUNE

Austria/Hungary, 1918. Dir: Mihaly Kertesz (Michael Curtiz) and Fritz Odon. With: Guyla Gal, Rozsi Szollosi, Jeno Torzs, Margit Lux, Kalman Kormendy, Geza Erdelyi. Phoenix. B&W.

Now apparently a lost film from Hungarian director Mihaly Kertesz, who eventually found fame in Hollywood as Michael Curtiz (*Doctor X* [1932]; *The Walking Dead* [1936], etc). In this version of the story by Hanns Heinz Ewers, the mad doctor fathers a demonic woman by forcing a prostitute to mate with a mandrake root. It is unlikely that a 1919 film entitled *Alraune und der Golem* (dir: Nils Chrisander) was ever made, although a publicity poster exists.

Remake: ALRAUNE (qv; 1928)

ALRAUNE

(USA: aka UNHOLY LOVE)
Germany, 1928. Dir: Henrik (Heinrich) Galeen. With: Brigitte Helm, Paul Wegener, Ivan Petrovich, Georg John, John Loder, Valeska Gert. Ama-Film/UFA. B&W.

Third version of Hanns Heinz Ewers' story, co-scripted by the writer and director Galeen (*Der Golem* [1914]). Wegener portrays mad doctor Ten Brinken, who uses the semen of a hanged man to inseminate a prostitute. The result is Alraune (Helm, the star of *Metropolis* [1926]), a beautiful but evil woman whose blatant sexuality fascinates and appalls her creator. This is probably the best version of the story, although Helm recreated the title role two years later.

Remake: ALRAUNE (qv; 1930)

DAS ANDERE ICH

Austria, 1918. Dir: Fritz Freisler. With: Raoul Aslan, Fritz Kortner, Magda Sonja. Sascha-Film. B&W.

A professor separates a soul from its body. The title translates as *The Other Self*.

THE DEVIL TO PAY

USA, 1920. Dir: Ernest C. Warde. With: Roy Stewart, Robert McKim, Fritzi Brunette, George Fisher, Evelyn Selbie, Joseph J. Dowling. Brunton Films. B&W.

Hanged for a crime he didn't commit, a man (Stewart) is brought back to life by a doctor (Mark Fenton) and haunts the wealthy banker (McKim) who framed him, until the latter commits suicide.

DOCTOR MAXWELL'S EXPERIMENT

USA, 1913. Lubin. B&W.

Seventeen minute short in which a doctor's operation transforms a criminal into an honest man.

DER DORFSGOLEM

(aka DES GOLEMS LETZTE ABENTEUER)
Austria, 1921. Dir: Julius Szomogyi. Sascha-Film. B&W.

Rural comedy in which the legendary man of clay is brought to life and used as cheap farm labour.

Remake: THE GOLEM (qv; 1936)

DR. CHARLIE IS A GREAT SURGEON

USA, 1911. Eclair. B&W.

Seven minute short. When Dr Charlie replaces McTouch's stomach with that of a monkey's, the recipient cavorts like an ape.

DR. HALLIN

Austria, 1921. Dir: Alfred Lampel. With: Franz Herterich, Traute Carlsen, Karl Schopfer, Paul Kronegg. Lampel-Film. B&W.

This apparently involves brain-transplanting.

THE ELECTRIC GIRL

USA, 1914. Eclair. B&W.

Fifteen minute short in which an electrified girl attracts metal objects.

THE ELECTRIC GOOSE

UK, 1905. Dir: Alf Collins. Gaumont. B&W.

Short in which an electric shock machine restores a Christmas dinner to life.

THE ELECTRIC VITALISER

UK, 1910. Dir: Walter D. Booth. Kineto. B&W.

Left: *Frankenstein.*

Short in which an electrical 'Vitaliser' restores historical characters to life.

THE ELECTRIFIED PIG

USA, 1911. Cosmopolitan. B&W.

Seven minute comedy short in which a large pig, being taken home from market, is struck by a loose power line. The pig becomes electrically charged and leads the farmer a merry chase until he dons a pair of rubber gloves to catch it. After being slaughtered, the pig is recreated alive when the electrically charged sausages are attracted to each other from various frying pans.

ELECTROCUTED

France, 1907 (1908). Pathe. B&W.

An electrician uses electrodes attached to a metal cap to animate a cook's body.

THE ELEVENTH DIMENSION

USA, 1915. With: William E. Welsh, Howard Crampton, Allen Holubar, Frances Nelson. Imp/Universal. B&W.

Produced by Raymond L. Shrock. Twenty-five minute short in which a mad professor attempts to revive a body to prove his theory of life after death.

ESTHER REDEEMED

UK, 1915. Dir: Sidney Morgan. With: Julian Royce, William Brandon, A. Harding Steerman, Mona K. Harrison, Cecil Fletcher. Renaissance. B&W.

Thirty-five minute short, based on the play *The Wolfe Wife* by Arthur Bertram. A woman's criminal nature is altered by a surgical operation.

THE FACE AT THE WINDOW

Australia, 1919. Dir: Charles Villiers. With: Agnes Dobson, D.B. O'Connor, Claude Turton. D.B. O'Connor Feature Films. B&W.

The first film version of F. Brooke Warren's stage play in which a killer distracts his victims with a monstrous face.

Remake: THE FACE AT THE WINDOW (qv; 1920)

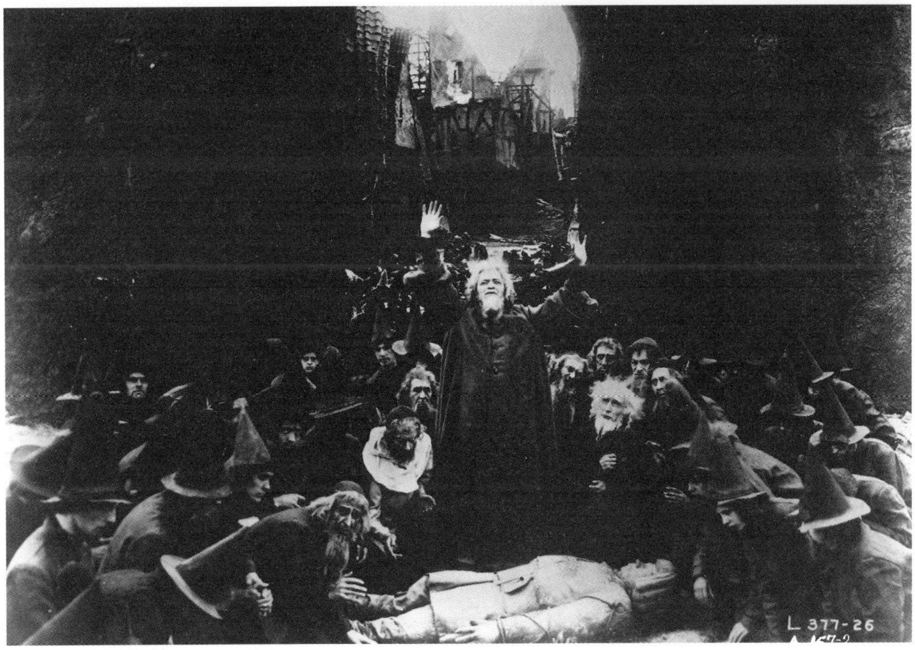

Above: The Golem.

THE FACE AT THE WINDOW

UK, 1920. Dir: Wilfred Noy. With: C. Aubrey Smith, Jack Hobbs, Gladys Jennings, Adrian Brunel. B&W.

Based on the play by F. Brooke Warren, previously filmed in Australia in 1919. The victims of a murderer are distracted by a hideous face peering through the window. In the end, a corpse is revived long enough to identify its killer.

Remake: THE FACE AT THE WINDOW (qv; 1932)

FRANKENSTEIN

USA, 1910. Dir: J. Searle Dawley. With: Charles Stanton Ogle, Augustus Phillips, Mary Fuller. Edison Film Company. B&W.

After numerous stage versions, this first short movie adaptation of Mary Shelley's novel is quite faithful to the story. Obsessed with creating the perfect human being, young medical student Dr Frankenstein (Phillips) produces a Monster (Ogle) from a cauldron of fiery chemicals. Standing before a mirror, the misshapen creature vanishes as it is finally defeated by its creator's better nature.

Remake: LIFE WITHOUT SOUL (qv; 1915)

GO AND GET IT

USA, 1920. Dir: M. (Marshall) Neilan and Henry R. Symonds. With: Pat O'Malley, Wesley Barry, Agnes Ayres, J. Barney Sherry, Charles Hill Mailes, Noah Beery. Marshall Neilan Productions/First National Pictures. B&W.

An executed convict's brain is transplanted into a gorilla, creating a hairy missing link-type creature, played by Bull Montana. Montana portrayed a similar-looking simian in *The Lost World* (1925), as his make-up for both films was created by Cecil Holland.

DER GOLEM

(USA: THE MONSTER OF FATE) Germany, 1914. Dir: Henrik (Heinrich) Galeen (and Paul Wegener). With: Paul Wegener, Lyda Salmonova (Wegener), Carl Ebert, Jacob Tiedtke, Rudolf Bluemner. Deutsche Bioscop. B&W.

Co-writer Wegener starred in three versions of the legend, this first one being set in modern times. The clay statue (Wegener) is uncovered by workmen and sold to an antiquarian, who brings it to life as his servant. When it falls in love with a woman (Salmonova), the creature rebels against its master and goes on the rampage until destroyed in a fall.

Remake: DER GOLEM (qv; 1916)

DER GOLEM

Denmark, 1916. Dir: Urban Gad. B&W.

It is questionable whether this version of the legend ever existed.

Remake: DER GOLEM UND DIE TANZERIN (qv; 1917)

THE GOLEM

(Orig: DER GOLEM WIE ER IN DIE WELT KAM)
Germany, 1920. Dir: Paul Wegener and Carl Boese. With: Paul Wegener, Albert Steinrück, Ernst Deutsch, Lyda Salmonova (Wegener), Hanns Sturm, Greta Schröder. Pagu/UFA. B&W.

When Rabbi Loew (Steinrück) reads in the stars that misfortune threatens the Jews, he creates a man of clay, the Golem (co-director Wegener, playing the creature for the third time). Calling upon the demon Astaroth to reveal the secret of life, Loew places a magic word in the star of David on his creation's chest. However, after saving the Jews of Prague from banishment by Rudolf II of Habsburg, the creature is revived by the Rabbi's assistant Famulus (Deutsch), who uses it to kidnap the beautiful Miriam (played by Wegener's wife, Salmonova). The clay giant goes on the rampage until a small child unknowingly removes the life-giving amulet. The scenes where the Golem is brought to life and the invocation of the demon are quite memorable. Future directors Karl Freund and Edgar G. Ulmer both worked on the cinematography. Many of the sequences first created here were later reworked in Universal's Frankenstein series.

Sequel: THE GOLEM (qv; 1936)
Remake: DER DORFSGOLEM (qv; 1921)

DER GOLEM UND DIE TANZERIN

Germany, 1917. Dir: Paul Wegener. With: Paul Wegener, Lyda Salmonova (Wegener), Rochus Gliese, Fritz Feld. Deutsche Bioscop. B&W.

Comedy in which Wegener plays himself, disguised as the man of clay to impress a beautiful dancer (Salmonova).

Remake: THE GOLEM (qv; 1920)

HOMUNCULUS

(aka DIE GEBURT DES HOMUNCULUS)
Germany, 1916. Dir: Otto Rippert. With: Olaf Fönss, Friedrich Kuehne, Ernst Ludwig, Albert Paul, Lore Rueckert, Max Ruhbeck. Deutsche Bioscop. B&W.

Six-part serial (401 minutes) in which Danish star Fönss portrays a 'perfect' man created by scientist Kuehne. When the creature discovers he has no soul, he revenges himself on mankind as a tyrant, relentlessly pursued by his creator, until destroyed by a bolt of lightning. This was reissued in 1920 by Decla-Bioscop in a three-part condensed (275 minutes) version.

HYDROTHERAPIE FANTASTIQUE

(aka THE DOCTOR'S SECRET)
France, 1909. Dir: Georges Méliès. With: Georges Méliès. Star/Méliès. B&W.

Thirteen minute comedy short. A patient in a hydro-therapy machine is blown apart and put back together again by doctors.

THE INSPIRATIONS OF HARRY LARRABEE

USA, 1917. Dir: Bertram Bracken. With: Clifford Gray, Margaret Landis, Winifred Greenwood, William Ehfe, Frank Brownlee. General Film Company. B&W.

When a girl (Landis) is killed by a ruthless jewel thief, a playwright (Gray) restores her to life with the Pulmoter machine, invented by a scientist friend. Based on a novelette by Howard Fielding.

LEGALLY DEAD

USA, 1923. Dir: William Parke. With: Milton Sills, Margaret Campbell, Claire Adams, Joseph Girard, Edwin Sturgis, Brandon Hurst. Universal. B&W.

When Will Campbell (Sills) is wrongly hanged for murder, brilliant scientist Dr Gelzer (Hurst) injects a large syringe of adrenalin into the heart of the dead man, bringing him back to life and a happy ending.

LIFE WITHOUT SOUL

USA, 1915. Dir: Joseph W. Smiley. With: Percy Darrell Standing, William A. Cohill, Lucy Cotton, George DeCarlton, Jack Hopkins, Pauline Curley. Ocean Film Corporation. B&W.

This second film version of Mary Shelley's novel (and the first feature-length adaptation) features English-born actor Standing wearing little or no make-up as the 'Brute Man', the creation of Dr William Frawley (Cohill). When the creature kills his sister, Frawley pursues the Monster across Europe and shoots it before dying from exhaustion. A framing device reveals that the story is being read from a book. This was reissued in a tinted version by Raver Film Corporation the following year, with added scientific documentary footage detailing the reproduction methods of fish.

Remake: IL MOSTRO DI FRANKENSTEIN (qv; 1920)

THE LOVE DOCTOR

USA, 1917. Dir: Paul Scardon. With: Earle Williams, Corinne Griffith, Patsy De Forest, Adele De Garde, Webster Campbell, Evart Overton. Vitagraph. B&W.

A doctor transfers the brain cells from a girl who loves him into the girl he loves. Based on the story 'Hashashin, the Indifferent' by George P. Dillenback.

THE MAGICIAN

USA/France, 1926. Dir: Rex Ingram. With: Alice Terry, Paul Wegener, Ivan Petrovich, Firmin Gemier, Gladys Hamer, Stowitts. Metro-Goldwyn-Mayer. B&W.

Based on an early novel by Somerset Maugham, inspired by the exploits of Aleister Crowley, this was thought a lost film for many years. Wegener plays Oliver Haddo, seeker of the homunculus, which needs the blood of a young maiden's heart to live. He uses magic to seduce heroine Terry on the eve of her wedding and, under hypnosis, she dreams of taking part in an orgiastic rite presided over by Pan (*Folies Bergère* dancer Stowitts). Michael Powell was the assistant designer. This probably influenced both of James Whale's Frankenstein movies.

***Below:** Homunculus. (RVB).*

METROPOLIS

Germany, 1926. Dir: Fritz Lang. With: Gustav Fröhlich, Brigitte Helm, Alfred Abel, Rudolf Klein-Rogge, Theodor Loos, Fritz Rasp. UFA. Tinted.
Lang's classic science fiction epic. Ignore Fröhlich's weak hero and Thea von Harbou's somewhat laboured script about class distinction between the dehumanised underground workers and the privileged upper classes. Instead, enjoy the often brilliant visuals, the impressive miniature futuristic city, the destruction of the giant subterranean machines and, best of all, Helm's spirited performance as the subversive robot Maria, created through science and sorcery by the insane Rotwang (Klein-Rogge, whose influence stretches all the way to Stanley Kubrick's *Dr Strangelove* [1963]). In 1984, music producer Giorgio Moroder restored missing sequences and added an appalling rock score. The result was a travesty.

(RVB).

THE MAN WITHOUT A SOUL

(USA: I BELIEVE)
UK, 1916 (1917). Dir: George Loane Tucker. With: Milton Rosmer, Edna Flugrath, Barbara Everest, Edward O'Neill, Charles Rock, Frank Stanmore. London/Jury/ Cosmotofilm/Sherman Pictures. B&W.
When a scientist brings a divinity student back to life, the latter has no soul. After praying, his soul is restored to him. Scripted by director Tucker, based on a story by Kenelm Foss.

THE MONKEY MAN

France, 1908. Pathe. B&W.
Eleven minute comedy short in which a surgeon transplants the brain of a monkey into his unconscious patient. The man then takes on the characteristics of the ape.

THE MONSTER

USA, 1925. Dir: Roland West. With: Lon Chaney, Gertrude Olmstead, Hallam Cooley, Charles A. Sellon, Walter James, Knute Erickson. Metro-Goldwyn-Mayer. B&W.
Comedy horror thriller based on the Broadway play by Crane Wilbur. Chaney Sr stars as the mad Dr Ziska, who, with the help of escaped lunatics, traps his victims with a large reflecting mirror and uses them for experiments in soul transference at his sinister sanatorium. The would-be detective hero (Johnny Arthur) bungles his way through the mystery and even gets the girl at the end. Director West (whose promising career ended with his involvement in the mysterious death of actress Thelma Todd) thankfully doesn't allow the humour to intrude too often, and Hal Mohr's atmospheric cinematography adds a certain flair to the more baroque sequences.

IL MOSTRO DI FRANKENSTEIN

Italy, 1920. Dir: Eugenio Testa. With: Luciano Albertini, Umberto Guarracino. Albertini Film/UCI. B&W.
The third silent version of Mary Shelley's novel is now apparently a lost movie. This includes a confrontation in a cave between Frankenstein (played by producer Albertini) and his Monster (Guarracino). Amazingly, it was the last Italian horror film for nearly forty years.
Remake: FRANKENSTEIN (qv; 1931)

ON TIME

USA, 1924. Dir: Henry Lehrman. With: Richard Talmadge, Billie Dove, Charles Clary, Stuart Holmes, Tom Wilson, Douglas Gerard. Carlos Productions/Truart. B&W.
A mad doctor attempts to transplant a gorilla's brain into the hero's head. In the end it turns out to be a trick to see if the man is capable of becoming a movie star. Scripted by Garrett Fort (*Frankenstein* [1931], etc).

THE RETURN OF MAURICE DONNELLY

USA, 1915. Dir: William Humphrey. With: Leo Delaney, Leah Baird, Anders Randolph, Mary Maurice, Denton Vane, Garry McGarry. Broadway Star/Vitagraph. B&W.
When Delaney is electrocuted for a crime he didn't commit, he is restored to life by a machine invented by physician Randolph and tracks down the real culprits. This thirty-five minute short was used as a propaganda film by groups advocating the abolition of capital punishment.

THE SECRET ROOM

USA, 1915. Dir: Tom Moore. With: Tom Moore, Ethel Clifton, Robert Ellis, Paton Gibbs, Marguerite Courtot, Betty Peterson. Kalem. B&W.
Twenty-five minute short in which a mad scientist plans to transfer a man's personality into the mind of his imbecilic son.

THE SURGEON'S EXPERIMENT

USA, 1914. With: Paul Scardon. Majestic. B&W.
Thirty minute short in which an operation turns a crook into an honest man.

WITHOUT A SOUL

(aka LOLA)
USA, 1916. Director: James Young. With: Clara Kimball Young, Alec B. Francis, Edward M. Kimball, Irene Tams, Mary Moore. Young Pictures/ World Film Corporation. B&W.
Based on the play *Lola* by Owen Davis. When his daughter Lola (the director's wife, Young) is killed in a car accident, her scientist father (Kimball) creates an electric ray which brings her back from the dead. However, when the girl's behaviour becomes selfish and wanton, her father realises that his daughter has been revived without her original soul. In the end she dies on the laboratory floor from a heart attack and he destroys his equipment.

The Gentle Monster

Boris Karloff was born William Henry Pratt on 23 November 1887 in Camberwell, South London. He was the youngest member of a family that comprised eight sons and one daughter.

In 1909, using a £100 legacy from his mother, he sailed to Canada, where he found employment as a farm labourer, workman, real-estate salesman and railway builder. At the end of the following year he applied for a job with a touring theatre company and, remembering a remote family name on his mother's side, he adopted 'Karloff' as a stage name. For a Christian name he pulled 'Boris' "out of the air".

His first role was playing a sixty year-old man in a play called *The Devil* by Ferenc Molnar. His starting pay was £4 per week. As his roles increased, so did his wages (to around £10 per week), and by the time he finally arrived in Los Angeles in December 1917, he had established himself as a popular stage villain.

***Right:** Boris Karloff, behind-the-scenes, The Ghoul (1933).*
***Below:** Karloff as the Monster, caricatured by Spanish-American bandleader Xavier Cugat. (FJA).*

His movie career began with appearances in crowd scenes and serials. As a 'guinea extra', he worked for a few days playing a Mexican soldier on the Douglas Fairbanks picture, *His Majesty, the American* (1919). In later years, Karloff would refer to this as his first film part. Other small roles followed, but by 1923 Karloff was broke. He became a lorry driver, taking an occasional day off to appear in movies. Nevertheless, he slowly began to establish himself and in 1929 made his first sound film, *The Unholy Night*, directed by Lionel Barrymore.

Karloff's film career alternated with his stage appearances, and in 1930 he landed the minor, but effective role of killer Ned Galloway in the play *The Criminal Code*. When Columbia decided to turn it into a film, director Howard Hawks cast the actor in the same part. Hollywood started to take notice. More substantial roles in such films as *Five Star Final* (1931) and *The Mad*

Genius (1931) followed, and it was while playing another gangster in *Graft* (1931) that his big break came.

"While I was eating lunch at the Universal Studio commissary," recalled Karloff, "someone tapped me on the shoulder and said that Mr Whale would like to see me at his table. Jimmy Whale was then the hottest director on the lot and told me he was getting ready to shoot the Mary Shelley classic, *Frankenstein*, and would like to test me for the Monster."

For Karloff, the worst thing about the original *Frankenstein* (1931) was not the arduous hours in Jack Pierce's make-up chair, but shooting the famous creation sequence. "I was never as nervous during the entire filming as when I lay half-naked and strapped to the operating table," said the actor. "Above me I could see the special effects men shaking the white-hot, scissor-like carbons that simulated the lightning. I prayed very hard that no one got butter fingers."

At the time, Karloff was considered subordinate to the film's three top-billed stars, Colin Clive, Mae Clarke and John Boles, and the name of the actor playing the Monster was only revealed in the closing credits. He wasn't even invited to attend the premiere in Santa Barbara, where ambulances were in attendance for anyone who could not stand the shock. After seeing the audience reaction to the Monster, Universal realised its mistake and quickly put Karloff under contract. When his agent called to break the news, Karloff told him: "After more than twenty years of acting, for once I'll know where my next breakfast is coming from!"

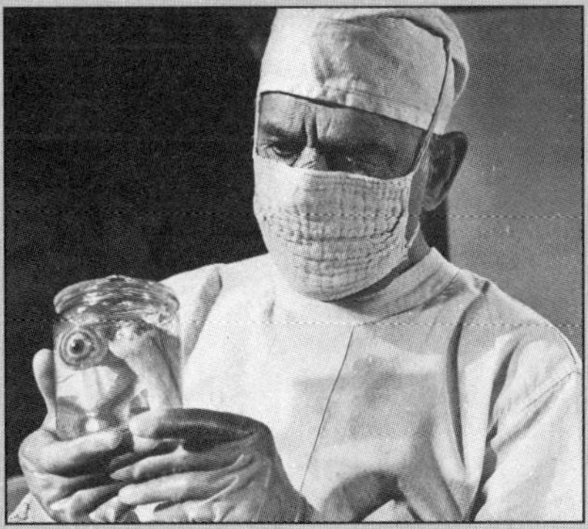

Above: *Son of Frankenstein.*
Below left: *Frankenstein (1931).*
Right: *Frankenstein 1970. (FJA).*

Karloff was always grateful for his role as the Monster: "One always hears of actors complaining of being typed — if he's young, he's typed as a juvenile; if he's handsome, he's typed as a leading man. I was lucky. Whereas bootmakers have to spend millions to establish a trademark, I was handed a trademark free of charge. When an actor gets in a position to select his own roles, he's in big trouble, for he never knows what he can do best. I'm sure I'd be damn good as little Lord Fauntleroy, but who would pay ten cents to see it?"

Much of Karloff's fan mail surprisingly came from youngsters. "The children have never fallen for my nonsense," he revealed. "They sit in the cinema with their eyes glued on the screen. The kiddies really sympathised with the Monster. They knew it wasn't the Monster's fault that he was so terrible. He just couldn't help it. So you see, they weren't actually frightened. I don't think anyone is, really — at least not for more than a minute or two at a time."

After portraying the Monster in *Bride of Frankenstein* (1935) and *Son of Frankenstein* (1939), Karloff vowed never to recreate the role on screen again. However, he later revealed: "The only time I really enjoyed playing the Monster was at the annual charity baseball game in Hollywood between a team of comedians and a team of leading men. I strode up to the plate for the occasion in my full make-up as Frankenstein's Monster, whereupon Buster Keaton, who was catching for the comedians, promptly shrieked at the sight of me, did a backward somersault and passed out cold behind the plate."

Although he went on to work steadily for another three decades, Karloff was often dismayed by the way the type of film he had made famous was being degraded. "There's so much needless violence," he lamented, "horror pictures have become ludicrous. Audiences are amused instead of frightened. Terror is the key, not bloodshed and fights. There was very little violence in *Frankenstein*; the Monster was gentle and a sympathetic character..."

Boris Karloff died of respiratory failure aged eighty-one, on 2 February 1969 in Midhurst, Kent. He was cremated at Guildford Crematorium in Surrey, and his memorial plaque in St Paul's Church, Covent Garden, includes a quote by Andrew Marvell: "He nothing common did, or mean / Upon that memorable scene." For millions of people around the world, Boris Karloff would always be remembered as 'The Gentle Monster'.

the

Perhaps the most important theatrical production of Mary Shelley's **Frankenstein** was the 1927 adaptation by Peggy Webling, which featured Hamilton Deane (who three years earlier had scripted the stage version of **Dracula**) as the Monster. It was so successful during its 1930 revival at the Little Theatre in London that it attracted the attention of Hollywood's ailing Universal Pictures.

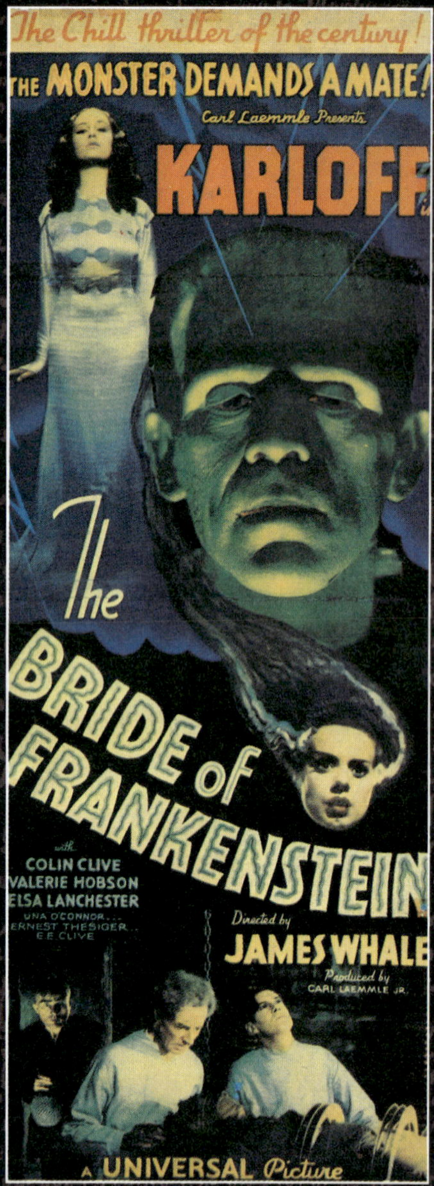

Despite the incredible box-office success of **Dracula** in 1930, Universal still had severe financial problems. Invited to develop a new horror project for the studio, thirty year-old, French-born writer-director Robert Florey (1900-1979) worked closely with Richard Schayer, head of the story department, to bring **Frankenstein** to the screen. Florey co-wrote a first draft screenplay with Garrett Fort and directed a twenty minute test reel featuring a disgruntled Bela Lugosi (1882-1956) in Jack Pierce's early make-up design for the Monster. The result did not impress producer Carl Laemmle Jr (1908-1979) and an outraged Florey was moved on to other projects while the search continued for a new director and an actor to portray Frankenstein's creature.

Boris Karloff (1887-1969) always insisted that it was a lucky encounter in the studio commissary which led to him being cast as the Monster. Following Florey's departure from the project, Universal hired James Whale (1886-1957), who had already directed acclaimed movie adaptations of R.C. Sherriff's play **Journey's End (1930)** and Robert Emmett Sherwood's **Waterloo Bridge (1931)**. After viewing his role as a killer in Howard Hawk's **The Criminal Code (1931)**, Whale offered fellow Englishman Karloff the part of the Monster, and with his square-shaped skull, corpse-like pallor and distinctive electrodes, it is Karloff's sympathetic interpretation of the creature which most people still remember.

Filming began on 24 August 1931, and of the $262,007 budget, $10,000 went on the electrical effects alone. The movie opened on 4 November at the Mayfair Theatre in New York's Times

1930s

Square and caused a sensation. In Kansas City, the State Board of Censors ordered thirty-two cuts, newspapers refused to run advertisements in Providence, Rhode Island, and the British censor excised the scene in which the hanged body of Fritz the hunchback is discovered. The notoriety boosted ticket sales and **Frankenstein** *earned more than $1,000,000 during its initial release (more than twice the take of* **Dracula***), becoming one of the highest grossing titles in Universal's history.*

Throughout the 1930s, the Monster was caricatured in cartoons and novelty films, although Universal waited four years before reuniting Whale, Karloff and Colin Clive for a sequel, **Bride of Frankenstein (1935)***, which despite being a superior film failed to quite match the box-office success of its predecessor. Karloff reprised his role for Universal one last time in 1939 for* **Son of Frankenstein***, this time under the direction of Rowland V. Lee (1891-1975).*

Son of Frankenstein.

By the end of the decade, the actor had become the undisputed King of Horror and vowed to never again play the Monster: "I owe him so much," Karloff explained, "that I owe him a little respect, a little rest.

Frankenstein (1931).

"There was not much left in the Monster to be developed," he later recalled, "we had reached his limits. I saw that from here on, he would become rather an oafish prop, so to speak, in the last act or something like that, without any great stature."

However, Universal did not share Karloff's sentiments. There was still plenty of mileage — and profit — to be exploited from Mary Shelley's creation. The second great cycle of American horror films was about to begin, and the studio was already grooming a new star to follow in his father's footsteps...

ALRAUNE

(USA: aka DAUGHTER OF EVIL)
Germany, 1930. Dir: Richard Oswald. With: Brigitte Helm, Albert Bassermann, Agnes Straub, Käthe Haack, Bernhard Götzke, Martin Kosleck. UFA. B&W.

The fourth film adaptation of Hanns Heinz Ewers' story suffers from Oswald's pedestrian direction. Helm (*Metropolis* [1926]) recreates her role from the 1928 version as the woman artificially created by mad scientist Ten Brinken (Bassermann), who inseminates a prostitute with the semen of a hanged man.

Remake: UNNATURAL (qv; 1952)

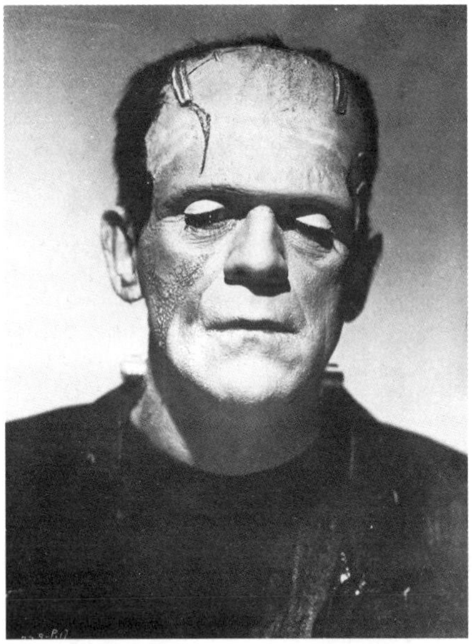

BETTY BOOP'S PENTHOUSE

USA, 1933. Dir: Dave Fleischer. Voices: Mae Questel, Jack Mercer. Paramount. B&W.

Seven minute cartoon in which Betty is menaced by a Frankenstein-like monster. When she sprays him with her perfume, the creature is transformed into a dancing flower! Produced by Max Fleischer. In the 1970s this was colourised and included in the compilation feature *The Betty Boop Follies*.

This page: *Bride of Frankenstein.*

BOO

USA, 1933. Universal. B&W.

Novelty short that includes clips from *Frankenstein* (1931).

BOSKO'S MECHANICAL MAN

USA, 1933. Dir: Hugh Harman. Harman-Ising/Warner Bros. B&W.

Six minute Looney Tunes cartoon. When Honey makes Bosko do the dishes, he builds a robot called Frankensteen, which goes on the rampage until he inserts a

BRIDE OF FRANKENSTEIN

USA, 1935. Dir: James Whale. With: (Boris) Karloff, Colin Clive, Valerie Hobson, Elsa Lanchester, Una O'Connor, Ernest Thesiger. Universal. B&W.

Finally convinced by Universal to make a sequel to his *Frankenstein* (1931), director Whale created this classic black comedy (filmed under the titles *The Return of Frankenstein* and *Frankenstein Lives Again!*). It benefits from a higher budget, excellent photography, an inventive script (co-writer John L. Balderston threatened to disown the film — he wrote it as a satire) and a superb cast: Karloff recreates his role as the sympathetic Monster, discovered still living in the ruins of the burned-out mill, who learns to talk, drink and smoke; Ernest Thesiger's marvellous Dr Septimus Pretorius (originally to have been played by Bela Lugosi or Claude Rains), with his bottled homunculi and a predilection for gin ("It's my only weakness"); and Lanchester, who appears as both creator Mary Shelley during the opening sequence and the shock-haired mate for the Monster. With solid support from Clive (who survives as Henry Frankenstein from the previous film), O'Connor's comedy relief Minnie, Dwight Frye's hunchbacked Karl, E.E. Clive's Burgomaster, and Mary Gordon, Walter Brennan and John Carradine in small roles. Franz Waxman's memorable score was later reused in Universal's *Flash Gordon* serials. Fifteen minutes were cut after previews and a happy ending — in which Henry and Elizabeth survive the laboratory explosion — was added.

Sequel: SON OF FRANKENSTEIN (qv; 1939)
Remake/sequel: THE BRIDE (qv; 1985)

(FJA).

record of 'Mary Had a Little Lamb' into it. This was Bosko's last film for Warners, although he survived for another five years at MGM.

CASTLE SINISTER

UK, 1932. Dir: Widgey R. Newman. With: Haddon Mason, Eric Adeney, Ilsa Kilpatrick, Wally Patch. Delta/ Filmophone. B&W.

Set in Devon, a mad scientist attempts to transplant a young girl's brain into the head of his apeman. Just fifty minutes long and not to be confused with the 1947 film with the same title.

CHARLIE CHAN IN HONOLULU

USA, 1938. Dir: H. Bruce Humberstone. With: Sidney Toler, Phyllis Brooks, (Victor) Sen Yung, Eddie Collins, John King, George Zucco. Twentieth Century-Fox. B&W.

When health problems forced Warner Oland to leave the popular series (he died the same year), Sidney Toler took over the role as Earl Derr Biggers' oriental sleuth in this enjoyable entry. As Chan and his entire family await the birth of his first grandchild, he investigates a murder on board a docked ship. Director Humberstone keeps the routine plot moving along, but the real surprise is Zucco's cameo spoofing his horror roles: as loony scientist Dr Cardigan, he keeps living criminal brains alive in glowing jars and helps catch the real killer! This was also the film that introduced (Victor) Sen Yung as Jimmy Chan, Number Two Son and resident comedy relief.

Sequel: CHARLIE CHAN IN RENO (1939)

DICK TRACY'S G-MEN

USA, 1939. Dir: William Witney and John English. With: Ralph Byrd, Irving Pichel, Ted Pearson, Phyllis Isley (Jennifer Jones), Walter Miller, George Douglas. Republic Pictures. B&W.

Third and probably best of Republic's four serials starring Byrd as the square-jawed detective hero of Chester Gould's comic strip. Over fifteen fast-paced chapters, Tracy battles master spy Zarnoff (the wonderful Pichel), who is brought back from the dead in the opening scenes after being executed in the gas chamber. In the end, Zarnoff is poisoned by drinking from an arsenic well. A two hour cut-down version was produced for television in 1973.

Sequel: DICK TRACY VS. CRIME, INC. (1941)

DOCTOR X

USA, 1932. Dir: Michael Curtiz (Mihaly Kertesz). With: Lionel Atwill, Fay Wray, Lee Tracy, Preston Foster, John Wray, Harry Beresford. First National Pictures/ Vitaphone. Colour.

Above right: Frankenstein (1931).
Below: Bride of Frankenstein.

During each full moon, a crazed cannibalistic strangler, who eats human glands, creates a functioning hand out of synthetic flesh (make-up created by Max Factor Co). Is it the mysterious Dr Xavier (Atwill in a rare starring role)? His devoted daughter Joanna (Wray), who screams every time she finds her father lurking around their lonely cliff-top mansion? Or perhaps it's one of the sinister scientists (Foster, Wray, Beresford and Arthur Edmund Carewe), who all have something to hide? It all adds up to a wonderfully gruesome pulp horror thriller, although the comedy antics of Tracy's wise-cracking reporter hero almost ruin the genuine chills. With regular Laurel and Hardy foil Mae Busch as a speakeasy madam. Originally filmed in the two-colour Technicolor process, it was restored in 1985 by UCLA.

THE FACE AT THE WINDOW

UK, 1932. Dir: Leslie Hiscott. With: Raymond Massey, Isla Bevan, Eric Maturin, Claude Hulbert. Radio B&W.

Based on F. Brooke Warren's stage play, previously filmed in Australia in 1919 and Britain in 1920. A hideous face distracts the victims of a murderer. In the end, a corpse is brought back from the dead long enough to identify the killer.

Remake: THE FACE AT THE WINDOW (qv; 1939)

THE FACE AT THE WINDOW

UK, 1939. Dir: George King. With: Tod Slaughter, Marjorie Taylor, John Warwick, Aubrey Mallalieu, Robert Adair, Wallace Evenett. British Lion/Ambassador. B&W.

FRANKENSTEIN

USA, 1931. Dir: James Whale. With: Colin Clive, Mae Clarke, John Boles, Boris Karloff, Dwight Frye, Edward Van Sloan. Universal. B&W.

Director Whale's dark, Gothic version of Mrs Percy B. Shelley's classic novel has some nice moments of humour and, along with *Dracula* (1930) from the same studio, kicked off the first great horror cycle. Still memorable for Clive's manic Henry Frankenstein ("It's alive!") and Frye's demented hunchback, Fritz. After Bela Lugosi and John Carradine both turned the role down because it involved no dialogue, the Monster (created by make-up artist Jack Pierce) made a star of forty-four year-old Karloff, who brought a unique child-like pathos to the role. In the 1980s it was re-released in its full version, which included the Monster throwing little Maria (Marilyn Harris) into the river to see if she would float like the flowers. With Lionel Belmore as the Burgomaster, and electrical equipment created and operated by Frank Grove, Kenneth Strickfaden and Raymond Lindsay. Some original release prints were apparently tinted green. Universal filmed two endings and, following previews, decided to use the one where Henry survives. A sequel announced in 1933, *The Return of Frankenstein,* stayed on the studio's tentative schedule until 1935.

Sequel: BRIDE OF FRANKENSTEIN (qv; 1935)
Remake: EL SUPERLOCO (qv; 1936)

The fourth version of F. Brooke Warren's stage play (previously filmed in 1919, 1920 and 1932) and one of Tod Slaughter's best horror melodramas. The nineteenth century Parisian setting is hardly convincing, but the star gives a marvellous barnstorming performance as the lecherous Chevalier Del Fardo, who is also a grisly knife murderer known as The Wolf. He is aided by his hideous half-brother (Harry Terry), whose bestial face appears at the window to hold the victim's attention. Director King also throws in white slavery and a mad professor (Evenett) involved with electrical experiments to revive the dead.

FRANKENSTEIN

USA, circa 1931. Dir: Robert Florey. With: Bela Lugosi, Edward Van Sloan. Universal. B&W.

Lost twenty minute test reel shot by Paul Ivano on the *Dracula* (1930) sets, with Lugosi playing the Monster. Universal didn't like the Golem-type make-up Lugosi and Jack Pierce designed, and Lugosi was not happy that the Monster was a non-speaking role. Although originally set to direct *Frankenstein* (1931), Frenchman Florey was replaced by James Whale and his significant contributions to the script went uncredited (except in France). Other cast members would have included Leslie Howard as Henry Frankenstein and Bette Davis as his fiancée Elizabeth.

G-MAN JITTERS

(aka GANDY GOOSE IN G-MAN JITTERS)
USA, 1939. Dir: Eddie Donnelly. Terrytoons/Twentieth Century-Fox. B&W.

Seven minute Paul Terry cartoon, in which Gandy Goose dreams he is a detective investigating a haunted house. He is pursued by the Frankenstein Monster, Dracula and ghosts. Colourised footage from this film later turned up in *Fortune Hunters* (1946) and *King Tut's Tomb* (1950).

THE GOLEM

(Orig: LE GOLEM. UK: THE LEGEND OF PRAGUE. USA: aka THE MAN OF STONE)
France/Czechoslovakia, 1936. Dir: Julien Duvivier. With: Ferdinand Hart, Harry Baur, Germaine Dussey, Roger Karl, Jany Holt, Gaston Jacquet. Metropolis Pictures/ Barrandov. B&W.

In 1933, Universal announced that Boris Karloff would star in a remake of *The Golem* (1920), to be directed by Karl Freund. It was never made, and this unofficial sequel to the 1920 adaptation became the first

(RVB).

sound version of the medieval legend, based on the play by Jan Werich and Jiri Voskovec. Following the death of Rabbi Loew, the living man of clay (Hart) once again saves the Jews of Prague from the tyranny of insane emperor Rudolf II (Baur) and his ruthless chancellor Lang (Karl) before turning to dust. Sequences from this film were used in the compilation *Dr. Terror's House of Horrors* (1943).
Remake: CISARUV PEKAR A PEKARUV CISAR (qv; 1951)

HAVE YOU GOT ANY CASTLES?

USA, 1938. Dir: Frank Tashlin. Voices: Mel Blanc. Vitaphone/ Warner Bros. Colour.
Seven minute Merrie Melodies cartoon about a number of book characters coming to life and singing the title song and 'Old King Cole' (both from *Varsity Show* [1937]) plus 'Swing for Sale'. Includes Frankenstein's Monster, Fu Manchu, Mr Hyde, the ghost from *Topper* and the Phantom of the Opera. With reused sequences from *Clean Pastures* (1937).

HOLLYWOOD CAPERS

USA, 1935 (1936). Dir: Jack King. Warner Bros. B&W.
Seven minute Looney Tunes cartoon set in a movie studio. When Beans the cat enters the set of a Frankenstein movie, he accidentally brings the mechanical Monster to life. The creature causes havoc until Beans chops him up with the blades of a wind machine. With a guest appearance by Porky Pig.

THE INVENTORS

USA, 1934. Dir: Al Christie. With: F. Chase Taylor, Wilbur Budd Hulick, Olive Borden, Harry Short, Evelyn Dall, Lucile Watson. Educational Pictures/Christie. B&W.
Twenty-two minute comedy short based on the *Stoopnagle and Budd* radio show. Colonel Lemuel Q. Stoopnagle (Taylor) and Budd (Hulick) build a 'Stoopenstein' (Frankenstein's second cousin) out of various spare parts collected by the students at a girls' school. However, the mechanical creature goes out of control, until a bell calms him down. This short was later included in the compilation *The Sound of Laughter* (1963).

LIFE RETURNS

USA, 1935. Dir: Eugen (Eugene) Frenke. With: Onslow Stevens, George Breakston, Lois Wilson, Valerie Hobson, Stanley Fields, Frank Reicher. Universal. B&W.
Based on the real-life exploits of Californian scientist Robert E. Cornish in 1934, Stevens (*House of Dracula* [1945]) plays Dr John Kendrick, who is experimenting with a fluid that restores life to the dead. In actual footage of Cornish's operation, Kendrick returns his son's dead dog to life. With Dr Cornish playing himself and future director Richard Quine in a supporting role. The director sued the studio and the film was banned in Britain for 'bad taste'.

THE LOST CITY

(aka CITY OF LOST MEN)
USA, 1935. Dir: Harry (C.) Revier. With: Wm. (Stage) Boyd, Kane Richmond, Claudia Dell, Josef Swickard, Sam Baker, Geo. F. (Gabby) Hayes. Sherman Krellberg/ Regal Pictures/Super Serial Productions. B&W.
Frenetic twelve chapter serial with such titles as 'Living Dead Men', 'Human Beasts' and 'The Mad Scientist'. Inventor

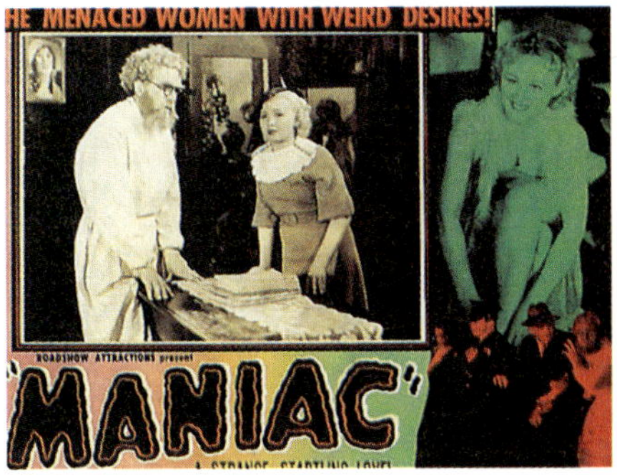

(RVB).

Bruce Gordon (Richmond) uses a magnetic detector to trace a series of world-wide electrical disasters to the lost city of the Ligurians in central Africa. His expedition discovers mad scientist Zolok (Boyd, in his last role) and his hunchbacked assistant Gorzo (Wm. Bletcher) using electromagnetic rays to create an army of giant black zombie slaves with shaggy afros who grunt at each other. Zolok's super-scientific laboratory includes television, a death ray and electrical effects created by Kenneth Strickfaden. This was later released in two feature versions.

MANIAC

(aka SEX MANIAC)
USA, 1934, Dir: Dwain Esper. With: Bill Woods, Horace Carpenter, Ted Edwards, Phyllis Diller, Thea Ramsey, Jennie Dark. Roadshow Attractions Company/Hollywood Producers & Distributors. B&W.
Low budget, adults only version of 'The Black Cat' by Edgar Allan Poe. A crazed vaudeville performer (Woods) kills and impersonates the wild-eyed Dr Meirschultz (silent screen veteran Carpenter), who is experimenting with bringing the dead back to life. Includes the eating of a cat's eye, a rapist who believes he's a gorilla, some mild nudity and clips from *Witchcraft Through the Ages* (1918/1921) and *Siegfried* (1923/1924). An unbelievable exploitation movie from the Hollywood husband and wife team of Dwain Esper and Hildegarde Stadie. Some prints add an instructional foreword about mental illness!

It's Alive!

Colin Clive(-Greig) was born to English parents on 20 January 1900 in Saint Marlo, France. He was related to Lord Robert Clive, founder of the British Empire in India and, at the urging of his family, enrolled in the Royal Military Academy at Sandhurst. Unfortunately, a riding accident ended his promising military career. Having always had a love for acting, he entered London's Royal Academy of Dramatic Art in 1919 and that same year made his first professional appearance in *The Eclipse* at the Garrick Theatre.

After touring for three seasons with the Hull Repertory Company, Clive's big break came in 1928 when playwright R.C. Sherriff and director James Whale cast him in the lead role of Captain Dennis Stanhope in the anti-war drama *Journey's End*.

The play opened at London's Savoy Theatre on 21 January 1929 and was an immediate hit, the unknown cast receiving nineteen curtain calls. However, rumours of alcoholism and bisexuality plagued the actor, and in June that same year he married French actress Jeanne de Casalis, a lesbian.

"To me, his face was a tragic mask," said David Manners, who later co-starred with Clive. "I know he was a tortured man. There seemed to be a split in his personality: one side that was soft, kind, and gentle; the other, a man who took to alcohol to hide from the world his true nature..."

When Hollywood's Tiffany Studios secured the film rights to *Journey's End*, Whale convinced them that Clive was the only actor capable of playing the role. After six weeks shooting in 1930, he returned to the London stage and also appeared in the British film *The Stronger Sex* (1930), along with a young Elsa Lanchester.

He made his Broadway début in William Bolitho's *Overture* that same year, but Clive was soon on his way to Hollywood in response to a cable from close friend James Whale, who wanted him to star as the slightly mad Henry in Universal's *Frankenstein* (1931).

"I chose Colin Clive for *Fran-*

Above: *Colin Clive in Frankenstein (1931). (FJA).*
Left: *Behind-the-scenes, Bride of Frankenstein.*

kenstein," explained the director, "because he had exactly the right kind of tenacity to go through with anything, together with the kind of romantic quality which makes strong men leave civilisation to shoot big game. There is also a level-headedness about Clive which keeps him in full control of himself even in his craziest moments in the picture."

"I think *Frankenstein* has an intense dramatic quality that continues throughout the play and culminates when I, in the title role, am killed by the Monster that I have created," revealed Clive. "This is a rather unusual ending for a talking picture, as the producers generally prefer that the play end happily with the hero and heroine clasped in each other's arms."

As it turned out, Universal changed its mind at the last minute and tacked on just such a happy Hollywood ending!

Following the success of *Frankenstein*, Clive returned to Britain to appear in *Lily Christine* (1932), where he told a reporter: "I used to hate film work at first. But now I prefer screen work to acting on the stage. There is something about the talkie business which fascinates me.

"The technical side is so interesting, and if ever I do master this part of making pictures I would like to produce pictures and give up acting altogether. You see, I'm little more than a puppet really as far as film work is concerned. The director does all the brain work. He is the man who *makes* the picture."

Clive next appeared opposite Katharine Hepburn in the title role of RKO's *Christopher Strong* (1933) and, following a minor appearance in MGM's *Looking Forward* (1933), turned down an offer from Whale to star in *The Invisible Man* (1933). Instead, he went on to appear in Monogram's *Jane Eyre* (1934, as Rochester), *The Key* (1934), *Clive of India* (1935, in which he portrayed the enemy of his own ancestor) and *The Right to Live* (1935).

He also reteamed with R.C. Sherriff and James Whale for Universal's *One More River* (1934), before recreating his role as Henry in Whale's *Bride of Frankenstein* (1935). Although his performance was overshadowed by those of Boris Karloff and Ernest Thesiger, the actor still brought his usual sensitivity to the role.

Following *The Girl from 10th Avenue* (1935) with Bette Davis, he portrayed Stephen Orlac, the victim of the diabolical Dr Gogol (Peter Lorre) in Karl Freund's *Mad Love* (1935). The same year he also appeared in *The Man Who Broke the Bank at Monte Carlo*.

In 1936, while appearing on the New York stage in *Libel*, Clive was admitted to hospital for a minor operation, but was soon back before the cameras in *History is Made at Night* (1937) and *The Woman I Love* (1937). The latter was to be his last film.

A few months later, Clive was taken ill with pneumonia and died of pulmonary tuberculosis on 25 June 1937. A public wake was held where friends and admirers paid their last respects and he was cremated on 29 June at Rosedale Crematory in Hollywood, where his ashes remained unclaimed.

"It isn't good for a player to be associated too closely with one role," the actor once said. "There are other roles to be played out there as good as Stanhope in *Journey's End*." As true as this may have been, in a career cut tragically short Colin Clive found precious few of them.

***Bottom:** Frankenstein (1931).*

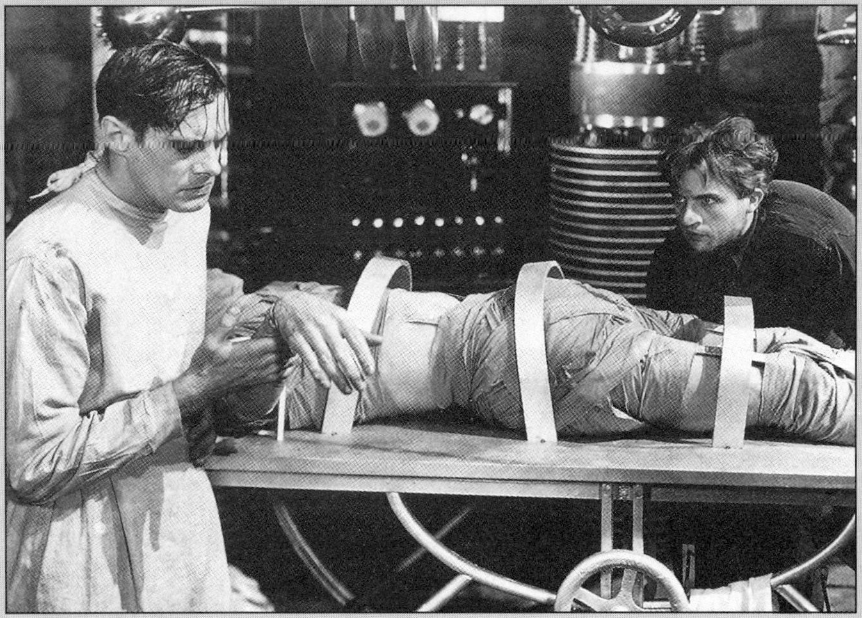

THE MAN THEY COULD NOT HANG

USA, 1939. Dir: Nick Grindé. With: Boris Karloff, Lorna Gray, Robert Wilcox, Roger Pryor, Don Beddoe, Ann Doran. Columbia/Favorite Films. B&W.

The first, and probably best, of five mad doctor movies Karloff starred in for Columbia during the late 1930s and early forties. After being unjustly executed for murder, Karloff's Dr Henryk Savaard has his assistant Lang (Byron Foulger) use a mechanical heart to bring him back from the dead. The crazed doctor, his neck broken by the hangman's noose, invites those he believes responsible for his death to a mansion, where he begins killing them off one by one. Karloff gives his usual fine performance, here supported by good production values and imaginative direction. This was cut by four minutes when originally released in Britain.

Below: *Frankenstein (1931).*
Bottom and right: *The Man Who Changed His Mind.*

THE MAN WHO CHANGED HIS MIND

(USA: THE MAN WHO LIVED AGAIN/THE BRAINSNATCHER/ DR. MANIAC)
UK, 1936. Dir: Robert Stevenson.

(RVB).

With: Boris Karloff, John Loder, Anna Lee, Frank Cellier, Donald Calthrop, Cecil Parker. Gainsborough/Gaumont-British. B&W.

One of Karloff's rare British films of the 1930s, this is an unexpected treat thanks to the often witty script by L. DuGarde Peach, Sidney Gilliat and John L. Balderston, stylish direction by Stevenson and good production values. When bluff tycoon Lord Haslewood (Cellier) withdraws his financial support for Dr Laurience's (Karloff) experiments, the dedicated scientist is driven insane by the ridicule of his colleagues and ends up swapping the brain of his patron with that of his cynical crippled assistant (Calthrop). Far superior to many of the mad doctor movies Karloff made during the late 1930s and early forties.

THE MAN WHO LIVED TWICE

USA, 1936. Dir: Harry Lachman. With: Ralph Bellamy, Marian Marsh, Thurston Hall, Isabel Jewell, Nana

(RVB).

(RVB).

Bryant, Ward Bond. Columbia. B&W.
Bellamy (*The Ghost of Frankenstein* [1942]) portrays a horribly scarred underworld killer, who has a brain operation that removes his memory and all criminal tendencies. After plastic surgery he becomes a famous doctor, but his past catches up with him.
Remake: MAN IN THE DARK (qv; 1953)

MICKEY'S GALA PREMIERE

USA, 1933. Dir: Burt Gillett. Walt Disney/United Artists. B&W.
Seven minute animated short, produced by Disney, in which Mickey Mouse dreams he is attending the première of his new movie. It features caricatures of numerous Hollywood stars, including the Frankenstein Monster, Count Dracula and Quasimodo. This was *Mickey Mouse* No 15.

ONE IN A MILLION

USA, 1936. Dir: Sidney Lanfield. With: Sonja Henie, Adolphe Menjou, Don Ameche, Ned Sparks, Jean Hersholt, The Ritz Brothers. Twentieth Century-Fox. B&W.
Début film of skating star Henie, built around the Winter Olympics. Al Ritz impersonates an ice skating Frankenstein Monster and joins brothers Jim and Harry singing 'Horror Boys of Hollywood', a number about movie villains Boris Karloff, Peter Lorre and Charles Laughton.

PORKY'S MOVIE MYSTERY

USA, 1939. Dir: Robert Clampett. Voices: Mel Blanc. Vitaphone/ Warner Bros. B&W.
Seven minute Looney Tunes cartoon. Porky Pig plays oriental detective 'Mr Motto' on the trail of studio vandal the Phantom, who turns out to be the Invisible Man. It also features a live action sequence and the Frankenstein Monster being given the third degree by police. This was colourised for release to television in the 1960s.

PORKY'S ROAD RACE

USA, 1937. Dir: Frank Tash (Tashlin). Voices: Mel Blanc. Vitaphone/Warner Bros. B&W.
Seven minute Looney Tunes cartoon. Despite the claim that 'Any resemblance to persons living or dead is the bunk,' Porky Pig takes part in a celebrity road race with caricatures of Freddie Bartholomew, Charlie Chaplin, W.C. Fields, Clark Gable, etc. Borax Karoff, looking like the Frankenstein Monster, tries to sabotage the race and Edna May Oliver wins. This was colourised in the late 1960s for release to television.

SING, BABY, SING

USA, 1936. Dir: Sidney Lanfield. With: Alice Faye, Adolphe Menjou, Gregory Ratoff, Ted Healy, Patsy Kelly, Tony Martin. Twentieth Century-Fox. B&W.
Madcap musical comedy with Menjou playing a wonderfully drunken Shakespearean actor. In their feature début, the aggravating Ritz Brothers (Al, Jim and Harry) perform a comedy skit (supposedly for radio!) in which Dr Jekyll's Mr Hyde meets the Frankenstein Monster.

SIX HOURS TO LIVE

USA, 1932. Dir: William Dieterle. With: Warner Baxter, Miriam Jordan, John Boles, George Marion, Beryl Mercer, Irene Ware. Fox. B&W.
Slow-moving drama based on the story 'Auf Wiedersehen' by Gordon Morris and Morton Barteaux. Stubborn Sylvarian diplomat Baxter is murdered at an international trade conference. Eccentric scientist Marion then uses a ray to bring him back to life for just six hours, giving him time to catch his murderer and destroy the life-giving machine before dying a second time.

SNIFFLES AND THE BOOKWORM

USA, 1939. Dir: Charles M. (Chuck) Jones. Voices: Mel Blanc. Vitaphone/Warner Bros. Colour.
Seven minute Merrie Melodies cartoon in which Sniffles the mouse enters a bookstore where various literary characters come to life and perform 'Mutiny in the

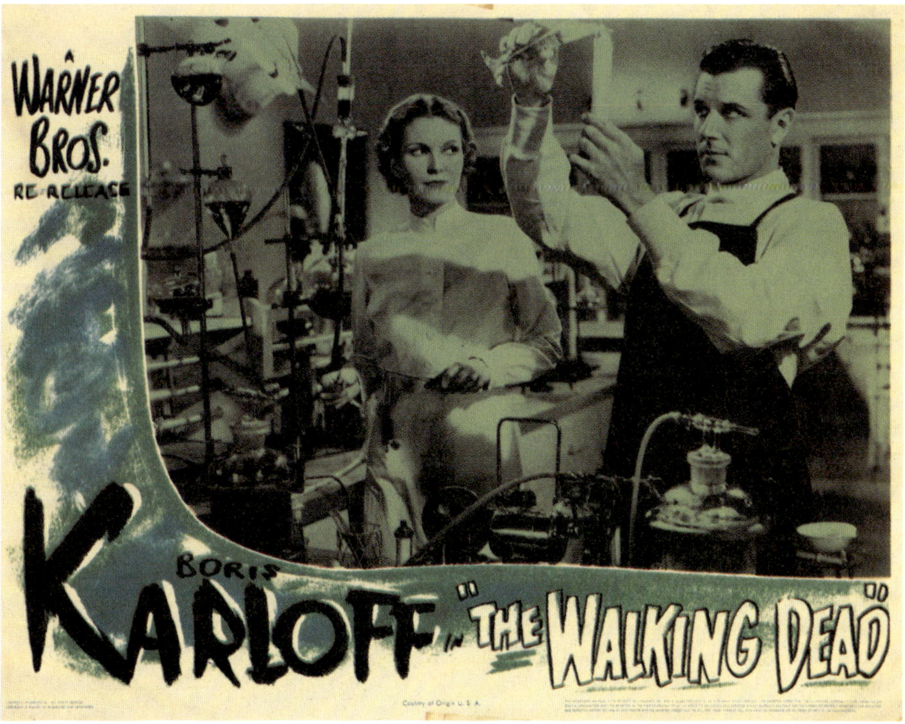

Above and below: *Son of Frankenstein.*

Nursery' (from *Going Places* [1938]). He is then chased by a Monster (beautifully animated by Robert McKimson) that steps out from the pages of Mary Shelley's *Frankenstein.*

STRANGE EXPERIMENT

UK, 1937. Dir: Albert Parker. With: Donald Grey, Ann Wemyss, Mary Newcomb, Ronald Ward, Henri de Vries, Alastair Sim. Fox British. B&W.

Low budget melodrama in which doctors perform a dangerous brain operation to reform a hardened criminal. Based on the play *Two Worlds* by Hubert Osborne and John Golden.

SULOCHANA

India, 1934. Dir: Chaudhury. With: Sulochana, D. Billimoria, Chandra, Zilloo, Hadi, Gulam Mahomed. Imperial. B&W.

An elixir brings a dead girl back to life. The title translates as *Temple Bells.*

EL SUPERLOCO

Mexico, 1936. Dir: Juan José Segura. With: Leopoldo Ortin, Carlos Villarias, Consuelo Frank, Ramón Armengod, Raul Urquijo, 'Indian' Fernandez. PCE. B&W.

Obscure comedy reworking of Mary Shelley's *Frankenstein,* in which the mad Dr Dyenis performs bizarre brain experiments on his Monster (Urquijo). This also apparently includes elements of *The Strange Case of Dr Jekyll and Mr Hyde* and *The Picture of Dorian Gray.*

Remake: FRANKENSTEIN (qv; 1940)

SWEET SPIRITS OF THE NIGHTER

USA, circa 1930s. With: El Brendel, Tom Kennedy. Columbia. B&W.

Two-reel short which was given an 'H' (for horror) certificate in Britain. The terrible comedy duo of Brendel and Kennedy investigate an old dark house where they encounter a mad doctor's experiments to revive the dead and a scary looking zombie.

TOYLAND PREMIERE

USA, 1934. Dir: Walter Lantz. Walter Lantz Productions/ Universal. Colour.

Six minute cartoon set in a department store at Christmas. A toy Frankenstein Monster comes to life and scares the Laurel and Hardy toys.

SON OF FRANKENSTEIN

USA, 1939. Dir: Rowland V. Lee. With: Basil Rathbone, Boris Karloff, Bela Lugosi, Lionel Atwill, Josephine Hutchinson, Donnie Dunagan. Universal. B&W.

Stylish follow-up to *Bride of Frankenstein* (1935). Rathbone (in a role originally planned for Peter Lorre) plays the eponymous Baron Wolf von Frankenstein, who returns to his father's castle with his family. There, at the bidding of the broken-necked Ygor (Lugosi, in one of his finest roles), he once again resurrects his father's creation (fifty-one year-old Karloff in his third and final film appearance as the Monster, now reduced to little more than a killing machine). In one scene, Rathbone's obsessive scientist complains that the name of his father and the Monster have become synonymous. With Atwill's memorable one-armed Inspector Krogh and strong support from Lionel Belmore, Gustav von Seyffertitz and Lawrence Grant. This was to be Universal's first Technicolor production, but after shooting began in October 1938, it was discovered that Karloff's make-up didn't photograph well in colour and the footage (which included Dwight Frye as an angry villager) was abandoned and reshot in black and white. The same year Universal announced a sequel, *After Frankenstein,* which was never made.

Sequel: THE GHOST OF FRANKENSTEIN (qv; 1942)

Top: *Son of Frankenstein. (FJA).*
Above: *Two Hearts in Wax Time. (FJA).*

TWO HEARTS IN WAX TIME

USA, 1935. With: Shirley Ross, Sid Saylor, Sam McDaniels. Metro-Goldwyn-Mayer. Colour.

Twenty minute Technicolor short in MGM's A Musical Revue series. A drunk imagines a number of store window figures coming to life, including Frankenstein's Monster, Fu Manchu and Mr Hyde. Filmed under the title *The Department Store.*

THE VAMPIRE BAT

USA, 1933. Dir: Frank Strayer. With: Lionel Atwill, Fay Wray, Melvyn Douglas, Maude Eburne, George E. Stone, Dwight Frye. Majestic Pictures. B&W.

Stars Atwill and Wray are teamed for the third time (after *Doctor X* [1932] and *Mystery of the Wax Museum* [1932]) in this low budget independent chiller, filmed on the Universal backlot. Atwill plays the mad Dr Otto van Niemann who uses hypnotism to create fake vampire deaths and obtain blood to feed the synthetic creature he has created. Douglas is miscast as the stiff police inspector, but there's always Lionel Belmore, recreating his Burgomaster from *Frankenstein* (1931), and a sleazy Dwight Frye as an idiot bat-lover.

THE WALKING DEAD

USA, 1936. Dir: Michael Curtiz (Mihaly Kertesze). With: Boris Karloff, Ricardo Cortez, Edmund Gwenn, Marguerite Churchill, Warren Hull, Barton MacLane. Warner Bros. B&W.

Combining both the horror and gangster genres, this is one of Karloff's best movies. He plays John Ellman, an ex-convict framed and executed for murder. When scientist Dr Beaumont (Gwenn) uses electricity to revive him, Ellman returns from the dead to seek revenge on those who framed him. The execution scene was originally cut from British prints. During shooting, author H.G. Wells visited the set and met Karloff and Gwenn.

Remake: INDESTRUCTIBLE MAN (qv; 1956)

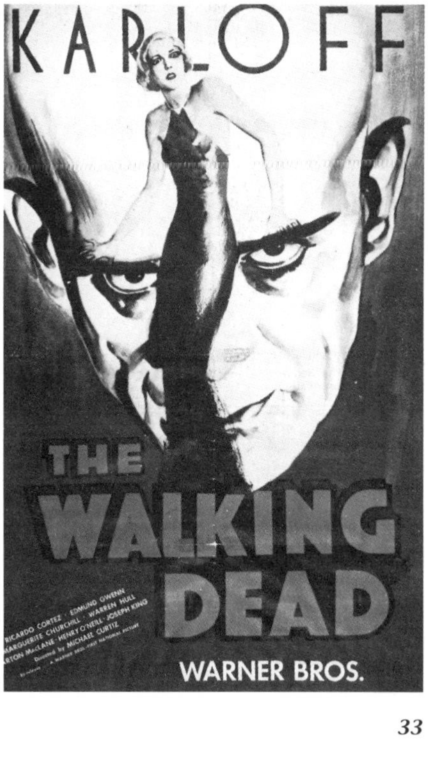

the

At the beginning of the 1940s, Universal was more than $2,000,000 in profit. Horror was a popular genre once again, but Boris Karloff had defected to Columbia, where he was making his series of 'mad doctor' movies.

Creighton Chaney (1906-1973), the son of one of the silent screen's most versatile performers, Lon Chaney (1883-1930), had made his movie début dancing in the chorus of RKO's **Girl Crazy (1932)**. *After appearing in numerous bit parts and supporting roles, the actor was forced to change his name to Lon Chaney Jr and began to make an impression in such films as* **Jesse James (1939)**, **Of Mice and Men (1939)** *and* **One Million B.C. (1940)**.

(RVB).

Universal offered the young actor a contract and began to groom him as its new horror star, initially casting him opposite Lionel Atwill in **Man Made Monster (1941)**. *With his starring role as the doomed lycanthrope Lawrence Talbot in* **The Wolf Man (1941)**, *Chaney Jr created a classic horror character and it was only natural that he should follow in Karloff's bootsteps. In 1942, the hard-drinking actor donned Jack Pierce's distinctive make-up as the Monster in* **The Ghost of Frankenstein**.

When the film made a healthy profit for the studio, it was inevitable that a sequel would be rushed into production. **Frankenstein Meets the Wolf Man (1943)** *was originally set to star Chaney Jr as* **both** *the Wolf Man and the Monster, but when this idea was scrapped at the last minute by producer George Waggner (1894-1984), Universal cast fifty-nine year-old Bela Lugosi in the role he had made the mistake of turning down twelve years earlier.*

All of the Monster's dialogue and references to the creature's blindness were cut by the studio prior to release, but the film still boasted a fine cast and good production values. It boosted Universal's profits and the studio decided that if two monsters together could reap box-office rewards, then surely a combination of four or five would result in even greater revenue. However, both **House of Frankenstein (1944)** *and* **House of Dracula (1945)** *proved the rule of diminishing returns.*

1940s

Both entries starred Chaney Jr as the Wolf Man, John Carradine as Count Dracula, and various hunchbacks and mad doctors. Karloff returned to the series, bringing a welcome touch of class to the first film, while western actor and stunt man Glenn Strange (1899-1973) became the fourth actor to play Universal's Frankenstein Monster.

By the time **House of Dracula** *opened on 6 February 1946, Universal had already dropped the troublesome Chaney and, despite profits of $4,600,000 that year, many other players lost their contracts when the studio officially merged with International Pictures on 1 October.*

During its first year, Universal-International almost went bankrupt and by 1948 the enormous popularity of the studio's comedy team Bud Abbott (1895-1974) and Lou Costello (1906-1959) was beginning to wane. In a desperate attempt to win back audiences, **Meet Frankenstein** *(Abbott and Costello's names are not included in the on-screen title) opened on 24 July 1948. Chaney and Strange were back in their usual roles, and Bela Lugosi triumphantly recreated the part of Dracula on screen for the last time. The film became the most successful in the series since the original* **Frankenstein** *seventeen years earlier, reviving the careers of the comedy duo and becoming one of the studio's top three box-office hits of the year.*

Meet Frankenstein.

The Ghost of Frankenstein.

Throughout the decade the Monster had also turned up in various cartoons and as a live-action character in the novelty short **Third Dimensional Murder (1940)** *and Universal's musical/comedy* **Hellzapoppin' (1941)**. *The character was already about as far removed from Mary Shelley's dignified creature as could be imagined.*

However, in the era of teenagers and rock 'n' roll, there were even worse indignities to come before a small British company would revitalise the saga in blood-dripping colour...

Piercing the Veil

When director James Whale cast Boris Karloff for the part of the Monster in *Frankenstein* (1931), he naturally turned to Universal's chief make-up artist, Jack P. Pierce, to create the look of the creature pieced together from corpses.

Pierce was born on 5 May 1889 in Greece. After immigrating to America, he became a promising 'shortstop' baseball player before moving from Chicago to California in 1910 to break into the Coast League baseball team. He was turned down for being too light, so became a cinema projectionist before joining Universal in 1914 as an assistant cameraman. Pierce eventually drifted into make-up and, after turning Jacques Lerner into an ape for Fox's *The Monkey Talks* (1926), rejoined Universal that same year.

Pierce had experienced problems with Bela Lugosi during the filming of *Dracula* (1930) and later on Robert Florey's test reel for *Frankenstein*, when the actor insisted on creating his own hairy make-up for the creature. However, Karloff genuinely cared about the "dear old Monster", and Pierce and the actor spent three hours every evening for three weeks coming up with a look that both Whale and producer Carl Laemmle Jr would accept. "This is going to be a big thing," Pierce told Karloff. He was right.

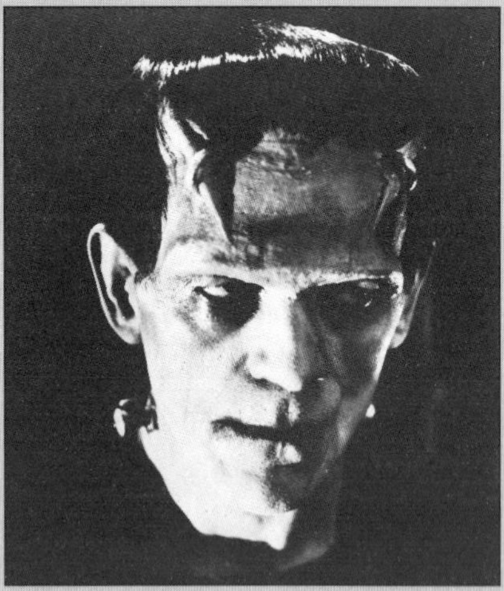

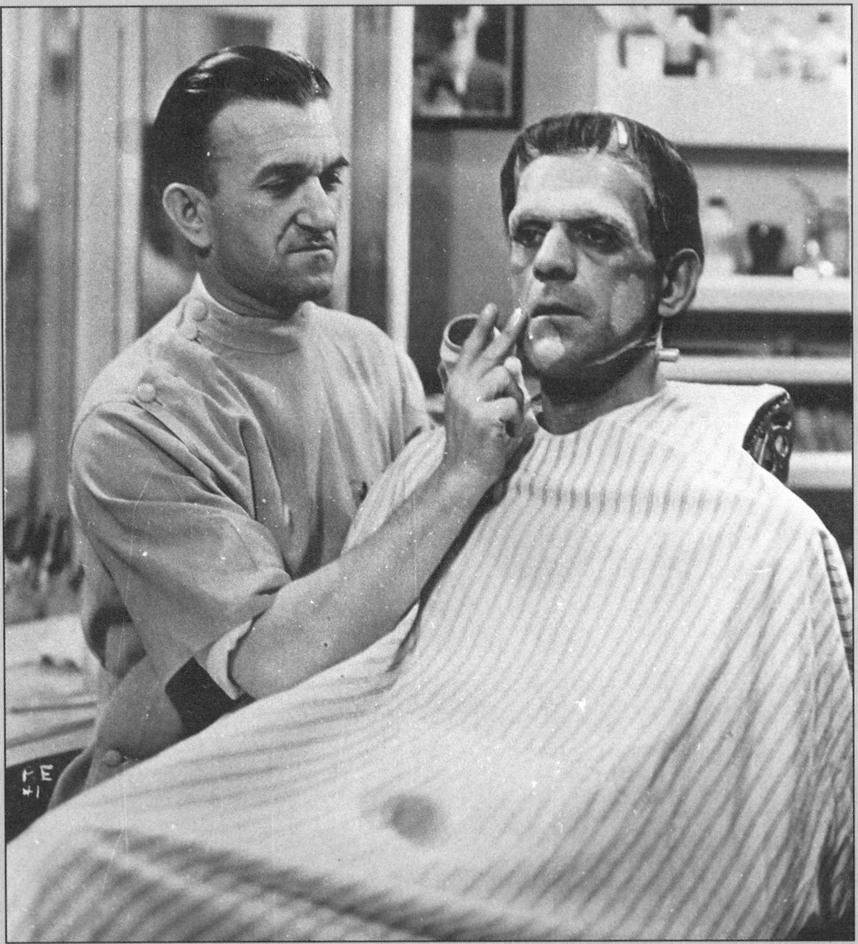

***Above:** Unused make-up design, Frankenstein (1931).*
***Left:** Jack Pierce creates the Monster, Frankenstein (1931).*

After reading Mary Shelley's novel, the make-up artist didn't rely on his imagination. He realised he would have to create his own, distinctive look for the Monster.

"I did three months of research in anatomy, surgery, criminology, ancient and modern burial customs, and electrodynamics," he later explained. "My anatomical studies taught me that there are six ways a surgeon can cut the skull in order to take out or put in a brain. I figured that Frankenstein, who was a scientist but no practising surgeon, would take the simplest surgical way. He would cut the top of the skull off straight across like a pot lid, hinge it, pop the brain in, and then clamp it on tight. That's the reason I decided to make the Monster's head square and flat like a shoe box and dig that big scar across his forehead with the metal clamps holding it together.

"I read that the Egyptians used to bind some criminals hand and foot and bury them alive. When their blood turned to water after death, it flowed

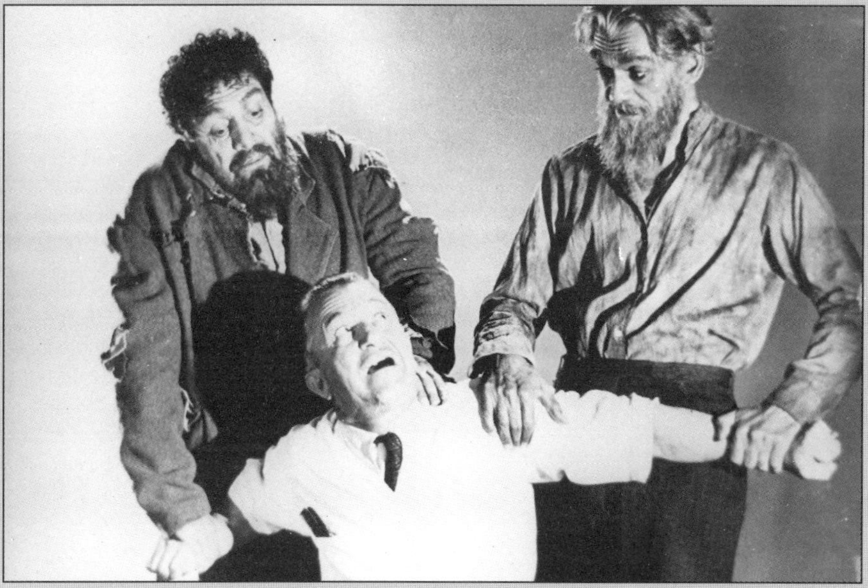

into their extremities, stretched their arms to gorilla length and swelled their hands, feet and faces to abnormal proportions. I thought this would make a nice touch for the Monster, since he was supposed to be made from the corpses of executed felons."

Pierce applied nose-putty on thin layers of cotton soaked in collodion to Karloff's face and hands, which he then coloured with blue-green greasepaint to photograph a corpse-like grey. An artificial, square-shaped skull was built to give the impression of, as Pierce put it, "a man whose brain had been taken from the head of another man." Wire clamps were fixed over his lips to distort the shape of his mouth and his eyelids were weighed down with several coatings of mortician's wax (a last-minute suggestion by Karloff).

"I made his arms look longer by shortening the sleeves of his coat," revealed the make-up artist, "and stiffened his legs with two pairs of pants over steel struts. His large feet were the boots asphalt-spreaders wear. I blackened his fingernails with shoe polish."

As a final touch, two electrodes were glued to the side of Karloff's neck (for some time afterwards, the actor's skin bore small scars where these conductors were attached). "Those two metal studs that stuck out of the sides of his neck were inlets for electricity," noted Pierce. "Remember, the Monster is an electrical gadget. Lightning is his life-force..."

In full make-up and costume, Karloff stood over seven feet tall and carried an extra forty-eight pounds (including boots weighing thirteen pounds each). After each day's shooting, which often lasted up to eighteen hours, the actor underwent massage and infra-red treatment to get his strained muscles back into shape.

"The make-up was quite an ordeal," recalled Karloff, "it was a rather horrible experience. I had to arrive at the studio every morning at 5.30am and spend three-and-a-half hours in the make-up chair getting ready for the day's work. The make-up itself was quite painful, particularly the putty used on my eyes. There were many days when I thought I would never be able to hold out until the end of the day, but somehow or other I always did."

Removing the make-up was even more painful, and it took a soaking in oils and acetones for up to two hours each night before the actor was himself again. Karloff's make-up for *Frankenstein* was a closely-guarded secret during shooting and his face was kept veiled when he made the journeys with Pierce between the dressing room and the sound stage.

"Jack Pierce did really feel that he *made* these people," remembered Elsa Lanchester, "like he was a *God* who created human beings. In the morning he'd be dressed in white, as if he were in a hospital to perform an operation."

Between 1926 and 1947, Jack Pierce created all of Universal's classic horror make-ups, working on every *Frankenstein* sequel except the last, *Meet Frankenstein* (1948). Considered too old and his time-consuming techniques obsolete, he was unceremoniously dropped by the studio in 1948, although he continued to freelance in films and television (including the popular TV series *Mr Ed* [1960-66]).

Bitter, bed-ridden with arthritis and living on a modest pension, seventy-nine year-old Jack Pierce died of uraemia on 19 July 1968. There were only twenty-three mourners at the funeral service. Upon learning of his old friend's death, Karloff sent an impressive floral wreath. "When you get right down to it, it was Jack Pierce who really created the Frankenstein Monster," said the actor. "I was merely the animation in the costume."

Above left: *Naish and Karloff revenge themselves on Pierce, behind-the-scenes, House of Frankenstein.*
Below: *James Whale adds a final touch, Bride of Frankenstein.*

BLACK FRIDAY

USA, 1940. Dir: Arthur Lubin. With: Boris Karloff, Bela Lugosi, Stanley Ridges, Anne Nagel, Anne Gwynne, Virginia Brissac. Universal. B&W.

Co-scripted by Kurt (Curt) Siodmak (*Donovan's Brain*, etc), Karloff stars as misunderstood scientist Dr Ernest Sovac (in a part originally intended for Lugosi), who performs an 'illegal' brain transplant to save the life of mild-mannered Professor Kingsley (an impressive performance by Ridges in the role Karloff was originally set to play). But after receiving part of the brain of a dead gangster, Kingsley undergoes a series of bizarre transformations as the new mind takes control. In a publicity stunt, Lugosi (who turns up in the thankless role of a rival crime boss) was hypnotised on the set by Dr Manley Hall for his death scene. The following year Universal announced that Karloff and Lugosi would co-star in *The Monster of Zombor*, but it was never made and this marked the fifth and final teaming of the two stars (who never share a scene) for the studio.

Remake: CRIMSON (qv; 1973)

ARSENIC AND OLD LACE

USA, 1941 (1944). Dir: Frank Capra. With: Cary Grant, Priscilla Lane, Jack Carson, Raymond Massey, Edward Everett Horton, Peter Lorre. Warner Bros. B&W.

Wonderfully ghoulish horror comedy, based on Joseph Kesselring's Broadway stage success. Although producer/director Capra shot the film in four weeks, it wasn't released until 1944, when the play had finished its original run. As Mortimer Brewster, Grant's split-second comedy timing results in some marvellous double-takes as he returns on his wedding night to the family home in Brooklyn Heights and discovers his spinster aunts, Martha and Abby (Jean Adair and Josephine Hull), are poisoning lonely old gentlemen, and uncle Teddy (John Alexander) is burying them in the cellar. To make matters worse, his psychotic brother Jonathan (Massey) also turns up with his own corpse and a horribly scarred face, modelled on the Frankenstein Monster by the drunken Dr Einstein (a scene-stealing Lorre). The gag worked better in the original stage play, where Jonathan was played by Boris Karloff (later by Bela Lugosi and Charles Laughton) in a role created for him. With a great Max Steiner score.

THE BOOGIE MAN WILL GET YOU

USA, 1942. Dir: Lew Landers (Lewis Friedlander). With: Boris Karloff, Peter Lorre, 'Slapsie' Maxie Rosenbloom, Jeff Donnell, Larry Parks, Don Beddoe. Columbia. B&W.

Karloff's fifth and final film under his Columbia contract and an attempt to recreate the comedy success of *Arsenic and Old Lace* (then starring Karloff and Lorre on the stage). Karloff plays Prof Nathaniel Billings, a slightly crazy old scientist trying to create a race of supermen to battle the Nazis. Parks and Donnell are the lovers who buy Billings' old inn and discover his failures buried in the cellar. With good support from Lorre as the scheming Dr Lorentz.

(RVB).

BOWERY AT MIDNIGHT

USA, 1942. Dir: Wally Fox. With: Bela Lugosi, John Archer, Wanda McKay, Tom Neal, Dave O'Brien, Wheeler Oakman. Monogram/ Astor Pictures. B&W.

One of Monogram's better low budget outings (which isn't saying much), produced by Sam Katzman and Jack Dietz. Lugosi stars as homicidal genius Karl Wagner, a college professor by day and a gangster by night, who uses a Bowery soup house as his cover. The real horror element comes from an old mad doctor-type who somehow brings Lugosi's victims back to life as zombies. It doesn't make a lot of sense.

CUDOTVORNI MAC

(USA: THE MAGIC SWORD)

Yugoslavia, 1949 (1952). Dir: Voislav Nanovic. With: Rade

Above: Frankenstein Meets the Wolf Man.

Markovich, Milvoye Zhivanovich, Vera Ilich Djukovich, Marko Marinkovitch. Zvezda/Avala. B&W.
Fairy tale fantasy about a demon who terrorises the lands around his castle. With a witch, a talking fish and the Golem-like giant Bas-Chelik, who is defeated by a shepherd.

DR. TERROR'S HOUSE OF HORRORS

USA, 1943. National Roadshow. B&W.
The producers of this compilation movie edited together sequences from five independent movies, including Dreyer's *Vampyr* (1932), *The Living Dead* (Germany, 1933; aka *Histoires Extraordinaires*), two Bela Lugosi features, *White Zombie* (1932) and *The Return of Chandu* (1934), and the 1936 version of *The Golem*.

THE FACE OF MARBLE

USA, 1946. Dir: William Beaudine. With: John Carradine, Robert Shayne, Claudia Drake, Maris Wrixon, Rosa Rey, Willie Best. Monogram. B&W.
Mad Professor Randolf (Carradine) experiments with reviving the dead, but his victims quickly expire again with rigid faces. When he resuscitates a Great Dane, the dog becomes semi-transparent, walks through walls and drinks blood. Low budget Monogram madness that includes voodoo love potions and the usual comedy relief from Best.

FORTUNE HUNTERS

(aka GANDY GOOSE IN FORTUNE HUNTERS)
USA, 1946. Dir: Connie Rasinski. Terrytoons/Twentieth Century-Fox. Colour.
Six minute Paul Terry cartoon in which the Frankenstein Monster pursues Gandy Goose through a haunted house. Colourised footage of the Monster is from *G-Man Jitters* (1939).

FRANKENSTEIN

USA, 1940. Dir: Glenn Alvey. Pixilated Pictures. B&W.
A real rarity: the earliest known amateur Frankenstein film (apparently a remake of the 1931 version), distributed through the Interstate Theatre Circuit in Texas.
Remake: THE CURSE OF FRANKENSTEIN (qv; 1957)

FRANKENSTEIN MEETS THE WOLF MAN

USA, 1943. Dir: Roy William Neill. With: Lon Chaney, Ilona Massey, Patric Knowles, Bela Lugosi, Lionel Atwill, Maria Ouspenskaya. Universal. B&W.
The forties horror boom was already failing when Universal decided to make this sequel to *The Wolf Man* (1941) and *The Ghost of Frankenstein* (1942), scripted by Curt Siodmak and atmospherically directed by B-movie veteran Neill. Chaney Jr recreates his role of the doomed lycanthrope Lawrence Talbot from the former, while a frail-looking Lugosi takes over as Frankenstein's creation (a role he originally turned down in 1931), with more than a little help from stunt double Eddie Parker. His stiff portrayal makes more sense when you realise that all references to the Monster's blindness (as a result of a brain transplant in the previous film) and his ability to speak were cut from the release print. After a great opening sequence in which the Wolf Man is accidentally revived by graverobbers, Talbot travels to Transylvania in the hope of discovering a cure for his affliction in the journals of Frankenstein. Instead, he discovers the Monster. The two creatures eventually confront each other and are finally washed away by an exploded dam. The impressive supporting cast includes Atwill as the Mayor, Ouspenskaya as the gypsy Maleva, Dennis Hoey as a police inspector, Dwight Frye and Jeff Corey as villagers, and Massey as Elsa, the daughter of Frankenstein.
Sequel: HOUSE OF FRANKENSTEIN (qv; 1944)

(FJA).

FRANKENSTEIN'S CAT

(aka MIGHTY MOUSE IN FRANKENSTEIN'S CAT)
USA, 1942. Dir: Mannie Davis. Terrytoons/Twentieth Century-Fox. Colour.

Seven minute Paul Terry cartoon in which Mighty Mouse battles a monster cat and knocks his head off, freeing a kidnapped baby bird.

GANG BUSTERS

USA, 1942. Dir: Ray Taylor and Noel Smith. With: Kent Taylor, Irene Harvey, Robert Armstrong, Ralph Morgan, Richard Davies, Grace Cunard. Universal. B&W.

Thirteen chapter serial based on the factual radio show. Scientist Morgan is the head of an organisation called The League of Murdered Men, who uses capsules to bring supposedly executed criminals back to life. In the end, he is killed by a speeding subway train while trying to escape.

THE GHOST OF FRANKENSTEIN

USA, 1942. Dir: Erle C. Kenton. With: Lon Chaney, Sir Cedric Hardwicke, Ralph Bellamy, Lionel Atwill, Bela Lugosi, Evelyn Ankers. Universal. B&W.

The fourth entry in Universal's Frankenstein cycle (following *Son of Frankenstein* [1939]) reduces the series to the level of a formula horror thriller utilising the studio's contract players. Hardwicke's Ludwig, the second son of Frankenstein (he also plays his father's ghost), is totally overshadowed by Atwill's mad Dr Bohmer and Lugosi's resurrected Ygor. Between them, they rescue the Monster from the lime pit

and restore his strength. Chaney Jr plays Frankenstein's creation as a dumb brute, despite a failed attempt to recapture Karloff's pathos in a scene where he kidnaps a little girl. With Barton Yarborough, Dwight Frye, Holmes Herbert, Lionel Belmore, Lawrence Grant, and Eddie Parker doubling for Chaney.

Sequel: FRANKENSTEIN MEETS THE WOLF MAN (qv; 1943)

THE GREAT PIGGY BANK ROBBERY

USA, 1946. Dir: Robert Clampett. Voices: Mel Blanc. Warner Bros. Colour.

Six minute Looney Tunes cartoon parody of the *Dick Tracy* comic strip. After being hit on the head while reading his favourite comic book, Daffy Duck dreams he is detective Duck Twacy, menaced by various bizarre villains, including Neon Noodle who looks exactly like Frankenstein's Monster. With a guest appearance by Porky Pig.

HARE CONDITIONED

USA, 1945. Dir: Charles M. (Chuck) Jones. Voices: Mel Blanc. Warner Bros. Colour.

Looney Tunes cartoon in which Bugs Bunny is chased around a department store until he scares the manager by doing an impersonation of the "horrible Frankencense Monster".

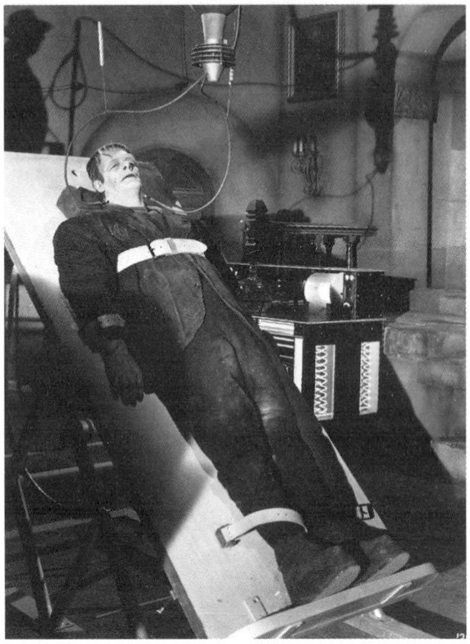

Top: *The Ghost of Frankenstein.*
Above: *House of Frankenstein.*
Left: *Meet Frankenstein.*

HARE TONIC

USA, 1945. Dir: Charles M. (Chuck) Jones. Voices: Mel Blanc, Arthur Q. Bryan. Warner Bros. Colour.

Looney Tunes cartoon in which Bugs Bunny impersonates Dr Killpatient and the Frankenstein Monster to torment Elmer Fudd, who is convinced he has 'rabbititus' and is turning into a rabbit.

HELLZAPOPPIN'

USA, 1941. Dir: H.C. Potter. With: Ole Olsen, Chic Johnson, Martha Raye,

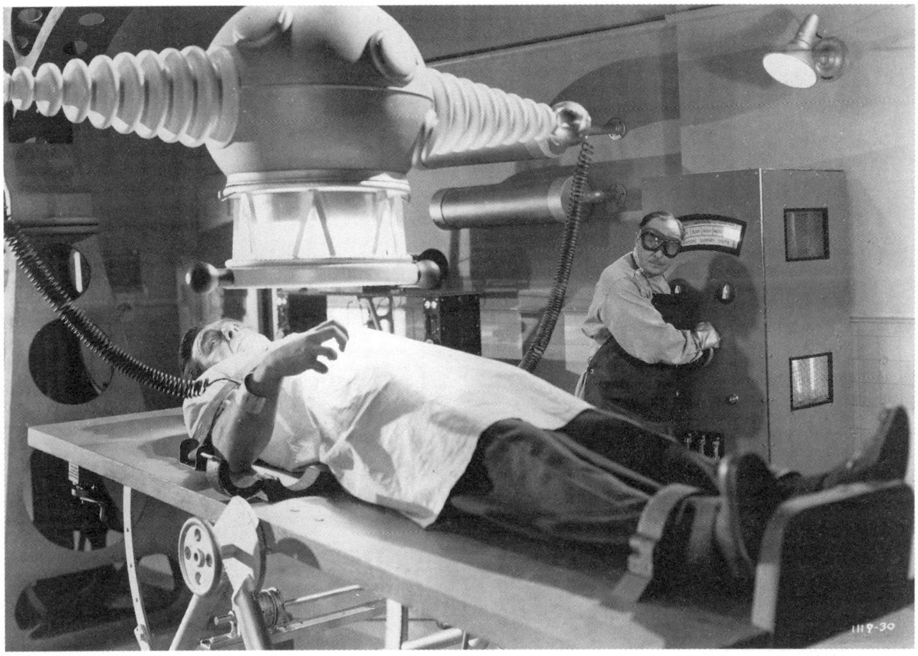

Hugh Herbert, Jane Frazee, Mischa Auer. Universal/Mayfair. B&W.
'Any similarity between *Hellzapoppin'* and a motion picture is purely coincidental' warns the opening caption of this near-plotless musical comedy based on the successful Broadway stage revue. The comedy duo of Olsen and Johnson try to help their friend Jeff (Robert Paige) put on a backyard show and win the hand of heiress Kitty (Frazee). Along the way there's a sequence set in Hell, *Citizen Kane* (1941) and *Here Comes Mr. Jordan* (1941) gags, John P. Fulton's invisible effects, a talking bear and an appearance by the Universal Frankenstein Monster (played by actor-stuntman Dale Van Sickel). With Elisha Cook Jr, Shemp Howard and midgets Angelo Rossitto (as a devil) and Billy Curtis.

HOLLYWOOD STEPS OUT

USA, 1941. Dir: Fred (Tex) Avery. Warner Bros. Colour.
Seven minute Merrie Melodies cartoon in which the Frankenstein Monster dances a conga in a posh Hollywood nightclub. With caricatures of Boris Karloff, Peter Lorre, the Three Stooges and numerous other movie stars.

HOUSE OF DRACULA

USA, 1945. Dir: Erle C. Kenton. With: Lon Chaney, Martha O'Driscoll, John Carradine, Lionel Atwill, Onslow Stevens, Glenn Strange. Universal. B&W.
Uninspired sequel to *House of Frankenstein* (1944). Dr Franz Edelmann (Stevens) attempts to cure the monsters with the aid of his scientifically-created mould! But Carradine's suave Count Dracula decides he enjoys being a vampire and turns Edelmann into one as well. The mad doctor tries to revive the Frankenstein Monster (Strange, who is given little to do) during the blazing climax (lifted from *The Ghost of Frankenstein* [1942]), while Lawrence Talbot (Chaney Jr) is finally 'cured' after changing into the Wolf Man only once. O'Driscoll portrays a beautiful hunchbacked nurse, Atwill turns up as another police inspector and Skelton Knaggs plays an angry villager. Worth catching for John P. Fulton's wonderful man-into-bat transformations. Clips from *Bride of Frankenstein* (1935) turn up in a nightmare sequence.
Sequel: MEET FRANKENSTEIN (qv; 1948)

HOUSE OF FRANKENSTEIN

USA, 1944. Dir: Erle C. Kenton. With: Boris Karloff, Lon Chaney, John Carradine, J. Carrol Naish, Anne Gwynne, Lionel Atwill. Universal. B&W.
Entertaining sequel to *Frankenstein Meets the Wolf Man* (1943), based on a story by Curt Siodmak. Karloff's mad Dr Gustav

Above left: *Man Made Monster.*
Below left: *Master Minds.*
Below: *Third Dimensional Murder.*

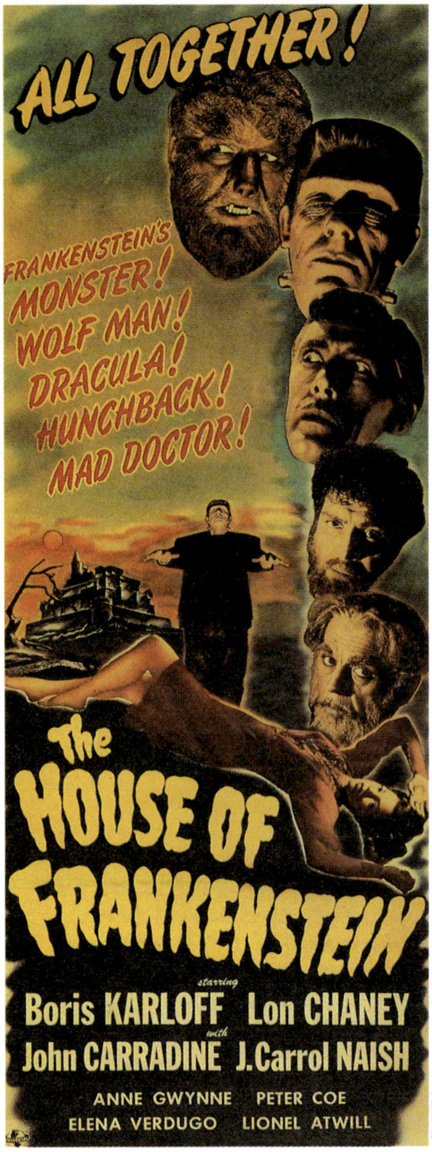

(RVB).

Niemann (the brother of a former assistant to the original Dr Frankenstein) and Daniel the homicidal hunchback (Naish) escape from a prison for the criminally insane and take over a travelling carnival. Pursued by Atwill's police inspector, they revive 'Baron Latos' (Carradine as Count Dracula, complete with top hat) before arriving at Castle Frankenstein, where they discover the Wolf Man (Chaney Jr as Lawrence Talbot, still trying to find a cure) and the Frankenstein Monster (Glenn Strange, who isn't given much to do, despite being coached in the role by Karloff). In the end, the villagers put a stop to it all and the Monster drags Niemann into the quicksands. Originally announced as *Chamber of Horrors* and *The Devil's Brood*, it also includes brief appearances by George Zucco, Frank Reicher and Sig Ruman.

Sequel: HOUSE OF DRACULA (qv; 1945)

THE JAILBREAK

(aka MIGHTY MOUSE IN THE JAILBREAK)
USA, 1946. Dir: Eddie Donnelly. Terrytoons/Twentieth Century-Fox. Colour.

Six minute Paul Terry cartoon in which the Frankenstein Monster and Count Dracula are prisoners on Alcatraz. This was a sequel to *Mighty Mouse Meets Bad Bill Bunion* (1945).

THE LADY AND THE MONSTER

(aka TIGER MAN. UK: THE LADY AND THE DOCTOR)
USA, 1944. Dir: George Sherman. With: Vera Hruba Ralston, Richard Arlen, Erich von Stroheim, Helen Vinson, Mary Nash, Sidney Blackmer. Republic. B&W.

The first attempt to film Curt Siodmak's 1943 novel *Donovan's Brain* features Czechoslovakian non-actress Ralston (then married to Herbert Yates, the head of Republic Studios), a Gothic castle in the Arizona desert and von Stroheim's mad Dr Franz Mueller. When renowned financier W.H. Donovan is killed in a plane crash, Mueller keeps his brain alive in the hope that it will reveal the secrets to a hidden fortune. The scene where the brain comes to life and controls hero Arlen is genuinely eerie, but a subplot involving blackmailers Vinson and Blackmer is simply forgotten. Atmospheric low budget chiller, only let down by a muddled screenplay. Not released until after World War Two in Britain, and then with ten minutes cut and a significant title change.

Remake: DONOVAN'S BRAIN (qv; 1953)

MAN MADE MONSTER

(aka THE ATOMIC MONSTER. UK: THE ELECTRIC MAN)
USA, 1941. Dir: George Waggner. With: Lionel Atwill, Lon Chaney Jr, Anne Nagel, Frank Albertson, Samuel S. Hinds, William Davidson. Universal. B&W.

Originally announced in 1937 to co-star Boris Karloff and Bela Lugosi under various titles, including *The Man in the Cab* and *The Mysterious Dr R*. Instead, it became a neat little B-feature, based on a story co-written by Harry J. Essex, which Universal used to launch Chaney Jr's horror film career. He plays 'Dynamo' Dan McCormick, the Electric Man, transformed by Atwill's gleefully insane Dr Paul Rigas into an electric zombie superman whose touch is lethal. Chaney's limited acting ability fails to convey any of the pathos which Karloff might have brought to the role, but any shortcomings are more than made up for by Atwill ("Mad! Of course I'm mad!"). Excellent John P. Fulton optical effects and an exciting climax where Chaney's power leaks out along a barbed wire fence.

THE MAN WITH NINE LIVES

(UK: BEHIND THE DOOR)
USA, 1940. Dir: Nick Grindé. With: Boris Karloff, Roger Pryor, Jo Ann Sayers, Stanley Brown, John Dilson, Hal Taliaferro. Columbia. B&W.

The second of five mad doctor movies Karloff made under contract to Columbia during the late 1930s and early forties. He portrays Dr Leon Kravaal, accidentally frozen in his subterranean ice chamber for ten years. When he is revived, he starts experimenting on those he believes responsible for upsetting his plans a decade before. This was cut by six minutes when originally released in Britain.

MASTER MINDS

USA, 1949. Dir: Jean Yarbrough. With: The Bowery Boys (Leo Gorcey, Huntz Hall, Billy Benedict, Gabriel Dell), Alan Napier, Jane Adams. Monogram. B&W.

Napier's mad doctor decides that Huntz Hall's brain is the perfect fit for his ape man, Atlas (Glenn Strange), in this typical Bowery Boys comedy. With Skelton Knaggs, Minerva Urecal and make-up created by the great Jack Pierce (*Frankenstein* [1931], etc).

THE MONSTER AND THE GIRL

USA, 1941. Dir: Stuart Heisler. With: Ellen Drew, Robert Paige, Paul

Lukas, Joseph Calleia, Onslow Stevens, George Zucco. Paramount. B&W.
This starts as a straight gangster thriller, with Scot Webster (a wooden performance by Phillip Terry) trying to stop his sister Susan (Drew) from being tricked into prostitution by crime boss Bruhl (Lukas) and his henchmen. In revenge, they frame Webster for murder and he's executed. The film then abruptly changes direction as Zucco's reasonably sane Dr Parry transplants the innocent man's brain into a gorilla. Under the control of the human mind, the beast (an impressive ape suit) escapes and kills the gangsters one by one. This unusual B-movie isn't as silly as it sounds and director Heisler creates some nicely atmospheric moments. An unbilled Edward Van Sloan turns up as the prison governor.

OLD MANOR HOUSE

UK, 1948. Dir: Harold F. Mack. British Animation Productions. Colour.
Seven minute cartoon in which Bubble and his talking taxi Squeaky encounter the Frankie Stein Monster in a haunted house.

SPOOK BUSTERS

USA, 1946. Dir: William Beaudine. With: The Bowery Boys (Leo Gorcey, Huntz Hall, Bobby Jordan, Gabriel Dell), Douglass Dumbrille, Charles Middleton. Jan Grippo Productions/ Monogram. B&W.
Typical Bowery Boys vehicle directed by William ('one shot') Beaudine. While investigating the supposedly haunted mansion of Menlo the Magician, the boys discover Dumbrille's mad scientist, who wants to transplant Huntz Hall's brain into a gorilla. Who would notice the difference? Filmed under the title *Ghost Busters*.

Above: The Lady and the Monster.

THIRD DIMENSIONAL MURDER

USA, 1940. Dir: George Sidney. With: Pete Smith, Ed Payson. Metro-Goldwyn-Mayer. B&W.
One of narrator Pete Smith's Metroscopix Specials, this seven minute short was originally released in 3-D. When a man enters the old Smith Mansion at midnight, he encounters ghosts, a witch, a skeleton, a masked archer and the Frankenstein Monster (Payson, in Jack Kevan's make-up inspired by Universal's *Son of Frankenstein* [1939]).

(RVB).

WHAT'S COOKIN' DOC?

USA, 1944. Dir: Robert Clampett. Voices: Mel Blanc. Warner Bros. Colour.
Seven minute Merrie Melodies cartoon set on Academy Awards night, in which Bugs Bunny does impressions of Edward G. Robinson, Jerry Colonna, Bing Crosby and the Frankenstein Monster to convince the committee he deserves an Oscar more than James Cagney. With clips from *Hiawatha's Rabbit Hunt* (1941) and the live-action *A Star is Born* (1937). This was later included in the feature compilation *Bugs Bunny Superstar* (1975).

MEET FRANKENSTEIN

(UK: ABBOTT AND COSTELLO MEET THE GHOSTS)
USA, 1948. Dir: Charles Barton. With: Bud Abbott, Lou Costello, Lon Chaney, Bela Lugosi, Glenn Strange, Lenore Aubert. Universal-International. B&W
Originally intended to be a serious entry in the series entitled *The Brain of Frankenstein*, this marked Universal's last outing for all its classic monsters. Bud and Lou (in probably their best film) team up with Chaney Jr's hero/Wolf Man to stop Dracula and a mad female scientist (Aubert) from transplanting Lou's brain into the Frankenstein Monster (Strange). For the climactic sequence, it's Chaney under the Monster make-up throwing Aubert's stunt double through a window, after Strange broke his foot. Director Barton plays the horror elements straight, thus emphasising the classic comedy routines, and an uncredited Vincent Price is heard as the Invisible Man. Costello apparently compiled his own collection of out-takes, many involving Strange's Monster.
Remake: CASTLE OF THE MONSTERS (qv; 1957)

Also Featuring...

Lionel (Alfred William) Atwill appeared in Universal's classic Frankenstein saga more than any other actor.

Born on 1 March 1885 in Croydon, England, he made his theatrical début on the London stage in 1905 as a footman in *The Walls of Jericho*. After theatrical tours in Britain and Australia, he arrived in America in 1915, making his Broadway début in 1917 in the title role of *The Lodger*. His first film was *Eve's Daughter* (1918), and he moved to Hollywood in 1932 to re-create his stage performance in *The Silent Witness*.

He soon achieved fame as a villain, starring in *Doctor X* (1932), *Mystery of the Wax Museum* (1932), *The Vampire Bat* (1933), *Murders in the Zoo* (1933), *The Devil is a Woman* (1935), *Captain Blood* (1935) and *The Three Musketeers* (1939).

"See — one side of my face is gentle and kind...the other profile is cruel and predatory and evil," explained the actor. "It all depends on which side of my face is turned toward you — or the camera."

Known as 'Pinky' by his associates, Atwill liked to attend sensational murder trials and drove around Hollywood in a Rolls Royce marked by bullet holes.

He played the memorable one-armed Inspector Krogh in *Son of Frankenstein* (1939) and the mad Dr Theodor Bohmer in *The Ghost of Frankenstein* (1942). However, after denying accusations of showing pornographic movies and holding orgies at his Pacific Palisades mansion to a Los Angeles County Grand Jury, Atwill finally confessed and was sentenced to five years' probation for perjury. Although the Hays office ordered studios not to hire the actor, Universal cast him as the Mayor of Vasaria in *Frankenstein Meets the Wolf Man* (1943).

"But for the courage and magnanimity of one particular studio, I guess I should be a dead egg now," said Atwill.

The actor publicly wept when he was absolved of his conviction in April 1943, and he appeared in the cameo role of Inspector Arnz in *House of Frankenstein* (1944). However, by the time he played the similar role of Inspector Holtz in *House of Dracula* (1945), the actor was fatally ill with bronchial cancer.

Atwill's other notable films include *Man Made Monster* (1941), *The Mad Doctor of Market Street* (1942), *Night Monster* (1942), *Sherlock Holmes and the Secret Weapon* (1942, as Professor Moriarty) and the serial *Lost City of the Jungle* (1946), in which a double had to be used to complete the actor's scenes.

Lionel Atwill died on 22 April 1946 from respiratory failure. His young wife and new son inherited most of the $250,000 estate.

Dwight (I) Frye was born on 22 February 1899 in Salina, Kansas. He made a film career out of playing bizarre characters, yet in the late 1920s was voted one of Broadway's ten finest actors and was also an accomplished concert pianist.

After touring with a vaudeville show, *The Plot Thickens* marked his

Right: *Lionel Atwill in Son of Frankenstein.*
Below: *Frankenstein (1931).*

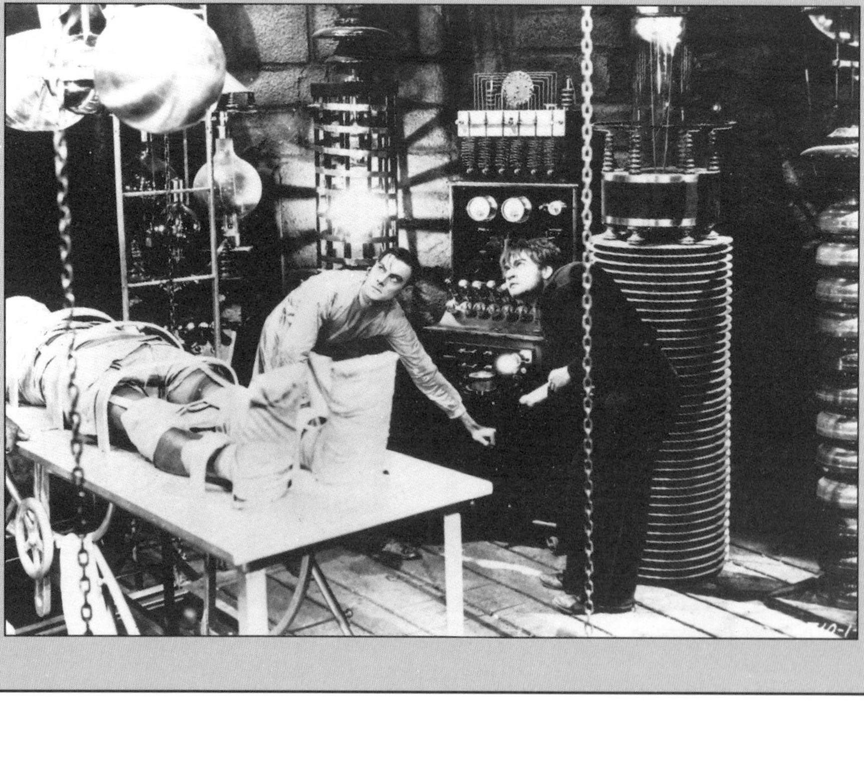

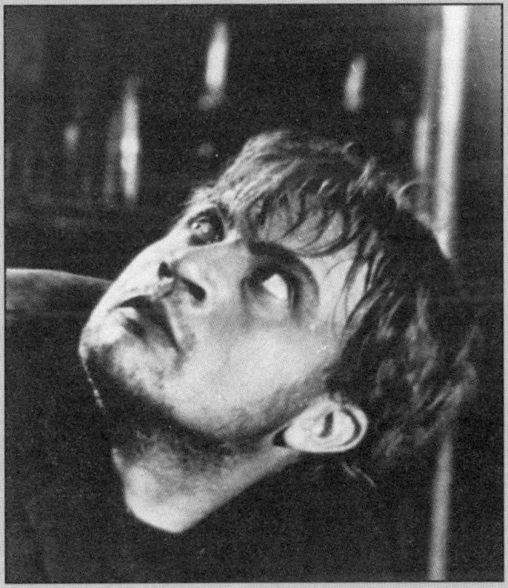

Broadway début in 1922. Entering films as an extra in *The Night Bird* (1928), he moved to Hollywood two years later with his wife and baby son.

After portraying the fly-eating Renfield in *Dracula* (1930), he turned up in often macabre roles in such films as the 1931 version of *The Maltese Falcon*, *The Black Camel* (1931), *The Vampire Bat*, *The Invisible Man* (1933), *The Crime of Dr. Crespi* (1935), *Dead Men Walk* (1943) and the serial *Drums of Fu Manchu* (1940).

"If God is good," the actor lamented, "I will be able to play comedy in which I was featured on Broadway for eight seasons and in which no producer of motion pictures will give me a chance! And please, God, may it be before I go screwy, playing idiots, half-wits and lunatics on the talking screen!"

Unfortunately, he never got his wish, and Universal was content to cast him as the sadistic hunchback Fritz in *Frankenstein* (1931) and the ghoulish Karl in *Bride of Frankenstein* (1935). In the latter film, two of his major scenes ended up on the cutting room floor, while his entire role as a villager in *Son of Frankenstein* was excised. After being reduced to playing a voyeur in a stag film, Frye turned up for a day's work as an angry villager in *The Ghost of Frankenstein*, and appeared as Rudi, yet another villager, in *Frankenstein Meets the Wolf Man*.

In an attempt to support his family, the actor spent his nights designing bombsights while by day he toured the casting offices. Frye had signed to play US Secretary of War Newton Baker in *Wilson* (1944) when he died from a heart attack on 7 November 1943. The death certificate listed his profession as 'tool designer'.

Ernest Thesiger only appeared in one Frankenstein movie, but in *Bride of Frankenstein* stole every scene he was in as the diabolical Dr Septimus Pretorius (a role director James Whale originally wanted Claude Rains to play).

"Ernest Thesiger was a delightful laugh for anybody who saw him or talked to him," recalled Elsa Lanchester, "a weird, strange character! Very acid-tongued — not a nasty person at all, just *acid!*"

Born in London on 15 January 1879, the actor made his stage début in 1909 at London's St James Theatre. He appeared in more than fifty movies on both sides of the Atlantic, including James Whale's *The Old Dark House* (1932, as the prissy Horace Femm), *The Ghoul* (1933, with Boris Karloff and Cedric Hardwicke), *The Man Who Could Work Miracles* (1936), *They Drive by Night* (1938), *A Place of One's Own* (1945), *Henry V* (1945), *The Ghosts of Berkeley Square* (1947), *The Man in the White Suit* (1951), *The Robe* (1953) and *Sons and Lovers* (1960).

An exhibited artist and accomplished crochet expert (he wrote a book on the subject, *Adventures in Embroidery*), he was awarded the Order of the British Empire in 1960. Ernest Thesiger died on 14 January 1961 in his London home.

Above left: *Lionel Atwill in Son of Frankenstein.*
Above centre: *Dwight Frye in Frankenstein (1931). (FJA).*
Above right: *Ernest Thesiger in Bride of Frankenstein.*
Below: *Bride of Frankenstein.*

the

Boris Karloff was unable to completely escape the comedy team of Bud Abbott and Lou Costello: In 1948, Universal Studios agreed to pay his hotel bill in New York City if he would pose outside Loew's Criteron Theatre for publicity shots with the advertising display for **Meet Frankenstein**. He agreed, adding "...as long as I don't have to see the movie!"

However, the actor's prediction that the Frankenstein Monster would become "rather an oafish prop" was proved depressingly accurate during the post-War era. Karloff made a return-of-sorts to the series in 1958 when he played the crippled Baron Victor Frankenstein experimenting with atomic energy and his great-great-grandfather's Monster in **Frankenstein 1970**. "I don't mind playing in another Frankenstein movie," revealed the actor, "because I have a sentimental attachment and a sorrow for the things done to the poor Monster in the other pictures which I didn't appear in...I feel I owe him a debt of gratitude and affection."

Around the same period, American International Pictures was enjoying remarkable success grinding out low budget product for the drive-in circuit, and **I Was a Teenage Frankenstein (1957)** was perhaps an inevitable mix of teens and terror. At least character actor Whit Bissell livened things up as the stuffy professor who berated Gary Conway's ugly monster: "I know you have a civil tongue in your head! I sewed it there myself!" Conway recreated his role the following year in another AIP cheapie, **How to Make a Monster (1958)**, while Donald Murphy managed to top even Bissell's arrogant scientist when he began experimenting on teenage girls in **Frankenstein's Daughter (1958)**.

Meanwhile, across the Atlantic, a small British company had already enjoyed some success adapting the BBC-TV **Quatermass** serials into two low budget science fiction movies. Then, in 1957, Hammer Films decided the time was right to produce a remake of Mary Shelley's classic novel in colour for the first time. **The Curse of Frankenstein** became the biggest grossing

I Was a Teenage Frankenstein.

1950s

movie in Britain that year.

Forty-three year-old television actor Peter Cushing (b 1913) starred as the ruthless Baron Victor Frankenstein, while hidden beneath the bandages and Philip W. Leakey's make-up, thirty-five year-old Christopher Lee (b 1922) portrayed the Creature. Universal owned the copyright to its Monster's appearance, so Hammer was forced to come up with another design, as director Terence Fisher (1904-1980) explained: "We wanted the Monster to fit Chris Lee's melancholy personality. We wanted a thing of shreds and patches, but in flesh and blood and organs."

The film was a huge hit around the world, becoming the highest dollar-earner produced by a British studio in 1957 and ushering in the Hammer Age of Horror. Looking to recreate its success, Hammer quickly reteamed the star duo in colour remakes of **Dracula (1958)**, **The Hound of the Baskervilles (1959)** *and* **The Mummy (1959)**.

The Curse of Frankenstein.

The Curse of Frankenstein.

Because Lee's Creature had been dissolved in a bath of acid, the studio ingeniously decided to make Cushing's Victor Frankenstein the recurring character in its series and so the Baron escaped the guillotine to continue his brain-swapping experiments in **The Revenge of Frankenstein (1958)**.

Together, Cushing, Fisher and Hammer embarked on a cycle of Frankenstein films that was set to rival the heyday of the Universal series...

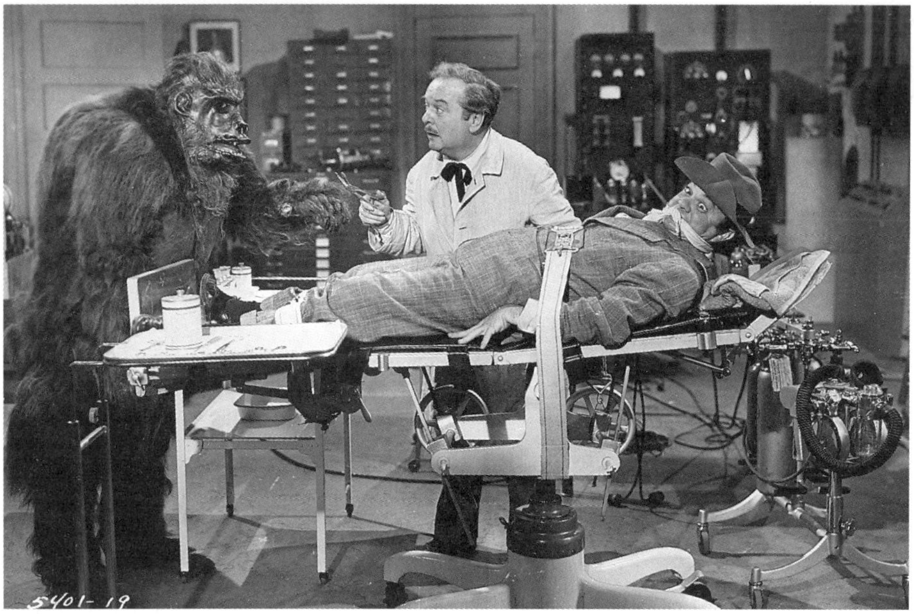

ABBOTT AND COSTELLO MEET DR. JEKYLL AND MR. HYDE

USA, 1953. Dir: Charles Lamont. With: Bud Abbott, Lou Costello, Boris Karloff, Craig Stevens, Helen Westcott, Reginald Denny. Universal-International. B&W.

Slapstick version of Robert Louis Stevenson's classic story. Bud and Lou (in the fifth *Abbott and Costello Meet...* movie) play two turn-of-the-century American policemen in London who are called in to help capture a monster which is terrorising the city. Although it doesn't have the polish of earlier Abbott and Costello vehicles, Karloff adds some much-needed class as Dr Jekyll, but stuntman Eddie Parker mostly plays Mr Hyde beneath an unconvincing mask. Includes an exciting roof-top chase and a sequence in a wax museum, where two uncredited actors portray the Frankenstein Monster and Count Dracula brought to life. Kids will enjoy it, despite originally being given an 'X' certificate by the British Board of Film Censors!

ANAK NG KIDLAT

Philippines, 1959. Dir: Mario Barri. With: Cacilia Lopez, Cesar Ramirez. Tamarawa-Hollywood Far East. B&W.

When a woman is struck by lightning, she becomes pregnant and gives birth to a daughter who can control electricity. The title translates as *Daughter of Lightning*.

THE BLACK SLEEP

(USA: aka DR. CADMAN'S SECRET) USA, 1956. Dir: Reginald Le Borg. With: Basil Rathbone, Akim Tamiroff, Lon Chaney, John Carradine, Bela Lugosi, Herbert Rudley. Bel-Air Productions/United Artists. B&W.

An impressive line-up of horror stars is mostly wasted in this low budget chiller set in nineteenth century England. Sir Joel Cadman (Rathbone, giving his usual fine performance) tries to cure his wife's coma by experimenting on the brains of victims he drugs with Nind Andhera — the Black Sleep. Among his failed experiments are the violent Mungo (Chaney Jr), the insane Borg (Carradine) and the gigantic Curry (Tor Johnson). In his last major performance, Lugosi (who had recently been cured of drug addiction and died the same year) plays Casmir, the mute butler. Producer Howard W. Koch went on to better things.

Above: *The Bowery Boys Meet the Monsters.*
Left: *Castle of the Monsters.*

BOOS IN THE NIGHT

USA, 1950. Dir: I. Sparber. Paramount. Colour.

Eight minute musical cartoon in the Screen Songs series. During the song 'Pack Up Your Troubles', Frankenstein's Monster and a Peter Lorre-type character discover an old house haunted by ghosts.

THE BOWERY BOYS MEET THE MONSTERS

USA, 1954. Dir: Edward Bernds. With: Leo Gorcey, Huntz Hall, Laura Mason, Ellen Corby, Lloyd

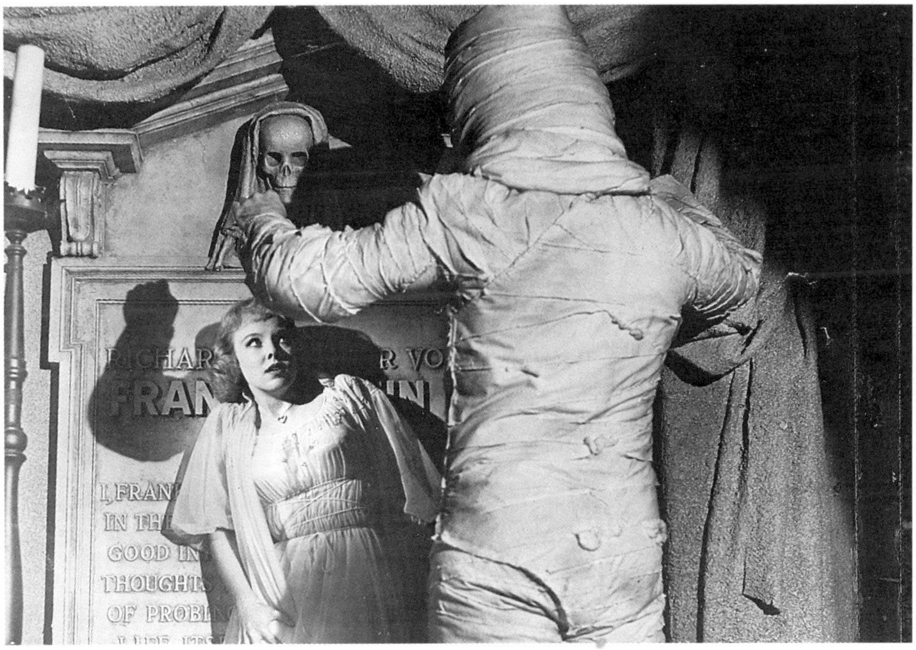

Above: Frankenstein 1970. (FJA).

Corrigan, John Dehner. Allied Artists. B&W.
B-movie comedy in the long-running Bowery Boys series. The boys approach the creepy Gravesend family about using their old dark house as a playground for local kids. Pretty soon a mad doctor wants to put Gorcey's brain into Cosmos the gorilla, Hall is turned into a werewolf, and they get involved with Gorog the robot, a carnivorous plant and a vampire (Paul Wexler).

BRIDE OF THE MONSTER

(aka BRIDE OF THE ATOM)
USA, 1954. Dir: Edward D. Wood Jr. With: Bela Lugosi, Tor Johnson, Tony McCoy, Loretta King, Harvey Dunn, William Benedict. Edward D. Wood Jr Productions/Exclusive. B&W.
In one of his last major performances, seventy-three year-old Lugosi hams it up as mad scientist Dr Vornoff trying to create a race of electronic supermen with the help of the monstrous Lobo (Johnson) and a particularly unconvincing giant octopus (left over from *Reap the Wild Wind* [1942]). With bottom-of-the-barrel production values and a hilarious script by Ed Wood Jr and Alex Gordon. Eddie Parker doubled for the supposedly superhuman Lugosi during the climax. Hero McCoy's father financed the film, but poor old Lugosi earned just $1,000 for this embarrassment!
Sequel: NIGHT OF THE GHOULS (1959)

CASTLE OF THE MONSTERS

(Orig: EL CASTILLO DE LOS MONSTRUOS)
Mexico, 1957. Dir: Julián Soler. With: 'Clavillazo' (Antonio Espino), Evangélina Elizondo, Carlos Orellana, Guillermo Orea, Germán Robles. Producciones Sotomayor/ Columbia. B&W.
Just what we needed, a Mexican version of (Abbott and Costello) *Meet Frankenstein* (1948). Comedians Clavillazo and Elizondo play newly-weds trapped in a castle with a gorilla, a mummy, a werewolf, a vampire (Robles), the Creature from the Black Lagoon and Frentenstein's (*sic*) Monster.
Remake: FRANKENSTEIN, EL VAMPIRO Y CIA (qv; 1961)

CISARUV PEKAR A PEKARUV CISAR

(aka THE EMPEROR'S BAKER)
Czechoslovakia, 1951. Dir: M. (Martin) Fric. With: Janem Werichem, Marie Vasova, Natasha Gollova, Bohuslav Zahorsky, Jiri Plachy, Zdenek Stepanek. Vypravny Film/Dvou Castech. Colour.
Comedic parable set in the Prague of 1610. While his subjects starve, Emperor Rudolph II (Werichem) uses the state treasury to finance attempts at transmuting lead into gold and building a Golem. However, a lowly baker (the Emperor's double, also played by Werichem) creates his own Golem which bakes bread for the whole country. The title translates as *Emperor's Baker, Baker's Emperor.*
Remake: THE GOLEM (qv; 1966)

THE COLOSSUS OF NEW YORK

USA, 1958. Dir: Eugène Lourié. With: John Baragrey, Mala Powers, Otto Kruger, Robert Hutton, Ross Martin, Charles Herbert. Paramount. B&W.
Juvenile science fiction adventure from

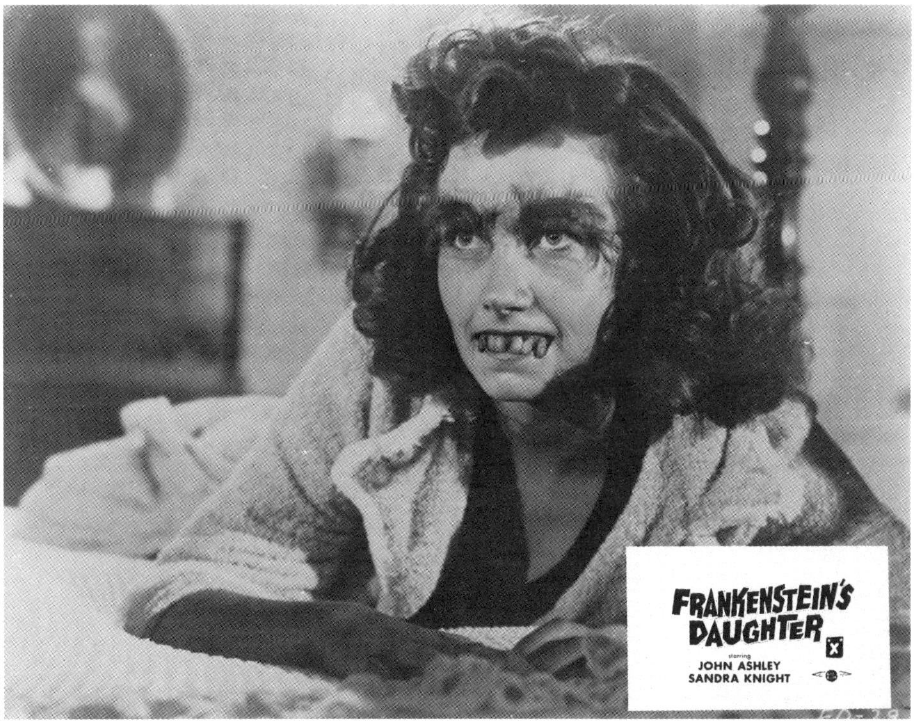

the director of *The Beast from 20,000 Fathoms* (1953). When Dr Jeremy Spensser (Martin) is killed in a car accident, his father (Kruger) transplants his brain into the body of a giant robot (played by seven-foot four-inch actor Ed Wolff). Although the script attempts to say something meaningful about life and death, the film soon becomes predictable as things go wrong and the robot rampages through New York's United Nations building.

CREATURE WITH THE ATOM BRAIN

USA, 1955. Dir: Edward L. Cahn. With: Richard Denning, Angela Stevens, Michael Granger, Linda Bennett, Harry Lauter, Tristram Coffin. Columbia/Clover. B&W.

Scripted by Curt Siodmak (*Donovan's Brain*). Denning plays a pipe-smoking police doctor who discovers that an ex-Nazi scientist (Gregory Gay) is replacing dead gangster's brains with atomic energy and turning them into radioactive zombie killers. More low budget madness from producer Sam Katzman.

THE CURSE OF FRANKENSTEIN

UK, 1957. Dir: Terence Fisher. With: Peter Cushing, Hazel Court, Robert Urquhart, Christopher Lee, Valerie Gaunt, Noel Hood. Hammer Films. Colour.

The film that launched the Hammer house of horror and made the names of Cushing, Lee and director Fisher synonymous with the horror genre. Jimmy Sangster's Gothic screenplay returns to Mary Shelley's original novel (with added gore and sex) as Baron Victor Frankenstein (Cushing) tries to convince his jailors that the murders for which he's been condemned to death were committed by a monster he created in his laboratory. Lee's features as the Creature are mostly hidden beneath Phil Leakey's scarred make-up (Universal controlled the rights to their traditional image) and he plays the role simply as a homicidal maniac, lacking any of the subtlety of Karloff's performance. However, it is Cushing who dominates the film as the obsessed and uncaring Victor,

and it was his character who became the focus of the sequels. Made for just $250,000, it grossed millions.

Sequel: THE REVENGE OF FRANKENSTEIN (qv; 1958)
Remake: THE HORROR OF FRANKENSTEIN (qv; 1970)

DONOVAN'S BRAIN

USA, 1953. Dir: Felix Feist. With: Lew Ayres, Gene Evans, Nancy Davis, Steve Brodie, Tom Powers, Lisa K. Howard. Dowling Productions. B&W.

Second movie version of Curt Siodmak's novel (adapted by Hugh Brooke and scripted by director Feist). Unsympathetic scientist Patrick Cory (Ayres) and drunken assistant Dr Frank Schratt (Evans) are experimenting with keeping animal tissue alive after death. However, when they preserve the brain of ruthless tycoon Donovan following a plane crash, Cory's attempts to establish a telepathic link with the disembodied mind result in the doctor taking on the characteristics of the dead businessman. With Nancy Davis (later Nancy Reagan) as Cory's suffering wife. Herbert L. Strock was the editor and assistant to producer Tom Gries.

Remake: VENGEANCE (qv; 1962)

DOS FANTASMAS Y UNA MUCHACHA

Mexico, 1958. Dir: Rogelio A. Gonzalez. With: 'Tin Tan' (Germán Valdes), Ana L. Peluffo, Manuel 'Loco' Valdez, Luis Aldas, Miguel Manzano. Producciones Sotomayor. B&W.

The musical adventures of a pair of disappearing ghosts who can turn into skeletons. Includes a scene being filmed on a movie set, which features the Frankenstein Monster, a gill man, a werewolf and a mummy. The title translates as *Two Ghosts and a Girl*.

EL FANTASMA DE LA OPERETA

Argentina, 1955. Dir: Enrique Carreras. With: Amelita Vargas, Alfredo Barbieri, Tono Andreu, Gogo Andreu, Inez Fernandez. Belgrano/Cine Argentine. B&W.

A horror comedy that includes a vampire and a Frankenstein-like monster. Not to be confused with the 1959 Mexican movie with the same title.

FOUR SIDED TRIANGLE

(USA: aka THE MONSTER AND THE WOMAN)
UK, 1953. Dir: Terence Fisher. With: Barbara Payton, James Hayter, Stephen Murray, Percy Marmont, John Van Eyssen, Glyn Dearman. Hammer Films. B&W.

American star Payton is loved by two scientists, but she only loves one of them (Van Eyssen). So rival Murray uses the machine he has invented to duplicate her, but the double also falls in love with the same man. Low budget adaptation of the novel by William F. Temple. Four years later Fisher directed Hammer's *The Curse of Frankenstein*.

FRANKENSTEIN 1970

USA, 1958. Dir: Howard W. Koch. With: Boris Karloff, Tom Duggan, Jana Lund, Donald Barry, Charlotte Austin, Irwin Berke. Allied Artists. B&W

Karloff returns to the saga as the crazy, crippled Baron Victor. So that he can afford a shiny new atomic reactor, he allows an American television crew to film a special celebrating the 230th(!) anniversary of Frankenstein at his castle in Germany. But the Nazi-hating Baron kills cast and crew members to restore vital organs to the body of his great-great-grandfather's preserved Monster (Mike Lane). In the end, they are both destroyed in a laboratory explosion and it is revealed that the creature has the features of a younger Victor (also Karloff). Co-scripted by George Worthing Yates, it was filmed in CinemaScope under the title *Frankenstein 1960*. Scenes from this film were later edited into a dream sequence in TV prints of *Daughter of Dr. Jekyll* (1957).

FRANKENSTEIN'S DAUGHTER

USA, 1958. Dir: Richard Cunha. With: John Ashley, Sandra Knight, Donald Murphy, Sally Todd, Harold Lloyd Jr, Felix Locher. Astor Pictures/Layton Film Productions. B&W.

Murphy is wonderful as arrogant scientist Oliver Frank (really the grandson of Frankenstein), who needs fresh organs to create the perfect being. Meanwhile, he uses a drug to periodically turn teenager Trudy Morton (Knight) into a monster with big teeth and ping-pong ball eyes, and creates his own female creature ("Frankenstein's daughter!") using the body of murdered good-time girl Suzy (Todd). In the end, Trudy's boyfriend Johnny (Ashley) throws acid in Frankenstein's face while the monster accidentally sets itself on fire! With Robert Dix and Page Cavanaugh and his Trio (who sing 'Daddy-Bird' and 'Special Date'). An underrated schlock classic, originally co-billed with the same director's *Missile to the Moon* (1958).

FRANK N. STEIN

(aka FEARLESS FOSDICK IN FRANK N. STEIN)
USA, 1951 (1952). Louis G. Cowan, Inc. B&W.

Twenty-four minute marionette short, the seventh in a series of Fearless Fosdick Adventures based on Al Capp's comic strip detective.

The Baron

"I was forty years old and a failure as an actor when the opportunity to play Baron Frankenstein was offered to me," Peter Cushing revealed.

Born in Surrey, England, on 26 May 1913, Cushing had wanted to be an actor since his early days at school. After working as a surveyor's assistant in his father's office for three years, he finally got a job for fifteen shillings a week with a repertory company in Worthing. Once he had saved £50, he bought a one-way ticket to Hollywood.

He found work playing Louis Hayward's stand-in in James Whale's *The Man in the Iron Mask* (1939) and went on to appear in the Laurel and Hardy comedy *A Chump at Oxford* (1939), *Vigil in the Night* (1940) and Whale's *They Dare Not Love* (1940), amongst others. With the outbreak of war, Cushing worked his way home to Britain, helping to entertain the troops with the Entertainments National Service Association (ENSA) in 1941, where he met and married Helen Beck.

A number of small film and television parts followed, including Osric in Laurence Olivier's 1947 adaptation of *Hamlet* (although he didn't share any scenes with another young featured actor named Christopher Lee). Then, in 1956, he gave an award-winning performance as Winston Smith in Rudolph Cartier's live television adaptation of George Orwell's *Nineteen Eighty-Four* for the BBC.

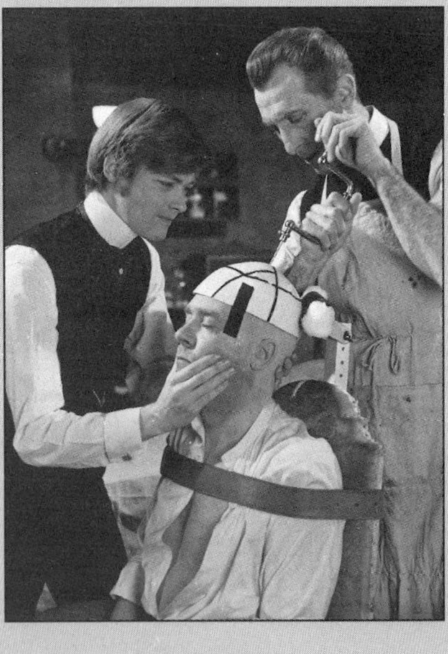

***Above:** The Curse of Frankenstein.*
***Left:** Frankenstein Must Be Destroyed.*

"It was *Nineteen Eighty-Four* which got me labelled 'The Horror Man'," recalled Cushing. "It was the scene with the rats that did it; nothing like that had been seen on TV before."

It was the actor's performance in that production which also attracted the attention of Hammer Films' Michael Carreras. Meanwhile, when Cushing heard that Hammer was considering a remake of *Frankenstein*, he asked his agent to contact the film company. "I'd seen the original many years ago with Boris Karloff and Colin Clive and had thought it was a wonderful film and a wonderful part," he explained.

"That's how it all happened. I had

no idea what I was beginning, though I soon found out that everything Christopher Lee and I did afterwards was described as a horror film, even the Sherlock Holmes film I did."

The Curse of Frankenstein (1957) was a huge box office success around the world and forever typecast Cushing and his co-star Lee as horror stars. However, the actor didn't mind being typed if it meant steady work, as he later revealed: "Despite years of endeavour both in America and in British television, I could see no future and was about to give up acting to design scarves for a living. My dear wife, Helen, was even reduced to taking in laundry."

Numerous films for Hammer and other studios followed. He went on to recreate his role as Baron Frankenstein in *The Revenge of Frankenstein* (1958), *The Evil of Frankenstein* (1964), *Frankenstein Created Woman* (1966), *Frankenstein Must Be Destroyed* (1969) and *Frankenstein and the Monster from Hell* (1973), as well as making a brief cameo appearance as the character in the comedy *One More Time* (1970).

"Frankenstein has tremendous style," explained the actor, "because he is always the same character. The writers do try and get some variety into the films, and you also try to create your character from what the scriptwriter has given you. And as he's always being frustrated, because there are always those beastly villagers knocking on his door, he perhaps becomes more ruthless in the way he goes about getting his materials.

"*Frankenstein* is about a man who has done the impossible in creating another man. He was really trying to prove something. For that reason I have never thought of him as being an essentially evil character, but one so single-minded and obsessed by what he is trying to achieve that any means will justify the end. He is indeed trying to be God, and in a sense, better than God."

Cushing's dedication to the role meant that whenever he was required to perform surgery on screen, he consulted his local doctor about which techniques he should use. "He spent about an hour explaining how to transplant a brain," said the actor. "I also believe that when you are involved with these pictures which are dealing with the impossible, you have to believe in them and love them yourself if you are going to get an audience to believe in them with you. But I don't think that Peter Cushing is all that much like Frankenstein."

Since the mid-1980s, the actor has remained semi-retired from the screen. However, he will always be indelibly linked in the minds of modern audiences with the role of Victor Frankenstein.

"At Hammer, our films had a certain style, a certain charm," Cushing observed, "even though they set out to shock. Really, they weren't so much horror films as fantasies. Too many of today's so-called horror films are crude in the extreme. They are not the sort of films I would want to be in.

"The strange thing is that when we first started these films back in 1957, everything that Frankenstein got up to was pretty impossible. But now Dr Barnard has caught up. He hasn't gone quite as far as me, because I have transplanted brains — not very successfully, I admit — but we all have to start somewhere. Then, transplants began to be shown on television and we thought that would be the end of the Baron, with his crude, do-it-yourself surgery. But he is more popular than ever."

***Above left:** The Curse of Frankenstein.*
***Below:** The Evil of Frankenstein.*

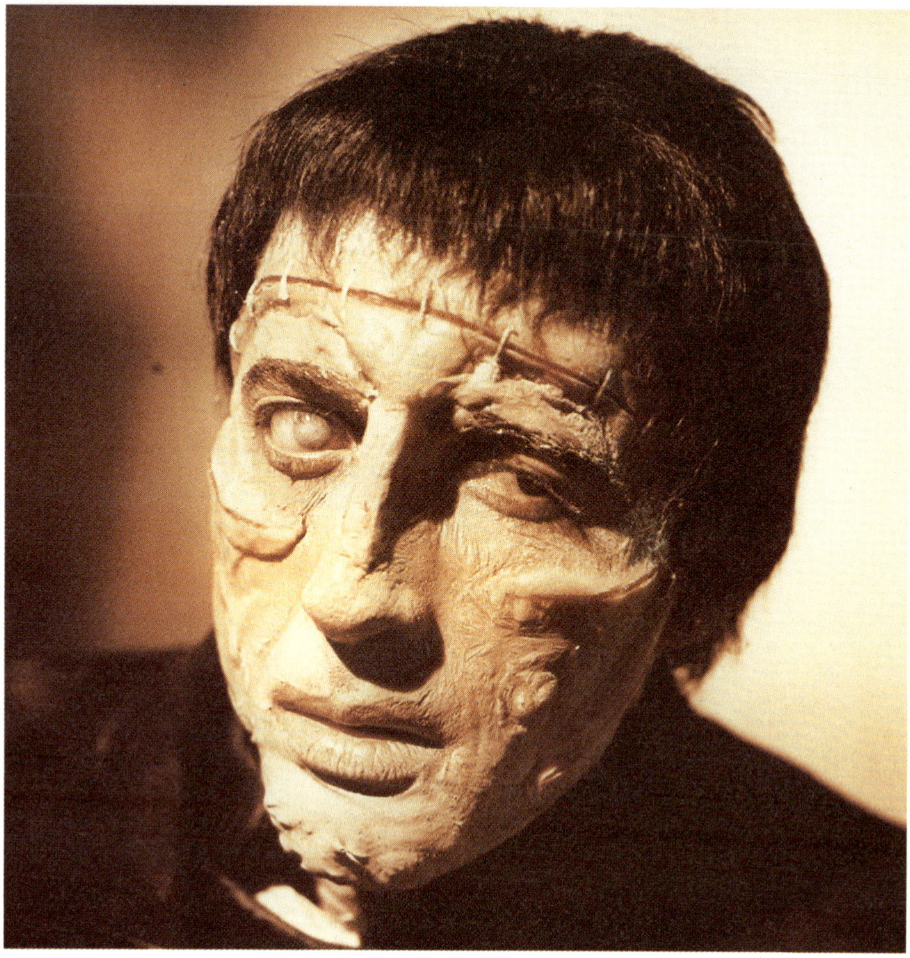

Left: *The Curse of Frankenstein.*

THE GHOST OF DRAGSTRIP HOLLOW

USA, 1959. Dir: William Hole Jr. With: Russ Bender, Jody Fair, Martin Braddock, Jack Ging, Leon Tyler, Paul Blaisdell. American International Pictures/Alta Vista. B&W.

Sequel to *The Hotrod Gang* (1958). Various kids in monster costumes turn up at a rock 'n' roll Halloween party in an abandoned old house, including a teenager dressed as the Frankenstein Monster and frustrated actor Paul Blaisdell in his costume from *The She-Creature* (1956). With music by The Renegades. Filmed under the title *Haunted Hotrod.*

GIANT FROM THE UNKNOWN

USA, 1957. Dir: Richard E. Cunha. With: Edward Kemmer, Sally Fraser, Buddy Baer, Morris Ankrum, Bob Steele, Joline Brand. Screencraft/Astor. B&W.

Professional boxer Baer portrays a Spanish conquistador revived by lightning in twentieth century California. Mineralogist Kemmer teams up with archaeologist Ankrum (giving the film's only decent performance) and his daughter (Fraser) to protect the superstitious townsfolk from the murderous menace. The giant's quite effective make-up was created by veteran Jack Pierce (*Frankenstein* [1931], etc). Producer Arthur P. Jacobs went on to make *Planet of the Apes* (1968), while director/photographer Cunha directed the low budget gem *Frankenstein's Daughter* (1958).

HARAM ALEK

Egypt, 1953. Dir: Issa Karama. With: Ismail Yassine. Studio Guiza. B&W.

Comedy in which Yassine encounters a Frankenstein-type monster, a mummy and a werewolf. The title translates as *Shame on You.*

THE HEAD

(Orig: DIE NACKTE UND DER SATAN)

West Germany, 1959 (1962). Dir: Victor Trivas. With: Horst Frank, Michel Simon, Karin Kernke, Christiane Maybach, Paul Dahlke, Helmut Schmid. Prisma-Wolfgang Hartwig/Rapid-Film/Trans-Lux. Colour.

Professor Abel (Simon) creates Serum-Z, which he uses to keep a dog's severed head alive. But he is decapitated by mad co-worker Dr Ood (Frank), who preserves Abel's living head with the serum and also transplants the head of beautiful hunchbacked nurse Irene (Kernke) onto the body of stripper Lilly (Maybach)! Art director Hermann Warm also designed the expressionist sets for *The Cabinet of Dr. Caligari* (1919).

HOW TO MAKE A MONSTER

USA, 1958. Dir: Herbert L. Strock. With: Robert H. Harris, Paul Brinegar, Gary Conway, Gary Clarke, Malcolm Atterbury, Dennis Cross. American International Pictures. B&W/Colour.

Inventive cheapie from producer Herman Cohen. Harris plays Hollywood make-up artist Pete Drummond, who gets fired when the studio decides to make rock 'n' roll films instead of *Werewolf Meets Frankenstein.* He dresses up as a caveman when he gets his revenge and uses drugged make-up to turn two actors into murderous teenage monsters (Conway, recreating his role from *I Was a Teenage Frankenstein* [1957], and Clarke, replacing Michael Landon from *I Was a Teenage Werewolf* [1957]). With a colour climax, Morris Ankrum, Robert Shayne and guest star John Ashley singing 'You've Got to

Have Ee-ooo'. Spot all the old props from AIP movies.

INDESTRUCTIBLE MAN

USA, 1956. Dir: Jack Pollexfen. With: Lon Chaney, Marian Carr, Casey Adams, Ross Elliott (Elliot), Stuart Randall, Kenneth Terrell. C.G.K. Productions/Allied Artists. B&W.

An unofficial remake of *The Walking Dead* (1936). Chaney Jr (whose career was already on the skids) stars in the mostly non-speaking role of 'Butcher' Benton, an executed psychopath who is accidentally brought back to life by scientist Robert Shayne's electrical experiments. Now a superhuman killer impervious to bullets, the Butcher seeks revenge on those gangland associates he believes double-crossed him. His face horribly burned by a flamethrower in the Los Angeles sewer system, he is finally killed by a massive charge of electricity. Elliott's risible *Dragnet*-style narration tries to make some sense out of this low budget madness.

I WAS A TEENAGE FRANKENSTEIN

(UK: TEENAGE FRANKENSTEIN) USA, 1957. Dir: Herbert L. Strock. With: Whit Bissell, Phyllis Coates, Robert Burton, Gary Conway, George Lynn, John Cliff. American International Pictures. B&W/ Colour.

AIP's follow-up to its box-office hit *I Was a Teenage Werewolf* (1957) is better than expected. Bissell stars as a stuffy Professor Frankenstein in modern Los Angeles, who creates an ugly monster (Conway) out of teenage auto wreck victims. When not ignoring his fiancée (Coates), he's throwing her to the alligator he keeps in the cellar. In the end, Frankenstein decides to give his monster a new face before it electrocutes itself during the predictable climax (which is in colour!). Produced by Herman Cohen. Some sequences later turned up in AIP's *Terror from the Year 5000* (1958).

Sequel: HOW TO MAKE A MONSTER (qv; 1958)

KING TUT'S TOMB

(aka HECKLE AND JECKLE, THE TALKING MAGPIES, IN KING TUT'S TOMB) USA, 1950. Dir: Mannie Davis. Terrytoons/Twentieth Century-Fox. Colour.

Seven minute Paul Terry cartoon in which an Egyptian cat dancer is magically transformed into the Frankenstein Monster (using colourised footage from *G-Man Jitters* [1939]). This also includes a flying carpet, ghosts and mummies.

LADRON DE CADAVERES

Mexico, 1956. Dir: Fernando Méndez. With: Columbia Dominguez, Crox Alvarado, Wolf Rubinskis, Carlos Riquelme, Arturo Maryinez, Eduardo Alcaraz. International Cinematografica/ Columbia. B&W.

Wrestler Guillermo Santa (Rubinskis) and Comandante Robles (Alvarado), the latter disguised as 'El Vampiro', team up to capture the mad Dr Ogden (Riquelme) who is transplanting animal brains into kidnapped athletes and corpses in an attempt to prolong human life. When Santa is killed and his brain replaced with that of a gorilla, he is transformed into an ugly ape monster. With wrestling heroes Lobo Negro (Guillermo Hernandez) and Black Shadow (future Blue Demon, Alejandro Cruz).

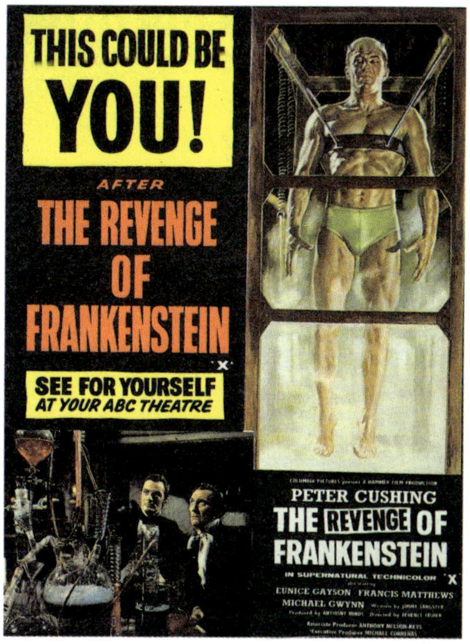

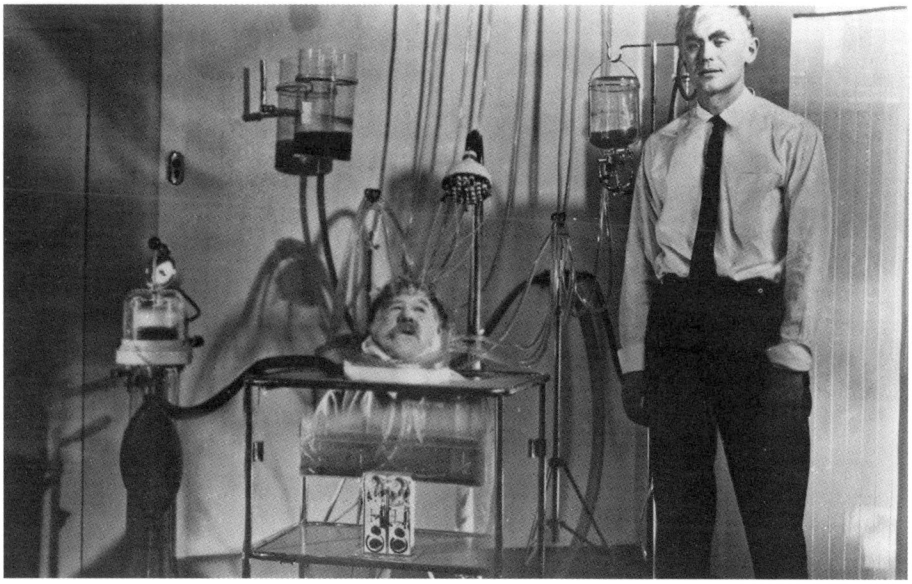

Left: *The Head.*
Below left: *I Was a Teenage Frankenstein.*
Below: *The Revenge of Frankenstein, (FJA).*

MAN IN THE DARK

USA, 1953. Dir: Lew Landers (Lewis Friedlander). With: Edmond O'Brien, Audrey Totter, Ted de Corsia, Horace McMahon, Nick Dennis, Dayton Lummis. Columbia. B&W.

Remake of *The Man Who Lived Again* (1936), with O'Brien as the convict who undergoes a brain operation which removes his memory and criminal tendencies. Unfortunately, the rest of his gang want to know where he stashed the loot. This was the first 3-D film from a major studio, photographed by Floyd Crosby and originally tinted in sepia.

THE MAN WITHOUT A BODY

UK, 1957. Dir: W. Lee Wilder and Charles Saunders. With: Robert Hutton, George Coulouris, Julia Arnall, Nadja Regin, Sheldon Lawrence, Michael Golden. Filmplays/Eros. B&W.

When ageing tycoon Karl Brussard (Coulouris) seeks a cure for a brain tumour he has developed, he steals the head of Nostradamus (Golden) from its crypt in France. However, Dr Philip Merritt (Hutton) and Jean Kramer (Arnall) end up transplanting the seer's reanimated head onto the body of dying laboratory assistant Lew Waldenhouse (Lawrence). As silly as it sounds, it was co-directed by Billy Wilder's less-talented brother.

EL MONSTRUO RESUCITADO

(aka DOCTOR CRIMEN)
Mexico, 1953 (1955). Dir: Chano Urueta. With: Miroslava, Carlos Navarro, José Maria Linares Rivas, Fernando Wagner, Alberto Mariscal, Stefan Berne. International Cinematografica. B&W.

Loosely based on the Frankenstein story and set in the Balkans. Misshapen mad scientist Dr Ling (Rivas) transplants a new brain into the resuscitated body of suicide Ariel (Navarro) and orders him to kidnap journalist Nora (Miroslava). But when Nora and Ariel fall in love, the zombie turns on his creator before being destroyed. The doctor has an apeman servant called Crommer (Berne).

NON PERDIAMO LA TESTA

Italy, 1959. Dir: Mario Mattoli. With: Ugo Tognazzi, Franca Valeri, Carlo Campanini, Xenia Valderi. Galatea. B&W.

Comedy in which a man is pursued by a mad scientist who wants to kill him and study his brain. The title translates as *Let's Not Lose Our Heads.*

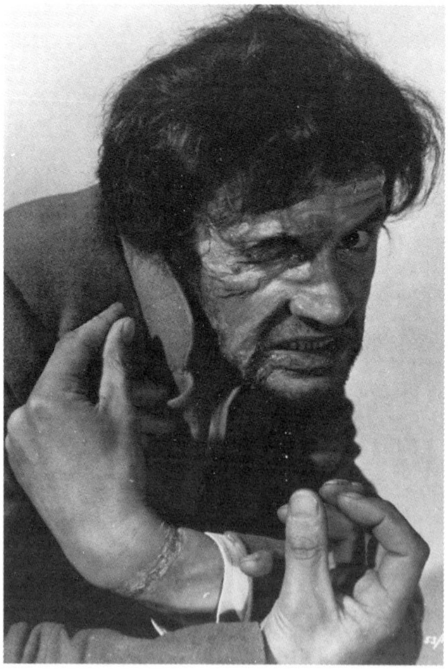

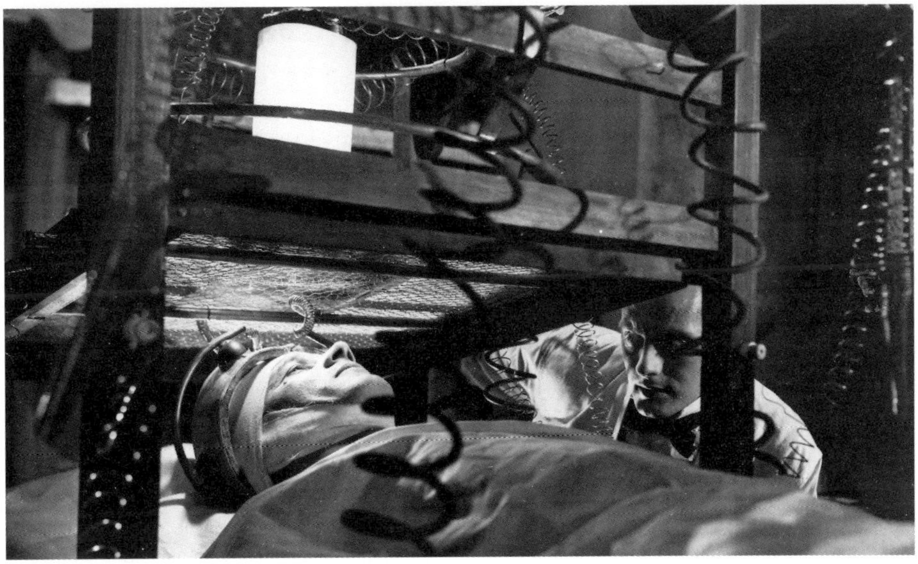

Above: *The Revenge of Frankenstein. (FJA).*
Below left and right: *Torticola contre Frankensberg. (FJA).*

THE REVENGE OF FRANKENSTEIN

UK, 1958. Dir: Terence Fisher. With: Peter Cushing, Eunice Gayson, Francis Matthews, Michael Gwynn, Lionel Jeffries, John Welsh. Hammer Films. Colour.

Good-looking sequel to *The Curse of Frankenstein* (1957), again scripted by Jimmy Sangster. When a pair of comic grave-robbers (Jeffries and Michael Ripper) make the mistake of plundering the 'grave' of Baron Frankenstein (Cushing), he escapes to begin his experiments in another town under the name Victor Stein. With the help of the idealistic Dr Kleve (Matthews), he transplants a dwarf's brain into the body of Karl (Gwynn), who gradually becomes a twisted, murderous cannibal. In the end, the Baron's own brain turns up in a new body. Originally announced as *The Blood of Frankenstein.*

Sequel: THE EVIL OF FRANKENSTEIN (qv; 1964)

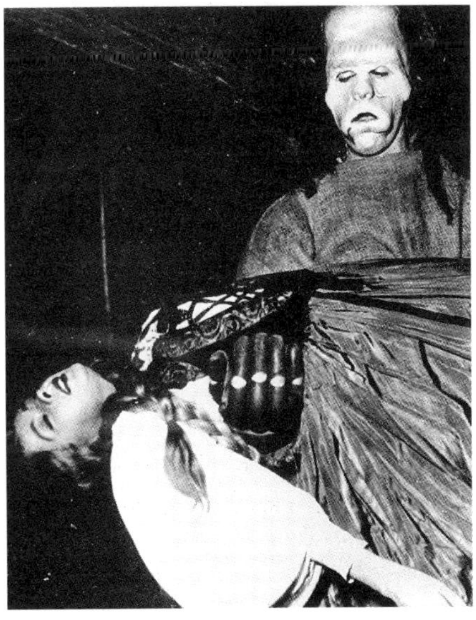

STASERA SCIOPERO

Italy, 1951. Dir: Mario Bonnard. With: Marisa Merlini, Clelia Mantania, Laura Gore, Virgilio Riento. Colamonici Montesi. B&W.

Comedy in which an oddball doctor combines two brains during an operation to create one perfect mind. The title translates as *Striking Tonight.*

TORTICOLA CONTRE FRANKENSBERG

France, 1952. Dir: Paul Paviot. With: Roger Blin, Michel Piccoli, Vera Norman, François Patrice, Helena Menson, Marc Boussac. Les Films Marceau. B&W.

Thirty-six minute short, comprising three segments ('Le laboratoire de l'epouvante', 'La proie du maudit' and 'Le monstre avait un coeur'). Dr Frankensberg (Blin), with the help of his assistant Furrespiegel (Boussac), plans to drain the blood of his niece, Lorelei (Norman). She is saved by Torticola (Piccoli), a monster the doctor has created from corpses. The title translates as *Twisted Neck vs. Frankensberg.*

TRES ERAN TRES

Spain, 1954 (1955). Dir: Eduardo G. Maroto. With: Manolo Moran, Antonio Riquelme, Gustavo Re, Manuel Arbo, Antonio Riquelme. Cooperative dei Cinema/Victory Films. B&W/Colour.

A trio of films based around the creation of a film company called Tiacapa. In the episode entitled 'Una de Miedo' ('A Horror Story'), Dr Salsamendi (Riquelme) creates his own Frankenstein-type monster (Arbo).

UNNATURAL

(Orig: ALRAUNE)
West Germany, 1952 (1956). Dir: Arthur Maria Rabenalt. With: Hildegarde Neff (Knef), Erich von Stroheim, Karl (Carl) Boehm (Karlheinz Böhm), Jula Koschka, Trude Hesterberg. Styria-Carlton/ DCA. B&W.

Fifth adaptation of Hanns Heinz Ewers' story, subtitled '...The Fruit of Evil'. Scientist Ten Brinken (von Stroheim) uses a hanged man's semen to artificially inseminate a prostitute. The result is a soulless woman (Neff) who is incapable of love. Director Rabenalt was better known for his Nazi propaganda films.

EL ZORRO ESCARLATA

Mexico, 1958. Dir: Rafael Baledón. With: Luis Aguilar, Fernando Fernández, Irma Dorantes, Fanny Schiller. Importadora. B&W.

Masked hero El Zorro Escarlata and his assistant arrive in a village plagued by a series of mysterious disappearances. They discover a mad scientist who has created his own monster and a witch he has brought back from the dead.

Sequel: EL ZORRO ESCARLATA EN LA VENGANZA DEL AHORCADO (1958)

the

Having ushered in the third great horror cycle during the late 1950s with its colour remakes of many Universal horror classics, Hammer Films continued to exploit its growing reputation as Britain's 'House of Horror' by teaming up with the American studio to make **The Evil of Frankenstein (1964)**. *Director Freddie Francis (b 1917) replaced Terence Fisher for this second sequel, but Peter Cushing returned as the Baron and the make-up for Kiwi Kingston's Monster resembled Karloff's original with permission.*

The Evil of Frankenstein.

Two years later, Cushing's Baron was himself revived by electricity and dabbled with soul transplants in **Frankenstein Created Woman (1966)**, *but he was still having problems exchanging brains in* **Frankenstein Must Be Destroyed (1969)**. *Both were directed by Fisher.*

In Mexico, Dr Carlos Frankenstein (Andres Soler) created a remote-controlled Monster in **Orlak, el Infierno de Frankenstein (1960)**, *while the comedy* **Frankenstein, el Vampiro y Cia (1961)** *was yet another remake of (Abbott and Costello)* **Meet Frankenstein (1948)**. *Santo, the legendary silver masked wrestler, encountered variations of the Frankenstein Monster in* **Santo contra el Cerebro Diabolico (1961), Samson in the Wax Museum (1963), Santo y Blue Demon vs. Los Monstruos (1968)** *and* **La Venganza de las Mujeres Vampiro (1969)**.

Further versions of the Monster appeared in the Spanish **El Testamento del Frankenstein (1964)**, *and the Japanese* **Frankenstein Conquers the World (1964)** *and its semi-sequel* **War of the Gargantuas (1966)**. *William Beaudine's* **Jesse James Meets Frankenstein's Daughter (1965)** *wasn't much of an improvement over the director's work for Monogram during the 1940s.*

1960s

while **Dracula vs. Frankenstein (1969)** *teamed up the two titular monsters with a werewolf, the mummy and alien invaders, achieving much the same results Universal had twenty-five years earlier.*

There were also plenty of monsters in **Mad Monster Party? (1966)**, *and at least Boris Karloff voiced a puppet version of himself as Baron Von Frankenstein, while Fred Gwynne donned the Universal Frankenstein Monster make-up for* **Munster, Go Home! (1966)**, *a comedy feature based on the popular TV series.*

As the decade came to an end, Boris Karloff was still working. Although he only had half a lung, a steel leg-brace and crippling arthritis which confined him to a wheelchair, he was determined to die "with my boots and my greasepaint on."

Munster, Go Home!

That time came on 2 February 1969, shortly after the eighty-one year-old actor had completed his roles in Peter Bogdanovich's **Targets (1967)**, **Curse of the Crimson Alter (1968**, *with co-star Christopher Lee) and four low-budget Mexican movies. "At my ridiculous age I'm lucky to be able to work," he said. "But I can't breathe and I can't walk. I've got this arthritic knee. Must have been the result of carrying too many bodies up stairs. Bronchitis I caught in California, so don't blame London."*

He died of respiratory problems at King Edward VII Hospital in Midhurst, England. "With his death," said Peter Cushing, "we come to a landmark in the history of cinema. If I ever came up to his shoulders I would be very very happy."

Karloff always credited his role in **Frankenstein (1931)** *for his success: "They tell me I'm typecast," he recalled. "Well, I've been fortunate. Actors are darned lucky to be typecast, like any tradesman who is known for speciality. Thanks to the Monster, I've worked steadily at the work I love best. God bless the old boy, without him I would have been nowhere..."*

THE ADVENTURES OF THE SPIRIT

USA, 1963. Dir: Don Glut. With: Don Glut, Glenn Strange, Billy Knaggs, Bob Burns, Dick Andersen, Jim Harmon, Lionel W. Comport. Colour.

Amateur twelve minute serial in five episodes ('The Phantom Avenger', 'Fangs of Death', 'It Lives Again!', 'Frankenstein's Fury', 'Human Targets') featuring comic book heroes the Spirit (Glut), Superman (Burns), the Phantom Avenger (Andersen) and the Shadow (Harmon). Only listed here because it marks Glenn Strange's return to the role of the Frankenstein Monster, revived by Dr Frankenstein (Knaggs) to battle the Spirit and Superman. It was a sequel to the equally amateur *Monster Rumble* (1961).

ANGELIC FRANKENSTEIN

USA, 1964. Dir: Bob Mizer. With: Ray Greig, Earl Dean. Athletic Models Guild. B&W.

Six minute gay short in which Frankenstein (Greig) creates a perfect male (Dean) who rebels when taught how to use a gun. This was apparently sold through magazines.

ANYBODY ANYWAY

(USA: aka BEHIND LOCKED DOORS)
USA, 1968 (1973). Dir: Charles Romine. With: Joyce Denner, Eve Reeves, Daniel Garth, Ivan Hagar, Irene Lawrence, Andrea Beatrice. Distribpix/SHB/Box Office International. Colour.

When their car runs out of petrol, two

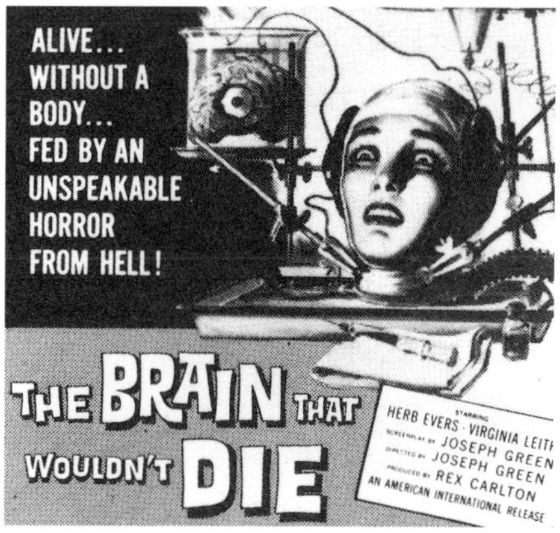

young girls (Denner and Reeves) are held captive in a hilltop mansion by mad scientist Mr Bradley (Garth) and his sinister sister Mina, who are experimenting with creating the perfect love object. In the end, Bradley's statuesque victims apparently return to life and attack him in his burning cellar. This low budget sexploitation movie was cut by eight minutes in Britain.

THE ASTRO-ZOMBIES

(USA: aka THE SPACE VAMPIRES/ SPACE ZOMBIES)
USA, 1968. Dir: Ted V. Mikels. With: Wendell Corey, John Carradine, Tom Pace, Joan Patrick, Tura Satana, Rafael Campos. Harris Enterprises/Ram Ltd. Colour.

'See berserk human transplants!' Wendell Corey (in one of his last films) plays a CIA chief pursuing Mexican-looking foreign agents led by ex-stripper Tura Satana. They are both after Carradine's mad Dr Demarco who, along with his hunchbacked assistant, is using stolen body parts to create an army of Astro-Zombies (wearing silly-looking skeleton masks). Carradine spends most of the film explaining to his deformed helper what's happening while his first zombie experiment (given a psychopath's brain by mistake) is tearing people apart. Made on a minuscule budget and written by Mikels and actor Wayne Rogers (TV's *M*A*S*H*), who also co-executive produced.

THE ATOMIC BRAIN

(aka MONSTROSITY)
USA, 1963. Dir: Joseph (V.) Mascelli. With: Marjorie Eaton, Frank Gerstle, Frank Fowler, Erika Peters, Judy Bamber, Lisa Lang. Emerson Film Enterprises. B&W.

Mascelli, the cinematographer of *The Incredibly Strange Creatures Who Stopped Living and Became Mixed-Up Zombies!!?* (1963) and other Ray Dennis Steckler movies, turned director for this low budget horror film about a mad doctor hired by a wealthy widow to transfer her brain into a younger body. During a test run, the incompetent doctor and his mutant assistant turn two girls into zombies and transplant a cat's brain into a third. The electrical effects were created by Kenneth Strickfaden (*Frankenstein* [1931], etc). Co-starring Xerxes the Cat.

ATTACK OF THE ROBOTS

(Orig: CARTAS BOCA ARRIBA/ CARTES SUR TABLE)
Spain/France, 1966. Dir: Jess (Jesús) Franco. With: Eddie Constantine, Françoise Brion, Fernando Rey, Alfredo Mayo, Sophie Hardy, Marcelo Arroita Jauregui. Hesperia Films/Speva Films/Cine-Alliance/ American International. B&W.

Secret agent Al Peterson/Al Pereira (Constantine) investigates a series of bizarre VIP murders and uncovers a plot by the diabolical Sir Percy (Rey) to create an army of robotised killers from kidnap victims with a certain blood-type. The director has a cameo as a pianist in a Go-Go bar.

Sequel: LES EBRANLEES (1972)
Remake: VIAJE A BANKOK ATAUD INCLUIDO (1985)

Below left: *Attack of the Robots.*
Below: *Carry On Screaming.*

BABAING KIDLAT

Philippines, 1964. Dir: Tony Cayado. With: Liza Moreno, Dolphy, Apeng Daldal, Tony Cayado, Ril Bustamante. Lea. B&W.

When a girl's parents are killed by lightning during her birth, she has the power to fly and electrocute with a touch. The title translates as *Lightning Woman*.

THE BLOOD BEAST TERROR

(USA: aka THE VAMPIRE BEAST CRAVES BLOOD)
UK, 1967. Dir: Vernon Sewell. With: Peter Cushing, Robert Flemyng, Wanda Ventham, Vanessa Howard, David Griffin, Glynn Edwards. Tigon British. Colour.

Cushing stars in the thankless role of a nineteenth century police inspector investigating a series of bizarre deaths. It turns out that Flemyng's Professor Mallinger has created a giant blood-sucking moth that seduces its prey in the guise of a beautiful woman (Ventham)! Basil Rathbone was originally signed to play the mad doctor, but died before filming began. During a student play, Cushing watches a parody of his Frankenstein role when the corpse of a train accident victim is revived by electricity. British comedian Roy Hudd livens things up as a mortuary attendant, but Sewell's direction is, at best, workmanlike. Apparently, Cushing considers this his worst film.

BLUE DEMON CONTRA CEREBROS INFERNALES

(aka BLUE DEMON VS. EL CRIMEN/EL CEREBRO INFERNAL)
Mexico, 1967 (1968). Dir: Chano Urueta. With: Blue Demon (Alejandro Cruz), David Reynoso, Ana Martin, Victor Junco, Barbara Angeli, Noé Murayama. Estudios America/Cinematografica RA. Colour.

The blue-clad hero battles a gang of zombie-like women who are killing scientists and male wrestlers and stealing their brain cells with the help of Dr Sanders (Junco). Co-scripted by ex-wrestler Fernando Oses. The title translates as *Blue Demon versus the Infernal Brain*.

Sequel: BLUE DEMON CONTRA LAS DIABOLICAS (1967)

THE BRAIN THAT WOULDN'T DIE

USA, 1960 (1962). Dir: Joseph Green. With: Herb (Jason) Evers, Virginia Leith, Leslie Daniel, Adele Lamont, Bonnie Sharie, Paula Maurice. Rex Carlton/American International Pictures. B&W.

Sleazy exploitation horror thriller with Evers as an obsessed surgeon who accidentally decapitates his fiancée in a car accident. He keeps her head alive while searching for a big-breasted stripper or photographic model whose body he can use for a transplant. During the gory climax, the mutant pinhead monster he keeps locked in the closet escapes and bites a chunk out of his throat. With plenty of footage of ugly near-naked women.

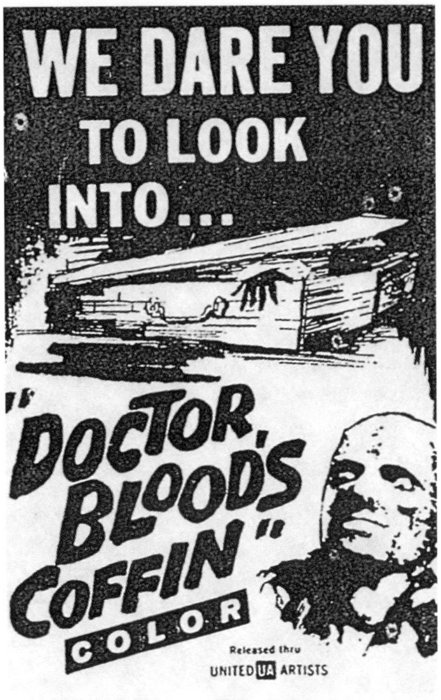

Below: The Creation of the Humanoids.

THE CANDIDATE

(aka PARTY GIRLS FOR THE CANDIDATE)
USA, 1964. Dir: Robert Angus. With: Mamie Van Doren, June Wilkinson, Ted Knight, Eric Mason, Rachel Roman. Cosnat Productions/ Morgan. B&W.

Exposé of political corruption in Washington DC. At a party, people wearing Frankenstein and other monster masks (created by Ellis Burman) try to frighten the guests. Photographed by the great Stanley Cortez.

CARRY ON SCREAMING

UK, 1966. Dir: Gerald Thomas. With: Harry H. Corbett, Kenneth Williams, Jim Dale, Charles Hawtrey, Fenella Fielding, Joan Sims. Anglo Amalgamated. Colour.

The vampish Valeria (Fielding) and her reanimated brother Dr Watt (Williams) are using their Frankenstein-like monster Odbodd (Tom Clegg) to kidnap nubile young girls so they can petrify them (literally!) into show window mannequins. When the creature loses a finger, it grows into Odbodd Jr (Billy Cornelius). This was the twelfth in the long-running British comedy series and one of the best.

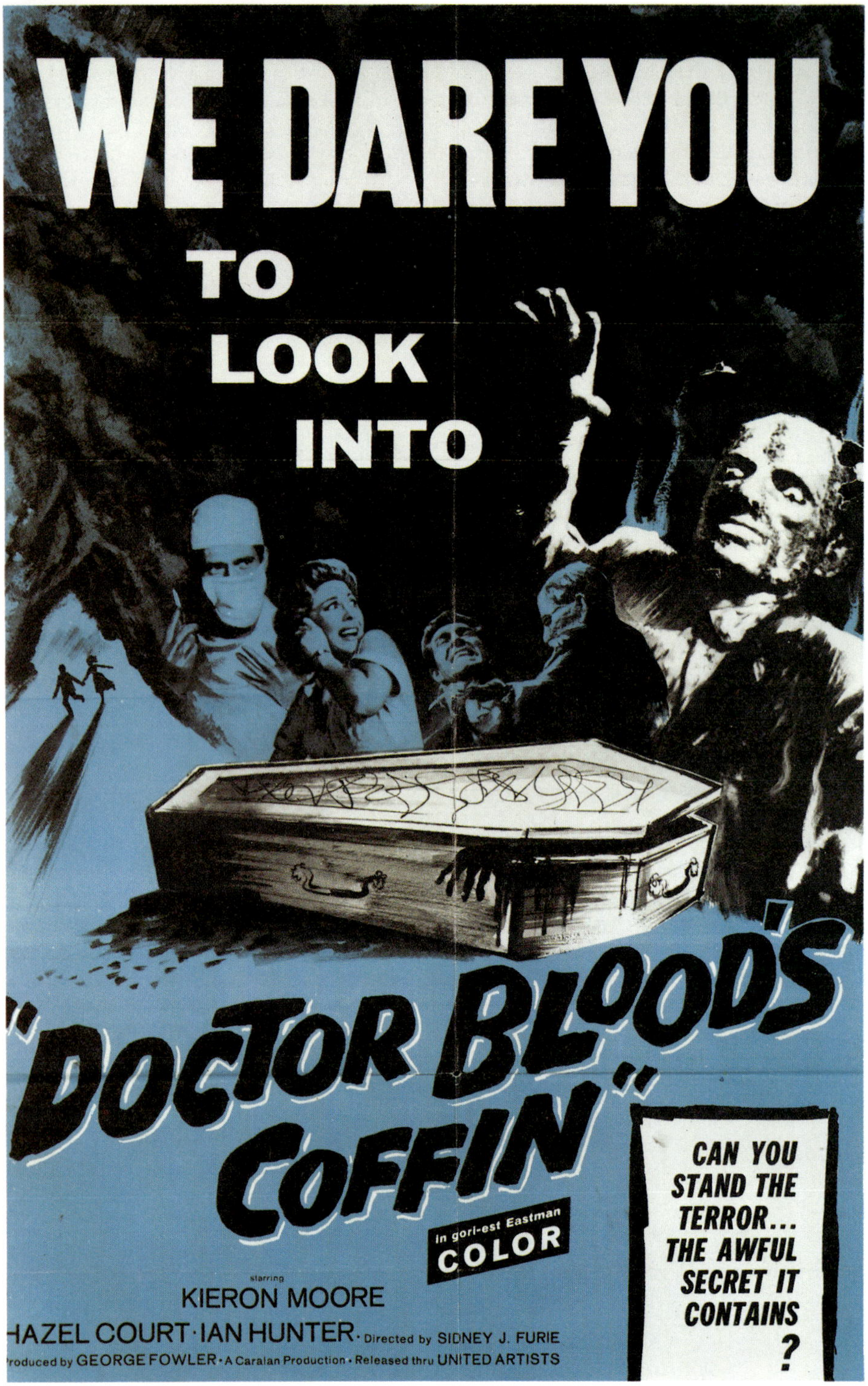

CASINO ROYALE

UK, 1967. Dir: John Huston, Ken Hughes, Val Guest, Robert Parrish and Joe McGrath. With: Peter Sellers, Ursula Andress, David Niven, Orson Welles, Joanna Pettet, Daliah Lavi. Columbia. Colour.

Over two hours of sci-spy mayhem. Ian Fleming's first James Bond novel was the only one not owned by the Saltzman and Broccoli partnership. Columbia kept the title, threw out the plot and turned it into an all-star hit-and-miss comedy. When Sir James Bond (Niven) is called out of retirement to battle SMERSH, he encounters a Caligari-like spy school run by a Dr Strangelove-like administrator (Ronnie Corbett), and Dave Prowse as the Frankenstein Monster. This took two years and five directors to make (and still needed Val Guest to shoot extra sequences with cinematographer Nicolas Roeg). With Woody Allen as the surprise villain, Deborah Kerr, William Holden, Charles Boyer, John Huston as M, Kurt Kasznar, George Raft as himself, Jean-Paul Belmondo, cameos by Peter O'Toole and racing driver Stirling Moss, and Dusty Springfield singing 'Look of Love'.

THE CASTLE OF LUST

(Orig: IM SCHLOSS DER BLUTIGEN BEGIERDE)

West Germany, 1968. Dir: Percy G. Parker. With: Janine Reynaud, Jan Hendriks, Howard Vernon (Mario Lippert), Elvira Berndorff, Michel Lemoine, Pier A. Caminneci. Aquila. Colour.

Gothic horror movie involving heart transplants and reviving the dead.

CATCH US IF YOU CAN

(USA: HAVING A WILD WEEKEND)

UK, 1965. Dir: John Boorman. With: The Dave Clark Five, Barbara Ferris, David Lodge, Robin Bailey, Yootha Joyce, David De Keyser. Warner Bros/Anglo Amalgamated. B&W.

Swinging sixties musical comedy featuring pop group The Dave Clark Five as disillusioned stuntmen searching for a dream island. In one scene, film buff Guy (Bailey) dresses up as the Frankenstein Monster and helps the boys escape from police at a movie masquerade party. This was Boorman's début as a director. With Ronald Lacey and Michael Gwynn.

***Below:** Doctor Blood's Coffin.*

CHARLY

USA, 1968. Dir: Ralph Nelson. With: Cliff Robertson, Claire Bloom, Lilia Skala, Leon Janney, Dick Van Patten, William Dwyer. Selmur/Robertson Associates. Colour.

Based on the novel *Flowers for Algernon* by Daniel Keyes. Robertson gives an Oscar-winning performance as Charly Gordon, a thirty year-old man with the mind of a child of six. When his brain is artificially matured by surgery, he develops into a genius only to discover that the effect is temporary and he will eventually revert to his original state. Often funny, sometimes tragic, but never mawkish science fiction. With an impressive nightmare sequence in which Charly's earlier self pursues the new man.

CHANGE OF MIND

Canada, 1969. Dir: Robert Stevens. With: Raymond St. Jacques, Leslie Nielsen, Susan Oliver, Cosette Lee, Janet MacLachlan, Donnelly Rhodes. Sagittarius/Cinerama. Colour.

The brain of a dying white district attorney is transplanted into the body of a dead black man (St. Jacques). The man in the newly revived body is rejected by his family and former associates, but solves the murder of the black mistress of a bigoted sheriff (Nielsen).

THE CREATION OF THE HUMANOIDS

USA, 1962. Dir: Wesley E. Barry. With: Don Megowan, Erica Elliot, Frances McCann, Don Doolittle, David Cross, Richard Vath. Genie Productions/Emerson Film Enterprises. Colour.

Following an atomic war, the few remaining humans use superintelligent robots called Clickers to do their work. However, vigilante Craigus (Megowan) discovers that renegade scientist Dr Raven (Doolittle) has been transplanting the essence of human brains into the humanoid duplicates in order to develop a new race capable of procreating. Featuring Dudley Manlove as a robot and impressive make-up effects by Jack Pierce (*Frankenstein* [1931], etc). This talky, moralistic little movie was apparently Andy Warhol's favourite film.

THE CURIOUS DR. HUMPP

(Orig: LA VENGANZA DEL SEXO) Argentina, 1967 (1970). Dir: Emilio Vieyra (and Jerald Intrator). With: Richard Bauleo, Gloria Prat, Aldo Barbero, Susana Beltran, Justin Martin, Michel Angel. Productores Argentinos Asociados/Unicorn Releasing/PAA. B&W.

Reporter Bauleo discovers that sadistic, sex-crazed scientist Barbero is kidnapping women to turn into robot slaves because he is controlled by a talking brain kept alive in his laboratory. The American version contains approximately ten minutes of extra softcore footage (featuring, among others, Kim Pope), directed by Intrator.

DOCTOR BLOOD'S COFFIN

UK, 1961. Dir: Sidney J. Furie. With: Kieron Moore, Hazel Court, Ian Hunter, Gerald C. Lawson, Kenneth J. Warren, Andy Alston. Caralan/United Artists. Colour.

Low budget horror chiller set in a small Cornish village. Moore plays Peter Blood, a mad doctor transplanting the hearts of living (but "worthless") bodies into corpses to bring them back to life. Nothing very exciting happens until the climax, when a green-faced rotting zombie takes grisly revenge. From the Canadian director of *The Snake Woman* (1961) and *Lady Sings the Blues* (1972).

Above left: *Charly.*

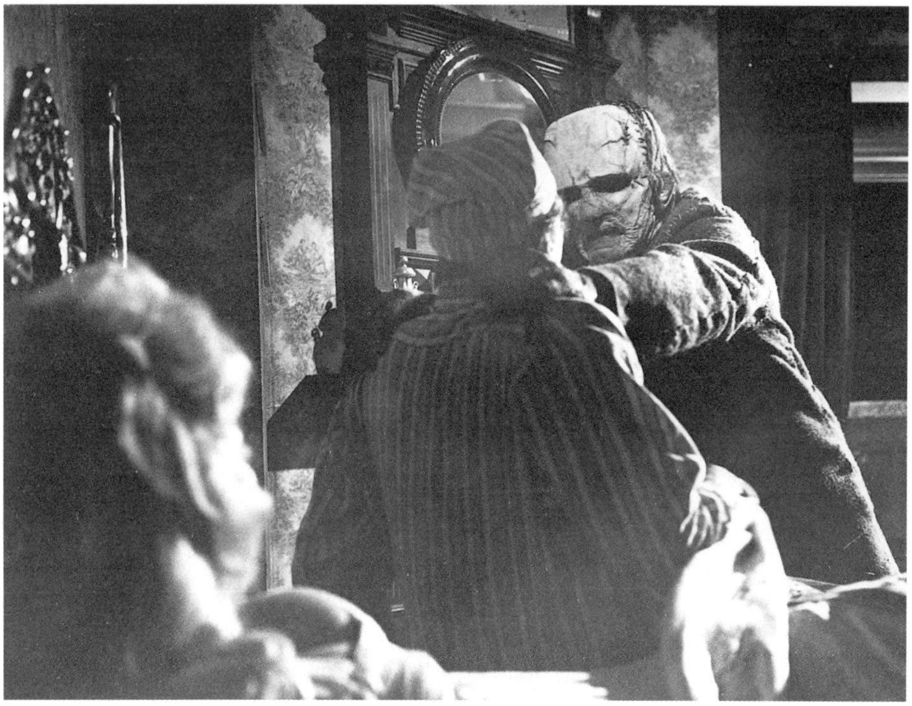

DOCTOR OF DOOM

(Orig: LAS LUCHADORAS CONTRA EL MEDICO ASESINO)
Mexico, 1962. Dir: René Cardona. With: Armando Silvestre, Lorena Velázquez, Elizabeth Campbell, Roberto Cañedo, Martha 'Guera' Solis, Irma Rodriguez. Cinematografica Calderon/K. Gordon Murray/American International. B&W.

Wrestlers Gloria Venus (former Miss Mexico Velázquez) and the Golden Ruby (Campbell) battle a masked mad doctor who transplants the brain of his sidekick, Gomar the apeman, into female wrestler Vendetta (Solis) and telepathically controls her in the ring. The first in the popular Wrestling Women series.

Sequel: THE WRESTLING WOMEN VS THE AZTEC MUMMY (1964)
Remake: NIGHT OF THE BLOODY APES (qv; 1968)

Top and above: The Evil of Frankenstein. (FJA).

DOUBLE TROUBLE

USA, 1967. Dir: Norman Taurog. With: Elvis Presley, Annette Day, John Williams, Yvonne Romain, Chips Rafferty, Michael Murphy. Metro-Goldwyn-Mayer. Colour.

A teenage heiress (Day) falls for pop star Guy Lambert (Presley) while he's performing in London. Elvis sings 'Old MacDonald' and 'Long Legged Girl'. Includes characters in Frankenstein Monster, Dracula and Phantom of the Opera masks.

DRACULA VS. FRANKENSTEIN

(Orig: EL HOMBRE QUE VINO DEL UMMO/DRACULA JAGT FRANKENSTEIN/LOS MONSTRUOS DEL TERROR. USA: aka ASSIGNMENT TERROR)
Spain/West Germany/Italy, 1969 (1971). Dir: Tulio Demichelli (and Hugo Fregonese and Peter Riethof). With: Michael Rennie, Karin Dor, Craig Hill, Paul Naschy (Jacinto Molina), Patty Sheppard (Shepard), Angel del Pozo. Jaime Prades/Eichberg-Film/International Jaguar. Colour.

The sequel to *Nights of the Werewolf* (1968). Michael (*Day the Earth Stood Still* [1951]) Rennie's last film stars him as Dr Varnoff, the leader of a group of aliens who have travelled from their dying planet, Ummo, to reanimate the world's legendary monsters — Frankenstein's creature (Naschy, who wrote the script under his real name, Jacinto Molina Alvarez), Dracula (del Pozo), Count Waldemar Daninsky the werewolf (Naschy again) and the Mummy — and conquer the Earth. Argentinian director Fregonese quit towards the end of production and was replaced by Demichelli. Despite being shot in just six days, the whole thing moves at a leaden pace, and Universal learned to stop doing this sort of thing twenty-five years earlier. Despite the title, Dracula and the Frankenstein Monster never actually meet!

Sequel: FURY OF THE WOLFMAN (1970)

DR. DEVIL AND MR. HARE

USA, 1964. Dir: Robert McKimson. Voices: Mel Blanc. Warner Bros. Colour.

Seven minute Merrie Melodies cartoon in which Bugs Bunny disguises himself as a mad scientist and creates a Frankenstein Monster to battle the always hungry Tasmanian Devil. Bugs sings 'By a Waterfall' (from *Footlight Parade* [1933]).

DR. ORLOFF'S MONSTER

(Orig: EL SECRETO DEL DR. ORLOFF)
Spain, 1964. Dir: Jess Frank (Jesús Franco). With: Agnes Spaak, Joseph Raven (José Rubio), Perla Cristal, Patrick Long (Pastor Serrador), Hugh White (Hugo Blanco), Mike Arnold (Marcelo Arroita-Jauregui). Leo Films/Nueva Films/American International. B&W.

Franco's first semi-sequel to *The Awful Dr. Orloff* (1962). Dr Conrad Fisherman (Arnold), a mad disciple of Dr Orloff, transforms the corpse of his adulterous brother Andros (Raven) into a radio-controlled zombie. Using supersonic beams, the doctor orders the creature to kill his unfaithful wife Inglud (Cristal) and various strippers. The director has a cameo playing the piano in a nightclub and also wrote the novel under his pen name David Khunne. In France, Italy and West Germany this was released as a Dr Jekyll movie!

Sequel: THE DIABOLICAL DR. Z (1965)

DR. TERROR'S GALLERY OF HORRORS

(aka THE BLOOD SUCKERS/ RETURN FROM THE PAST/ALIEN MASSACRE/GALLERY OF HORRORS)
USA, 1967. Dir: David L. Hewitt. With: Lon Chaney, John Carradine, Rochelle Hudson, Roger Gentry, Karen Joy, Vic McGee. Dora-Borealis/ American General. Colour.

Inept five-part horror anthology, shot on cardboard sets and featuring the same small group of performers, plus clips from AIP's Poe movies. Carradine introduces the segments and plays a warlock in 'The Witch's Clock'. A vampire terrorises Victorian London in 'King Vampire', Mitch Evans is the eponymous 'Count Alucard' who fights a werewolf, and a dead man returns from the tomb in 'Monster Raid'. Inspired by Eric von Frankenstein, poor old Chaney Jr (who still had worse roles to come) plays Dr Mendel, who brings a crazed murderer back to life in 'Spark of Life' (set in the nineteenth century, although all the laboratory equipment is modern!). Filmed under the title *Gallery of Horrors.*

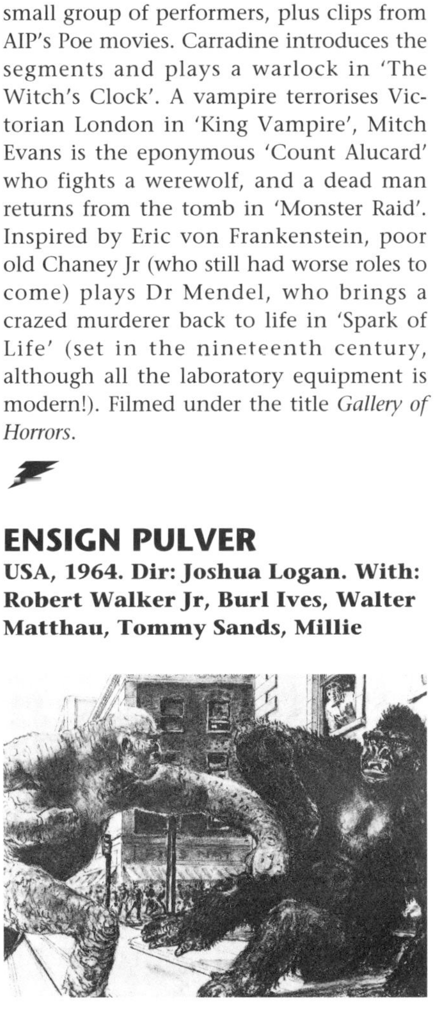

Above: *The Evil of Frankenstein. (FJA).*
Below left: *Dr Orloff's Monster.*
Below right: *Willis O'Brien sketch for his unrealised 1960's King Kong vs Frankenstein project.*

ENSIGN PULVER

USA, 1964. Dir: Joshua Logan. With: Robert Walker Jr, Burl Ives, Walter Matthau, Tommy Sands, Millie Perkins, Kay Medford. Warner Bros. Colour.

Disappointing sequel to *Mister Roberts* (1955) in which Walker Jr takes over Jack Lemmon's Oscar-winning role as the titular seaman. Ives' Captain Morton keeps screening a film for the crew entitled *Young Dr Jekyll Meets Frankenstein* (combining scenes from *The Walking Dead* [1936] with new footage). Includes early appearances by Larry Hagman, Al Freeman Jr, James Farentino, James Coco and Jack Nicholson.

THE EVIL OF FRANKENSTEIN

UK, 1964. Dir: Freddie Francis. With: Peter Cushing, Peter Woodthorpe, Sandor Eles, Kiwi Kingston, Duncan Lamont, Katy Wild. Hammer Films/Universal. Colour.

The third and probably weakest in Hammer's Frankenstein series. Director Francis took over from Terence Fisher for this one entry and Cushing's Baron appears more humane. This time the real villain is Woodthorpe's drunken hypnotist, Zoltan, who uses the revived Monster (ex-wrestler Kingston in make-up closely resembling Karloff's original) to revenge himself on the authorities of Carlstaad. The screenplay by John Elder (Anthony Hinds) contains few surprises and has no connection with the previous films, while a confused flashback sequence only adds to the muddled narrative. American TV prints include extra sequences filmed at Universal Studios (featuring William Phipps, Steven Geray, Patrick Horgan, Tracy Stratford

FEARLESS FRANK

USA, 1967 (1969). Dir: Philip Kaufman. With: John Voigt, Monique Van Vooren, Severn Darden, Joan Darling, Lou Gilbert, Nelson Algren. Jeriko Film/ American International Pictures. Colour.

Filmed in Chicago under the title *Frank's Greatest Adventure*. When naive country boy Frank (Voigt) is murdered by gangsters, he is revived by the Good Doctor (Darden) and becomes a bullet-proof crimefighter with the ability to fly. However, the Good Doctor's evil brother, Claude (also Darden), creates False Frank (also Voigt), a Frankenstein Monster-like double. The two Franks battle each other until they find themselves taking on the other's characteristics. Director Kaufman moved on to better things.

FRANKENSTEIN CONQUERS THE WORLD

(Orig: FURANKENSHUTAIN TAI BARAGON)

Japan/USA, 1964 (1965). Dir: Inoshiro Honda. With: Nick Adams, Tadao Takashima, Kumi Mizuno, Yoshio Tsuchiya, Takashi Shimura, Haruo Nakajima. Toho/Henry G. Saperstein Enterprises/American International Pictures. Colour.

A boy eats the radioactive heart of the Frankenstein Monster and begins to grow into an ugly giant who watches Japanese teenagers do the twist! Stealing Willis

and Maria Palmer) in which the mute beggar girl meets the Monster as a child. Scenes from *The Evil of Frankenstein* also turn up in *Kiss of Evil*, the American TV version of Hammer's *The Kiss of the Vampire* (1962).

Sequel: FRANKENSTEIN CREATED WOMAN (qv; 1966)

FANNY HILL MEETS DR. EROTICO

USA, 1967. Dir: Barry Mahon. With: Sue Evans. Chancellor. Colour.

Nudie sequel to *Fanny Hill Meets Lady Chatterley* (1967). Fanny Hill (Evans) discovers that Dr Erotico has created a monster in his castle laboratory. When she accidentally brings the creature to life, it falls in love with her before being burned to death by the villagers.

Sequel: FANNY HILL MEETS THE RED BARON (1968)

O'Brien's concept of a fifty foot tall Frankenstein Monster from his proposed *King Kong vs Frankenstein* (aka *King Kong vs Prometheus*), Toho pitted their towering version of Mary Shelley's creation against a fire-breathing prehistoric reptile called Baragon (played by stuntman Nakajima in a silly-looking rubber suit). With a giant crawling hand and imported American actor Nick Adams looking confused. The original ending, with the Monster being dragged into the sea by a bizarre giant octopus (which walks on land!), was replaced in Western prints with an alternative sequence in which the Monster is killed when a mountain collapses.
Sequels: WAR OF THE GARGANTUAS (qv; 1966) and DESTROY ALL MONSTERS (1968)

Above: Frankenstein Must Be Destroyed.

FRANKENSTEIN CREATED WOMAN

UK, 1966. Dir: Terence Fisher. With: Peter Cushing, Susan Denberg, Thorley Walters, Robert Morris, Duncan Lamont, Peter Blythe. Hammer Films. Colour.
This fourth outing for Cushing's Baron (following *The Evil of Frankenstein* [1964]) marks the welcome return of director Fisher, but the screenplay by John Elder (Anthony Hinds) seems unsure of how to vary the formula. As a result, Frankenstein and his bumbling assistant Dr Hertz (Walters) are experimenting with cryogenic suspension when they end up transplanting the soul of a young man falsely executed for murder into the body of the once-crippled Christina (1966 *Playboy* pin-up Denberg). He/she then revenges herself on the real killers. For a change, Frankenstein survives at the end to continue his experiments.
Sequel: FRANKENSTEIN MUST BE DESTROYED (qv; 1969)

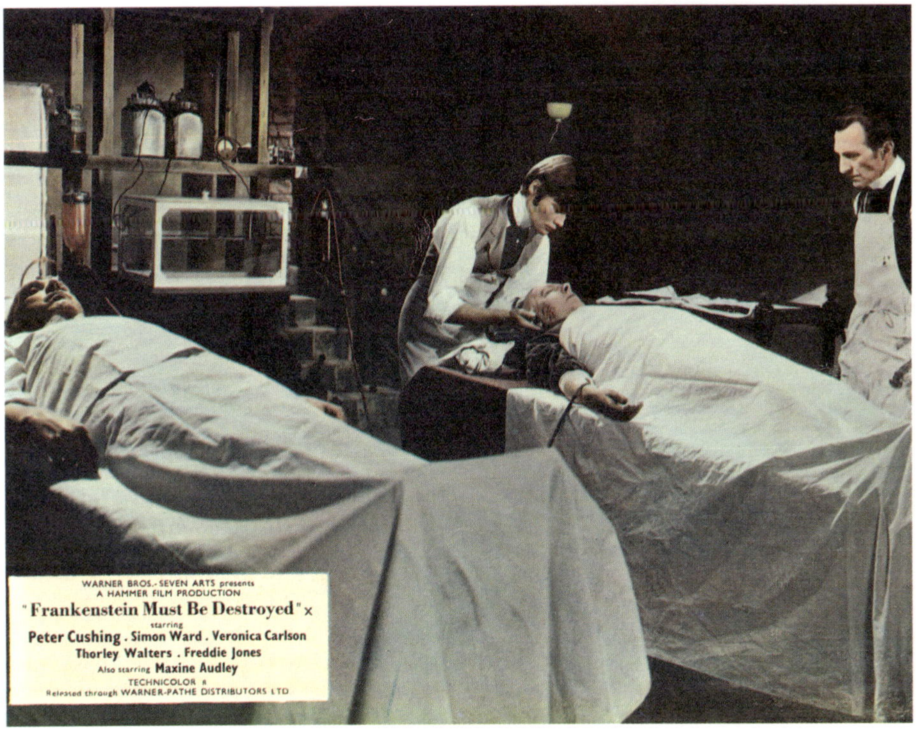

FRANKENSTEIN CUM CANNABIS

Holland, 1969 (1970). Dir: Niko Paape. B&W.
Nineteen minute non-monster short about drugs.

FRANKESTEIN, EL VAMPIRO Y CIA

Mexico, 1961 (1963). Dir: Benito

Alazraki. With: Manuel 'Loco' Valdés, José Jasso, Joaquin Garcia Vargas (Borolas), Martha Elena Cervantes, Nora Veryán, Roberto G. Rivera. Cinematografica Calderon. B&W.

After *Castle of the Monsters* (1957), here's another Mexican version of (Abbott and Costello) *Meet Frankenstein* (1948). The comedy team of 'Loco' Valdés and José Jasso are employed to deliver wax figures of the Frankestein (*sic*) Monster and a vampire (Quintin Bulnes) to a mysterious castle. When the figures come to life, the vampire tries to convince female scientist Dr Sofia (Veryán) to transplant Valdes' brain into the Monster so that it can conquer America! This also includes a werewolf.

Remake: LEENA MEETS FRANKENSTEIN (qv; 1993)

Top and above: Frankenstein Created Woman.
Left: Frankenstein Conquers the World.

FRANKENSTEIN MEETS THE SPACEMONSTER

(aka MARTE INVADE A PUERTO RICO. UK: DUEL OF THE SPACE MONSTERS)

USA, 1965. Dir: Robert Gaffney. With: Marilyn Hanold, Jim (James) Karen, Lou Cutell, Nancy Marshall, David Kerman, Robert Reilly. Vernon Films/Seneca/Futurama Entertainment. B&W.

Right: *Frankenstein Meets the Spacemonster.*

Dr Adam Steele (Karen) creates an astronaut, Col Frank Saunders (Reilly), out of corpses and machinery. However, when his brain is damaged by the henchmen of sexy alien Princess Marcuzan (Hanold), who are kidnapping Earth women, Saunders is transformed into a monster. In the end, 'Frankenstein' battles the space creature Mull before destroying the aliens and himself with a laser. Padded with plenty of documentary space footage, this was filmed (apparently without synchronised sound) in Puerto Rico and New York. With incredible sixties songs by The Distant Cousins and The Poets.

FRANKENSTEIN MUST BE DESTROYED

UK, 1969. Dir: Terence Fisher. With: Peter Cushing, Simon Ward, Veronica Carlson, Thorley Walters, Freddie Jones, Maxine Audley. Hammer Films. Colour.

Unpleasant fifth entry in Hammer's Frankenstein series. Bert Batt's ill-judged screenplay presents Cushing's Baron as a totally irredeemable character — the film's true monster. His blackmailing of the hapless Karl Holst (Ward) and rape of Anna Spengler (Carlson) — originally cut from American prints — results in the sadistic destruction of the young couple. Freddie Jones brings some much-needed sympathy to the film as the tragic Dr Brandt, who awakens to discover his brain has been transplanted into another body, and veterans Thorley Walters and Geoffrey Bayldon add a welcome touch of comedy to their investigations of the gory killings.

Sequel: FRANKENSTEIN AND THE MONSTER FROM HELL (qv; 1973)

FRANKENSTEIN'S BLOODY TERROR

(Orig: LA MARCA DEL HOMBRE LOBO. UK: HELL'S CREATURES) Spain, 1967 (1971). Dir: Henry Egan (Enrique L. Eguiluz). With: Paul Naschy (Jacinto Molina), Diane Konopka (Dianik Zurakowska), Julián Ugarte, Rossana Yanni, Michael Manz (Manuel Manzanaque), Joseph Morton (José Nieto). Maxper/Independent-International. Colour.

American audiences were promised a free burial to anyone who died of fright during performances of this film — a pretty safe bet. Werewolf Count Waldemar Daninsky (Naschy, who also scripted under his real name) appeals to a pair of weird occultists for help. Unfortunately, they turn out to be vampires. Originally released in Spain in 3-D, this was a box-office smash there and led to a series of films with Naschy as Daninsky. Frankenstein's Monster (which changes into a werewolf!) only appears in Gray Morrow's cartoon prologue for the American version, which was totally re-edited (by F. Neumann) and released in 'Super 70mm Chill-O-Rama'.

Sequel: NIGHTS OF THE WEREWOLF (1968)

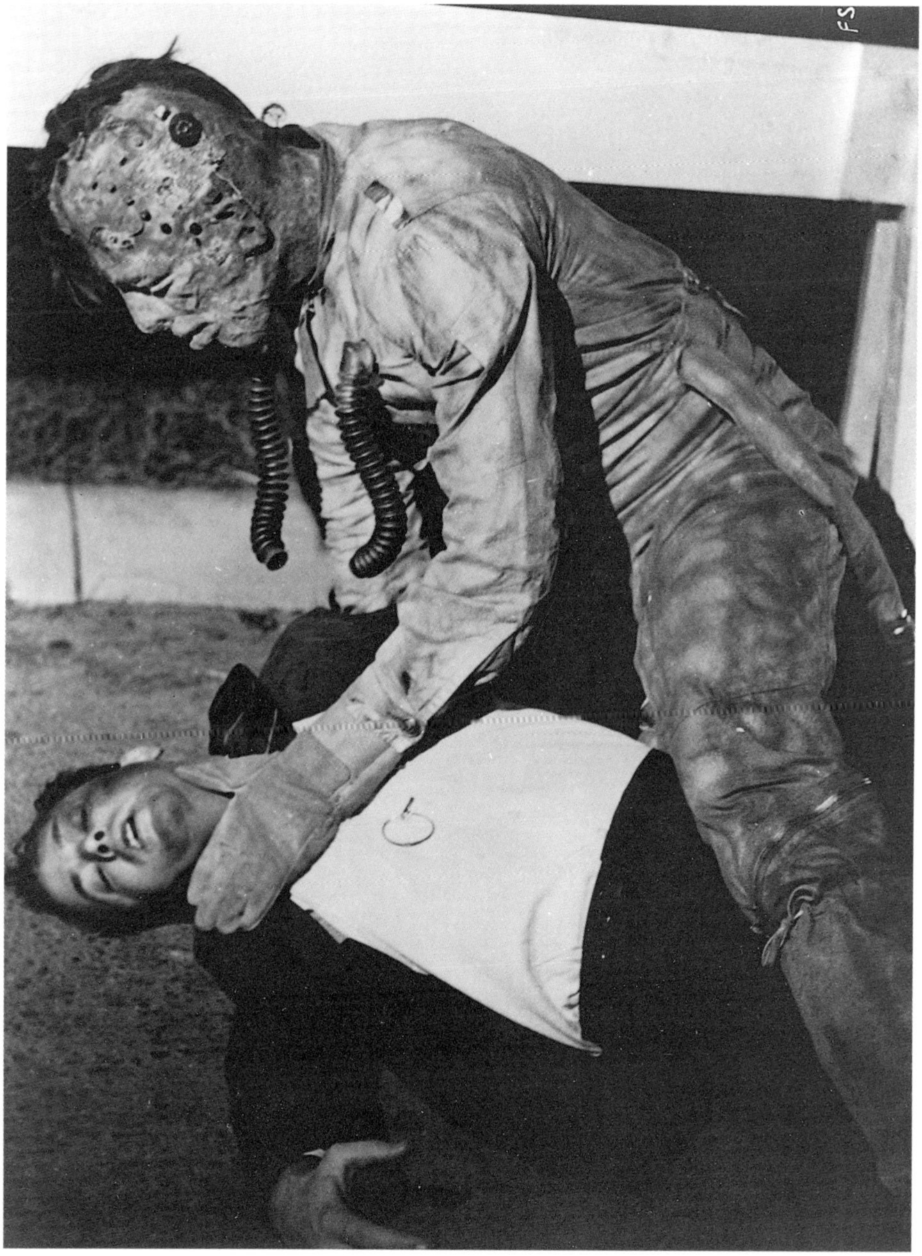

The Fisher King

Terence Fisher was born in London in 1904. After five years in the Merchant Navy and a stint working in the rag trade, he entered the film industry at the age of twenty-eight ("the oldest clapper boy in the business"), moving up the ranks to tea boy, third assistant director, assistant editor and editor.

In 1947 he went to Highbury Studios as part of a training scheme for potential directors run by the Rank Organisation. He made his directing début with *Colonel Bogie* that same year.

His first film for Hammer was *The Last Page* (1951), but such projects for the studio as *Stolen Face* (1952), *Four-Sided Triangle* (1953) and *Spaceways* (1953) were more indicative of the course his career would take after Hammer offered him *The Curse of Frankenstein* (1957).

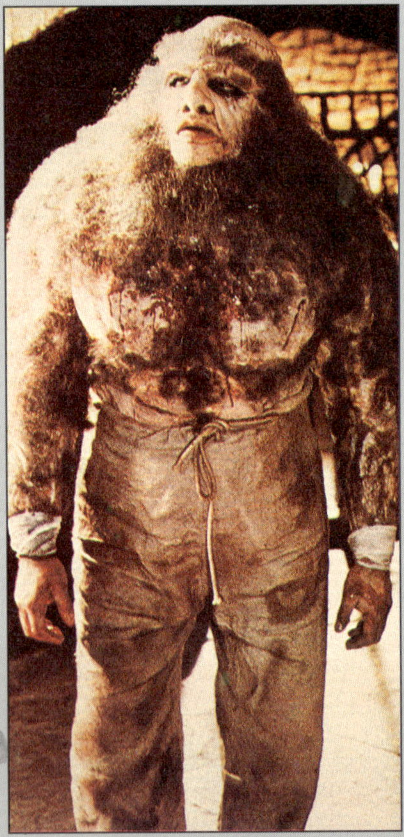

"I tried to forget the idea that I was continuing the central horror tradition of the cinema," he later recalled. "I wanted the film to grow out of personal contact with the actors and out of the influence of the very special sets. I have never read Mary Shelley's original book, and I don't think I ought to read it."

Fisher also admitted that "*The Curse of Frankenstein* put my career into perspective." The film grossed $7,000,000 around the world, at that time making it the most successful British film ever produced in proportion to its cost. It was a remarkable collaboration between the director and his twenty-two year-old scriptwriter, as Fisher acknowledged: "The greatest credit ought to go to Jimmy Sangster, who wrote the script and managed to make the original story so cinematic."

Fisher and Sangster continued to work together on *Dracula* (1958), *The Revenge of Frankenstein* (1958), *The Mummy* (1959), *The Man Who Could Cheat Death* (1959) and *The Brides of Dracula*, (1960), until Sangster decided to concentrate on more contemporary subjects.

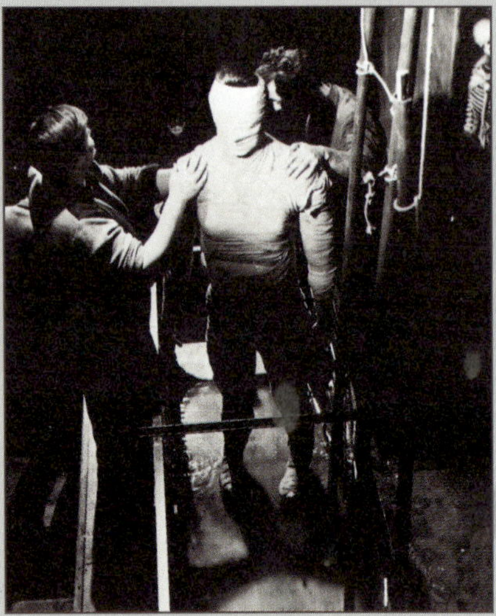

On average, a Hammer film would cost £200,000 and took six weeks to shoot. "He doesn't waste six inches of film," revealed actor Shane Briant, who

Top: *Terence Fisher directs Frankenstein and the Monster from Hell.*
Above: *Behind-the-scenes, The Curse of Frankenstein.*
Left: *Frankenstein and the Monster from Hell.*

appeared in *Frankenstein and the Monster from Hell* (1973). "He knows how he plans to cut it, and rather than do a master shot and then cover the various angles and close-ups, he shoots sparingly what he requires."

"I am not an intellectual director — I am an emotional director," admitted Fisher. "My pre-planning is knowing the story completely and absolutely, knowing the set I am going to work in completely and absolutely, knowing the content of the scene which I am going to direct within the context of the story."

However, following the box-office disappointment of *The Phantom of the Opera* (1962), Hammer dropped its star director. Fisher returned to the studio for *The Gorgon* (1964), *Dracula Prince of Darkness* (1965) and, after being replaced by Freddie Francis for *The Evil of Frankenstein* (1964), was reunited with Cushing's Baron for *Frankenstein Created Woman* (1966).

"I've always been fascinated by Baron Frankenstein," he revealed. "He is either an atheist who doesn't believe in God and believes he can really create man better than God ever has, or he is a deep religionist who sold his soul to the Devil, forsaking the fundamental religious belief that God creates man.

"Baron Frankenstein is a complete idealist. He is consecrated to one thing and one thing only, and that is to perfect the human body, the human mind. Like most consecrated people, he is single-minded and completely ruthless in what he does. As the physical barriers in life go, Frankenstein will have to concentrate on the mind. That's where the real barriers are and the possibilities are endless."

Fisher admitted that the film he most enjoyed making, and was most proud of, was the next in the series, *Frankenstein Must Be Destroyed* (1969): "That was probably the first time within the Frankenstein series that you had a really emotional, character approach to brain transplants. Freddie Jones was in that and he is someone for whom I have the greatest respect as an actor."

Just after finishing *The Devil Rides Out* (1967), Fisher was hit by a car while crossing the road and broke his right leg. Soon after completing *Frankenstein Must Be Destroyed*, he broke the same leg in an identical accident. "I am very careful now to look for pedestrian crossings," he quipped. However, as a result, he didn't direct again for three years, and *Frankenstein and the Monster from Hell* turned out to be his final credit.

"The real task of the fantasy film director is to bring integrity of intention to his film-making," Fisher stated. "I always ask for a similar response from my actors, and I rarely fail to get it, especially from Peter Cushing and Christopher Lee.

"I have been abused, from the moment I made the first Frankenstein, by practically every critic and every newspaper. But that doesn't worry me at all. It worried me at first — but the films have survived and still create interest. I've always felt that the object of film-making is not a self-indulgent one. It's not to please critics, it is to please cinema audiences.

"If my films reflect my own personal view of the world in any way, it is in their showing of the ultimate victory of good over evil. It may take human beings a long time to achieve this, but I do believe that this is how events work out in the end."

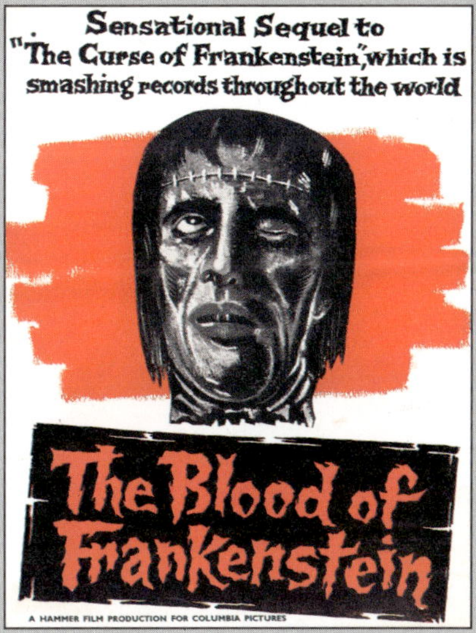

Seventy-six year-old Terence Fisher died on 18 June 1980 following a long bronchial illness. At the time, he was planning to direct a television film for Hammer. His short obituary in *Variety* dismissed him as "an international cult *auteur* via the low budget horror genre for Hammer Films."

Always a pragmatist, he saw his career in even simpler terms: "I make what I'm offered, and I make them as well as I can."

Above left: *The Curse of Frankenstein.*
Below: *The Revenge of Frankenstein.*

Above: Frankenstein Must Be Destroyed.

FRANKEN-STYMIED

USA, 1961. Dir: Jack Hannah. Voices: Grace Stafford. Walter Lantz Productions/Universal-International. Colour.

Six minute Woody Woodpecker cartoon in which the character is pursued by Franky, a mechanical chicken-plucker created by a mad scientist.

THE FROZEN DEAD

UK, 1967. Dir: Herbert J. Leder. With: Dana Andrews, Anna Palk, Karel Stepanek, Kathleen Breck, Basil Henson, Philip Gilbert. Goldstar/Seven Arts. Colour.

Low budget horror thriller with imported American star Andrews as Nazi scientist Dr Norborg, attempting to revive an army of top Nazis frozen alive at the end of World War Two and hidden in caves. He also keeps the severed head of a female victim (Breck) alive in a box. With Edward Fox in a small role as a murderous zombie.

THE GHOST IN THE INVISIBLE BIKINI

USA, 1966. Dir: Don Weis. With: Tommy Kirk, Deborah Walley, Basil Rathbone, Patsy Kelly, Susan Hart, Boris Karloff. American International Pictures. Colour.

Mindless AIP comedy/horror/musical variation on their *Beach Party* series. In what look like tacked-on sequences, Karloff plays Hiram Stokely (billed as 'The Corpse' on prints), who is told by his dead girlfriend (Hart) that he must do a good deed to go to Heaven. This involves helping Kirk and his teenage friends stop scheming lawyer Reginald Ripper (Rathbone) killing the heirs to a hidden fortune. It all ends with a frenetic chase through a chamber of horrors that includes a dummy of the Frankenstein Monster. With veterans Patsy Kelly, Jesse White and Francis X. Bushman, Harvey Lembeck as Eric von Zipper, Nancy Sinatra (who sings), some unconvincing monsters and a gorilla. Not released in Britain until 1989. You've got to see it to believe it!

Sequel: BACK TO THE BEACH (1987)

THE GOLEM

(Orig: LE GOLEM. aka MASK OF THE GOLEM)

France, 1966. Dir: Jean Kerchbron. With: Andre Reybaz, Pierre Tabard, Michel Etchevery, Marika Green, Francois Vibert, Robert Etchevery. ORTF. B&W.

Reybaz portrays the stone-faced creature magically brought to life in this TV movie based on the book by Gustav Meyrink, adapted from the medieval Jewish legend.

Remake: IT! (qv; 1966)

GOOF ON THE LOOSE

USA, 1962. Dir: Ray Dennis Steckler. With: Rich Dennis. Morgan-Steckler Productions. B&W.

Comedy short from the director of *The Incredibly Strange Creatures Who Stopped Living and Became Mixed-up Zombies!!?* (1963). The Frankenstein Monster carries off a young female victim.

HOLLOW-MY-WEANIE, DR. FRANKENSTEIN

USA, 1969. Colour.

Gay porno movie in which Dr Frankenstein and his hunchbacked assistant create a well-endowed Monster in their base-

ment laboratory. This was apparently advertised as *Frankenstein De Sade*.

HOUSE ON BARE MOUNTAIN

USA, 1962. Dir: (R.) Lee Frost. With: Bob Cresse, Laura Eden, Angela Webster, Ann Meyers, Hugh Cannon, Jeffrey Smithers. Olympic International. Colour.

Nudie film from the makers of *One Million AC/DC* (1969). Co-producer Cresse plays a bootlegger who runs Granny Good's School for Good Girls in drag. His assistant is Krakow the werewolf (Cannon), and a fake Frankenstein Monster (Warren Ames) and Dracula (Smithers) turn up and do the twist at a costume ball. This cost $72,000 and was one of the most expensive adult movies made at the time.

HOW TO SUCCEED WITH GIRLS

(aka THE PEEPING PHANTOM)
USA, 1964. Dir: Edward A. Biery. With: Paul Leder, Leon Schrier, Marrisa Mathes, Patty Leigh, Helen Goodman. B&W/Colour.

Silly nudie comedy in which introverted salesman Harvey Brubaker (Leder) has various sexual daydreams (in colour!) which include guest appearances by Frankenstein's Monster, King Kong, the Phantom of the Opera and the Invisible Man. With Marrisa Mathes (*Playboy*'s Miss June 1962) as Harvey's busty secretary and the actress now known as Rue McClanahan (TV's *The Golden Girls*). Filmed under the title *Harvey's Girls*.

INVASION OF THE ZOMBIES

(Orig: SANTO CONTRA LOS ZOMBIES)
Mexico, 1961. Dir: Benito Alzraki. With: Santo (Rodolfo Guzman Huerta), Lorena Velázquez, Carlos Agosti, Armando Silvestre, Dagoberto Rodriguez, Irma Serrano. Tec/Filmadora Panamerica/Azteca. B&W.

The first true starring vehicle for Santo, the silver masked wrestler, who battles a mad scientist and his army of radio-controlled zombie gangsters. With former Miss Mexico Lorena Velázquez.

Sequel: SANTO CONTRA EL CEREBRO DIABOLICO (qv; 1961)

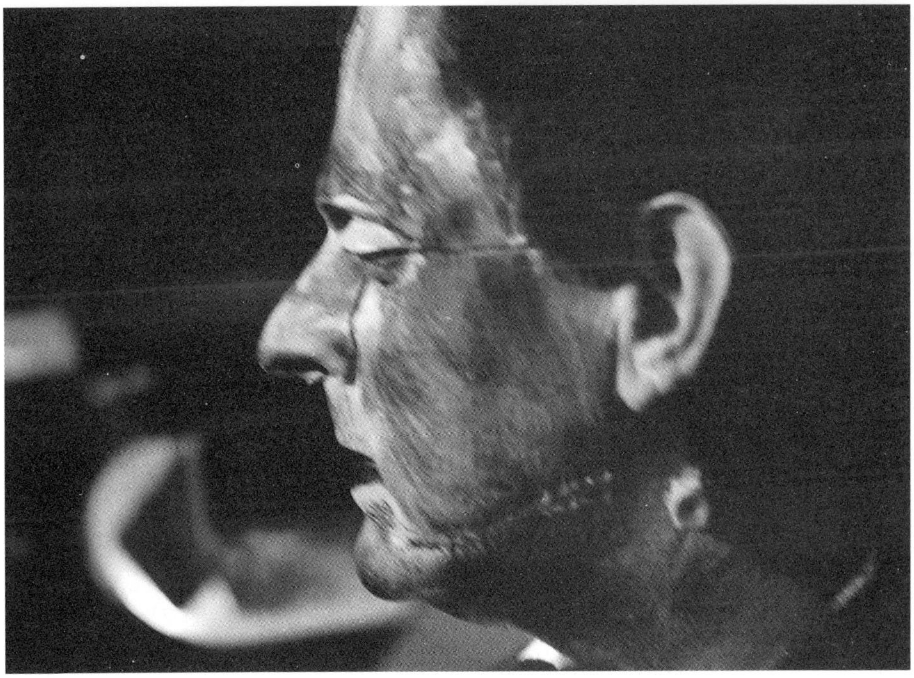

Above: Behind-the-scenes, Kiss Me Quick. (FJA).

ISABELL, A DREAM

Italy, 1968. Dir: Luigi Cozzi.

In a dream sequence, women hunt Frankenstein's Monster, Dracula and the Mummy (actors wearing Don Post masks) through a forest. Footage from this also turned up in Cozzi's *Il Tunnel Sotto Il Mondo* (1968) and *Il Vicino di Casa* (circa 1970s).

ISLAND OF TERROR

(USA: aka THE CREEPERS)
UK, 1966. Dir: Terence Fisher. With: Peter Cushing, Edward Judd, Carole Gray, Eddie Byrne, Sam Kydd, Niall MacGinnis. Planet Films. Colour.

This fun science fiction/horror thriller, set on Petrie's island off the Irish coast, reunites Hammer veterans Fisher and Cushing. While trying to discover a cure for cancer, a group of scientists create a silicate creature which multiplies and sucks the bones out of the locals. Cushing gives his usual fine performance as an investigating pathologist who loses a hand when Judd has to hack it off to save him from the blob monsters!

IT!

UK, 1966. Dir: Herbert J. Leder. With: Roddy McDowall, Jill Haworth, Paul Maxwell, Noel Trevarthen, Ernest Clark, Ian McCulloch. Goldstar/Seven Arts. Colour.

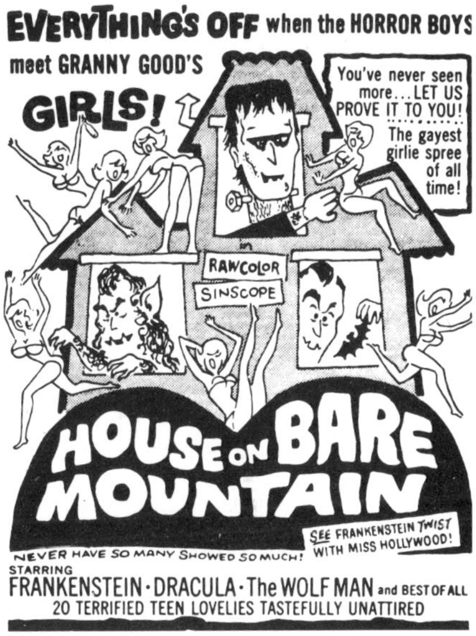

McDowall plays Arthur Pimm, a disturbed museum curator who keeps his dead mother around the house (*a la Psycho* [1960]) and discovers the original Golem (Alan Sellers), which he brings back to life and commands to kill. This could have been a neat black comedy without the Golem subplot, which involves the living clay statue toppling London's Hammersmith bridge and surviving a 'small' atomic bomb blast. When writer/producer/director Leder (*The Frozen Dead* [1967]) can't think of a way to end the film, he has the Golem walk off into the sea. Filmed under the title *The Curse of the Golem*.

Remake: PRAZSKE NOCI (qv; 1968)

JESSE JAMES MEETS FRANKENSTEIN'S DAUGHTER

USA, 1965. Dir: William Beaudine. With: Narda Onyx, John Lupton, Cal Bolder, Estelita, Jim Davis, Nestor Paiva. Embassy Pictures/ Circle. Colour.

Despite the title, it's Frankenstein's *granddaughter* (Onyx) who, along with her weak brother (Steven Geray), transplants a synthetic brain into Jesse James' sidekick (Bolder) and turns him into Igor, a monster. Lupton as outlaw Jesse and Davis as a sympathetic sheriff play this as a straight western, while Estelita's Mexican heroine has to be seen to be believed! The last film from veteran director William ('one shot') Beaudine, this is actually slightly better than its companion release, *Billy the Kid Versus Dracula* (1965), which is hardly a recommendation.

KILLING FRANKESTAYNA KARSI

Turkey, 1967. Dir: Nuri Akinci. With: Oktay Gursel, Oya Peri, Gultekin Ceylan, Ferhan Tanseli, Aynur Aydan, Yasar Sener. Omur Film. B&W

A master criminal known as Killing apparently battles the Frankenstein Monster.

KISS ME QUICK

(aka DR. BREEDLOVE OR HOW I LEARNED TO STOP WORRYING AND LOVE)
USA, 1964. Dir: Seymour Tuchas (Pete Perry and Max Gardens). With: Mannie Goodtimes (Sexton Friendly), Fatty Beltbuckle (Frank Coe), Natasha, Jackie (DeWitt), Althea Currier, Claudia Banks. Fantasy Films. Colour.

Nudie comedy filmed on a single laboratory set. Sterilox (Beltbuckle, doing a Stan Laurel impression), an alien from the all-male planet Droopiter in the Buttless galaxy, arrives on Earth looking for the 'perfect woman' to breed servants from. He visits the mad Dr Breedlove (Goodtimes, in a spoof of Peter Sellers' Dr Strangelove with a Bela Lugosi accent) who uses his sex machine to create various strippers and topless Go-Go dancers. In the end, the alien leaves with a vending machine. Includes a Karloffian sex-change Monster called Frankie Stein (Beltbuckle again), Dracula, Selfish the Mummy and a Peter Lorre-type narration. Lester (Laszlo) Kovacs was the cinematographer, while the direction is often mistakenly attributed to Russ Meyer. All the credits are spoken.

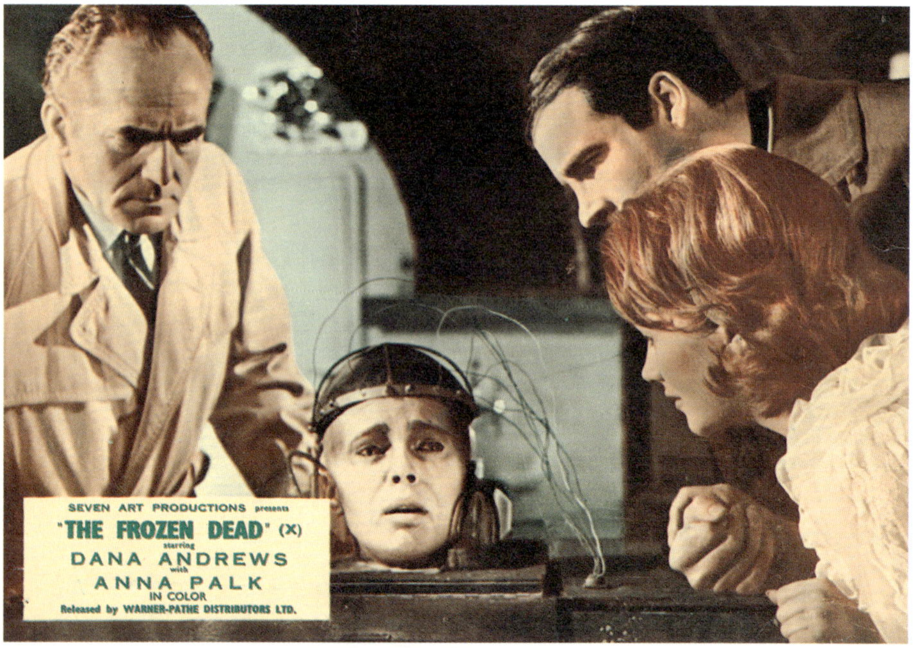

LATITUDE ZERO

(Orig: IDO ZERO DAI-SAKUSEN)
Japan, 1969. Dir: Inoshiro Honda. With: Joseph Cotten, Cesar Romero, Akira Takarada, Masumi Okada, Richard Jaeckel, Patricia Medina. Toho. Colour.

Co-scripted by Ted Sherdeman, based on his own stories, this juvenile science fiction adventure looks like a filmed comic book. Veteran Cotten plays the Captain Nemo-like leader of a futuristic scientific community beneath the sea, menaced by Romero's evil genius, Malic the Murderer. The super-scientific plot is simple (as is Richard Jaeckel's journalist hero), while Eiji Tsuburaya's special effects look terrible — particularly the monstrous rats and Malic's giant gryphon with the brain of his former mistress (Medina). Small children might enjoy it.

LOLITA

UK, 1962. Dir: Stanley Kubrick. With: James Mason, Shelley

Winters, Peter Sellers, Sue Lyon, Marianne Stone, Diana Decker. Metro-Goldwyn-Mayer. B&W.
Adapted by Vladimir Nabokov from his own novel. Lyon plays the sexually precocious titular teenager who seduces Mason's stolid professor and Sellers' bizarre lover. This includes clips from Hammer's *The Curse of Frankenstein* (1957).

LURK

USA, 1964 (1965). Dir: Rudy Burckhardt. With: Red Grooms, Mimi Grooms, Edwin Denby, Yvonne Burckhardt, Neil Welliver, Jacob Burckhardt. Film-makers Coop/Canyon Cinema. B&W.
Thirty-eight minute underground spoof of the 1931 *Frankenstein*, narrated by Edwin Denby and featuring Red Grooms as the Monster.

MAD MONSTER PARTY?

USA, 1966 (1969). Dir: Jules Bass. Voices: Boris Karloff, Alan Swift, Gale Garnett, Phyllis Diller, Ethel Ennis. Embassy/Videocraft International. Colour.
Animated children's puppet film, shot in a process dubbed 'Animagic'. Karloff voices a puppet version of himself as Baron Von Frankenstein (and even sings one of the better musical numbers), who holds a convention of all the monsters to reveal the secret of total destruction. Among the guests are the Frankenstein Monster and his mate (Diller), Count Dracula, the Werewolf, the Hunchback, the Mummy, Dr Jekyll and Mr Hyde, and It (King Kong). Also includes voice impersonations of Bela Lugosi, Peter Lorre, James Stewart, Charles Laughton and Sidney Greenstreet (as the Invisible Man). Overlong, but often amusing. *Mad* magazine's Harvey Kurtzman co-wrote the script (along with Len Korobkin and an uncredited Forrest J Ackerman).

MAGOO MEETS FRANKENSTEIN

USA, 1960. Dir: Gil Turner. Voices: Jim Backus. UPA. Colour.
Six minute cartoon in which the near-sighted Mr Magoo arrives at Professor Frankenstein's castle thinking it's a European hotel. The Professor, who has given his Monster the brain of a chicken, tries to transfer Magoo's mind into his creation.

MAJIN, MONSTER OF TERROR

(Orig: DAIMAJIN. USA: aka MAJIN, THE HIDEOUS IDOL)
Japan, 1966. Dir: Kimiyoshi Yasuda. With: Miwa Takada, Yoshihiko Aoyama, Jun Fujimaki, Ryutaro Gomi, Tatsuo Endo. Daiei/American International. Colour.
Japan's own version of the Golem. In the eighteenth century, the giant statue of a samurai warrior comes to life to save a young prince and princess (Takada and Aoyama) from an evil usurper (Gomi). The giant creates an earthquake and ends up impaling the villain on a huge spike before returning to stone. Special effects created by Yoshiyuki Kuroda.
Sequel: THE RETURN OF MAJIN (qv; 1966)

MAJIN STRIKES AGAIN

(Orig: DAIMAJIN GYAKUSHU)
Japan, 1966. Dir: Issei Mori. With: Hideki Ninomiya, Masahide Kizuka, Shinji Hori, Shiei Iizuka, Muneyuki Nagatomo. Daiei/American International. Colour.
Second and final sequel to *Majin, Monster of Terror* (1966). The giant stone statue rescues three children from a tyrannical villain. As usual, Yoshiyuki Kuroda created the miniature floods and earthquakes.

THE MAN CALLED FLINTSTONE

USA, 1965. Dir: Joseph Barbera and William Hanna. Voices: Alan Reed, Mel Blanc, Jean Vanderpyl, Gerry Johnson, Janet Waldo, Don Messick. Hanna-Barbera/Columbia. Colour.
Feature-length cartoon version of the popular TV series, inspired by the success of the James Bond films. Fred is the double of caveman super-spy Rock Slag and uses all kinds of ingenious Stone Age gadgets against the villainous Green Goose, who, in one sequence, turns himself into the Frankenroc Monster.

THE MAN WHO THOUGHT LIFE

(Orig: MANDEN, DER TAENKTE TING)
Denmark, 1969. Dir: Jens Ravn. With: Preben Neergaard, John Price, Lotte Tarp, Lars Lunoe, Kirsten Rolffes. Asa/Palladium. B&W.

Below: *Munster, Go Home!*

Obscure Danish film, based on the novel by Valdemar Holst. A wealthy tycoon named Steinmetz (Price) uses his superhuman mental powers to create an organic double of brain surgeon Max Holst (Neergaard). As Holst's identity is gradually usurped by his more intelligent *doppelgänger*, he realises that he has no alternative but to kill Steinmetz.

THE MIND OF MR. SOAMES

UK, 1969. Dir: Alan Cooke. With: Terence Stamp, Robert Vaughn, Nigel Davenport, Christian Roberts, Donal Donnelly, Vickery Turner. Amicus/Columbia. Colour.

Based on the novel by Charles Eric Maine, this thoughtful science fiction film shares certain similarities with *Charly* (1968). Stamp gives a sympathetic performance as John Soames, who has been in a coma since birth. Thanks to a successful brain operation by Dr Michael Bergen (Vaughn) he awakens with the mind of a new-born baby and the body of a fully-grown man. But when Soames escapes from his protective environment, tragedy inevitably follows.

MONSTER OF CEREMONIES

USA, 1966. Dir: Paul J. Smith. Voices: Grace Stafford. Walter Lantz Productions/Universal. Colour.

Seven minute cartoon in which Woody Woodpecker is transformed into a monster robot by a mad scientist trying to create a Frankenstein-like creature.

MR. MAGOO, MAN OF MYSTERY

USA, 1965 (1967). Voices: Jim Backus. UPA. Colour.

Cartoon feature film, re-edited from the mid-sixties TV series, in which the near-sighted Mr Magoo plays Sherlock Holmes, Dr Frankenstein (from *Famous Adventures of Mr. Magoo* [1965]) and appears with Dick Tracy.

MUNSTER, GO HOME!

USA, 1966. Dir: Earl Bellamy. With: Fred Gwynne, Yvonne De Carlo, Al Lewis, Butch Patrick, Debbie Watson, Terry-Thomas. Universal. Colour.

Based on *The Munsters* TV series, this was originally made for television but released theatrically at the last minute. The weird family travel to Britain to claim the Frankenstein Monster-like Herman's (Gwynne) inheritance. The humour is laboured (although there are a couple of nice *Car 54 Where Are You?* and *Batman* in-jokes) and guest stars like Terry-Thomas and Hermione Gingold just look embarrassed. Only John Carradine, hidden under a red wig and sideburns as Cruikshank, the doddering butler, makes anything out of his small role. The film quickly runs out of steam and ends with a tedious car chase.

Sequel: THE MUNSTERS' REVENGE (qv; 1981)

Above: *Mad Monster Party?*

NIGHT OF THE BLOODY APES

(Orig: LA HORRIPLANTE BESTIA HUMANA/HORROR Y SEXO) Mexico, 1968 (1970). Dir: René Cardona. With: José Elias Moreno, Carlos López Moctezuma, Norma Lazareno, Agustin Mtz. (Martinez) Solares, Armando Silvestre. Unistar Pictures/Jerand Films/Calderon. Colour.

Cardona's semi-remake of his own *Doctor of Doom* (1962) is actually better than most Mexican monster movies. During gory footage of real open-heart surgery (mostly cut from British prints), scientist Dr Krellman (Moreno) transplants a gorilla's heart into his dying son (Silvestre). The resulting blue-faced ape monster rapes and murders his victims until stopped by the policeman boyfriend of cat-suited female wrestler Lucy (Lazareno, who is totally superfluous to the plot). An export version, titled *Horror y Sexo*, includes more nudity.

THE NINE AGES OF NAKEDNESS

UK, 1969. Dir: George Harrison Marks. With: George Harrison Marks, Max Wall, Max Bacon, Julian Orchard, Cardew Robinson, Big Bruno Erlington. Token Films. Colour.

Photographer Marks produced, scripted, directed and starred in this nudie comedy in which he reveals to a psychiatrist his family's problems with women throughout history. This involves a Frankenstein spoof (he plays Frankenstein Marks), a prehistoric sequence and a futuristic segment. Narrated by Charles Gray.

ORLAK, EL INFIERNO DE FRANKENSTEIN

Mexico, 1960. Dir: Rafael Baledon. With: Joaquin Cordero, Armando Calvo, Rosa de Castilla, Irma Dorantes, Andres Soler, Pedro de Aguillon. Filmadora Independiente/ Columbia. B&W.

At the turn of the century, convicted bodysnatcher Jaime (Cordero) uses Orlak (also Cordero), the remote-controlled monster of Dr Carlos Frankenstein (Soler), to kill those who found him guilty. Low budget thrills, filmed in three weeks and comprising four episodes (to get around Mexican union restrictions). The misleading poster art depicts a werewolf, a vam-

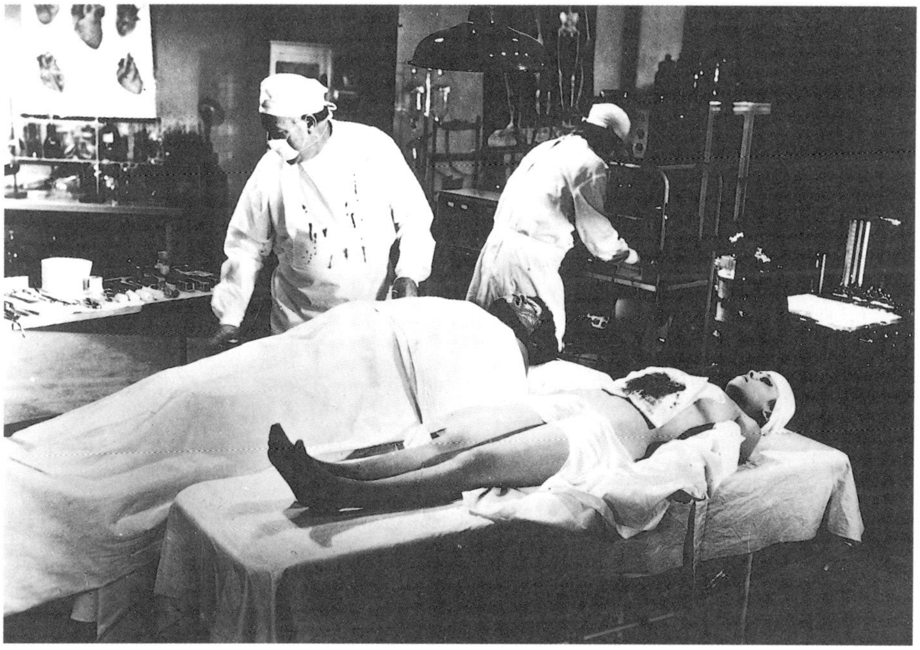

Above and below: *Night of the Bloody Apes.*

pire, an apeman, the Creature from the Black Lagoon and Frankenstein's Daughter! The title translates as *Orlak, the Hell of Frankenstein.*

PRAZSKE NOCI

Czechoslovakia, 1968. Dir: Jiri Brdecka, Evald Schorm and Milos Makovek. With: Jana Brezkova, Jan Klusak, Teresa Tuszynska, Josef Somr, Josef Abrham, Lucie Novot. Felix Broz Unit. Colour.

Omnibus film featuring three tales of Prague. The first two, 'The Bread Shoes' and 'The Poisoned Poisoner', are both set in the Middle Ages and directed, respectively, by Schorm and Makovek (the latter also responsible for the framing story, 'Fabricus'). The third legend is a reworking of 'The Golem' by Brdecka (better known as an animator). Rabbi Loew discovers that Emperor Rudolf II asked a Polish rabbi, Chaim (Klusak), to create a Golem for him. Loew uses his own artificially-created woman (Brezkova) to remove the magic formula from the Golem's forehead and destroy the creature.

THE RETURN OF MAJIN

(Orig: DAIMAJIN IKARU. USA: aka THE RETURN OF GIANT MAJIN)
Japan, 1966. Dir: Kenji Misumi. With: Kojiro Hongo, Shiho Fujimura, Tara Fujimura, Taro Murui, Jutaro Hojo, Takashi Kanda. Daiei/ American International. Colour.

Sequel to *Majin, Monster of Terror* (1966). When villains attempt to destroy the giant effigy of Majin, the living statue rises from the middle of a lake to wreak havoc. In the end, the heroine's (Fujimura) tears persuade the stone samurai to return home. Special effects once again created by Yoshiyuki Kuroda.

Sequel: MAJIN STRIKES AGAIN (qv; 1966)

ROSTRO INFERNAL

(USA: THE INCREDIBLE FACE OF DR. B)
Mexico, 1961 (1963). Dir: Alfredo B. Crevenna. With: Eric Del Castillo, Rosa Carmina, Jaime Fernández, Elsa Cárdenas. Tec/Clasa-Mohme/ Azteca. B&W.

Over three episodes ('Rostro Infernal', 'Error Fatal' and 'La Trampa') a police inspector investigating a series of bizarre kidnappings discovers a mad scientist cursed with eternal life and the female automaton he has created.

SAMSON IN THE WAX MUSEUM

(Orig: SANTO EN EL MUSEO DE CERA)
Mexico, 1963 (1964). Dir: Alfonso Corona Blake. With: Santo (Rodolfo Guzman Huerta), Claudio Brook, Rubén Rojo, Norma Mora, Roxana Bellini, Fernando Oses. Filmadora Panamerica/Azteca/Clasa-Mohme/ American International. B&W.

Santo the silver masked wrestler (called Samson in this dubbed version) battles mad scientist Dr Karol (Brook), who transforms sleepwalkers into monsters and displays them in his spooky wax museum. On display are a Frankenstein-like creature, Quasimodo, Landru (Bluebeard), the Phantom of the Opera and a yeti.

Sequel: SANTO CONTRA EL ESTRANGULADOR (1963)

SANTO CONTRA EL CEREBRO DIABOLICO

Mexico, 1961 (1962). Dir: Federico Curiel. With: Santo (Rodolfo Guzman Huerta), Fernando Casanova, Ana Bertha Lepe, Roberto Ramirez, Augustino Benedico, Luis Aceves Castañeda. Peliculas Rodriguez. B&W.

A Frankenstein-type mad scientist creates

a monster to battle Santo, the silver-masked wrestling hero. In the end, the creature turns on its creator and destroys him. Filmed in three parts ('Santo contra el Cerebro diabolico', 'Pueblo Sin Ley' and 'La Lucha Final'), the title translates as *Santo vs. the Diabolical Brain.*

Sequel: SANTO CONTRA EL REY DEL CRIMEN (1961)

SANTO CONTRA LOS CAZADORES DE CABEZAS

Mexico, 1969. Dir: René Cardona. With: Santo (Rodolfo Guzman Huerta), Nadia Milton, René Cardona, Freddy Fernández, Enrique Lucero. Zacarias/Azteca. Colour.

Santo, the silver masked wrestler, sets out to stop the mad Dr Mathus using the blood of the living to revive the dead. The title translates as *Santo vs. the Head Hunters.*

Sequel: SANTO CONTRA LOS ASESINOS DE LA MAFIA (1969)

SANTO Y BLUE DEMON VS. LOS MONSTRUOS

(aka CONTRA LOS MONSTRUOS/ SANTO Y BLUE DEMON CONTRA LOS MONSTRUOS/SANTO CONTRA LOS MONSTRUOS DE FRANKENSTEIN) Mexico, 1968 (1969). Dir: Gilberto Martinez Solares. With: Santo (Rodolfo Guzman Huerta), Blue Demon (Alejandro Cruz), Jorge Rado, Carlos Ancira, Raul Martinez Solares Jr, Hedy Blue. Cinematografica Sotomayor/Azteca/Clasa-Mohme. Colour.

During the late 1960s and early seventies, as their respective series reached a peak of popularity, Mexico's two greatest wrestling heroes, Santo and the Blue Demon, teamed up for a number of adventures. This is probably the best, in which they not only have to confront the mad Dr Bruno Halder (Ancira) who is revived by his evil dwarf assistant, but also battle a vampire (David Alvizu) with pointy ears and a top hat, the Mummy (Fernando Rosales), the bearded Franquestain/ Frankestein (*sic*) Monster (Manuel Leal), a black wolfman (Vincente Lare 'Cacama'), two vampire women (Elsa Maria Tako and Yolanda Ponce), a glowing-eyed Cyclops (Gerardo Cepeda), a big-brained blue alien, a quartet of zombies and a deadly double of the Blue Demon! It all ends in an incredible battle between the wrestlers and all the monsters that has to

SECONDS

USA, 1966. Dir: John Frankenheimer. With: Rock Hudson, Salome Jens, John Randolph, Will Geer, Jeff Corey, Richard Anderson. Paramount/Joel Productions. B&W.

Chilling medical thriller, based on the book by David Ely. Middle-aged businessman Randolph is 'reborn' by a mysterious corporation into the body of Hudson (giving perhaps his finest dramatic performance). When he decides he prefers his previous life, he discovers that it is too late to go back. This is the third in Frankenheimer's loose science fiction trilogy (along with *The Manchurian Candidate* [1962] and *Seven Days in May* [1963]), with an excellent supporting cast (including Murray Hamilton) and James Wong Howe's remarkable cinematography. The ending is truly disturbing.

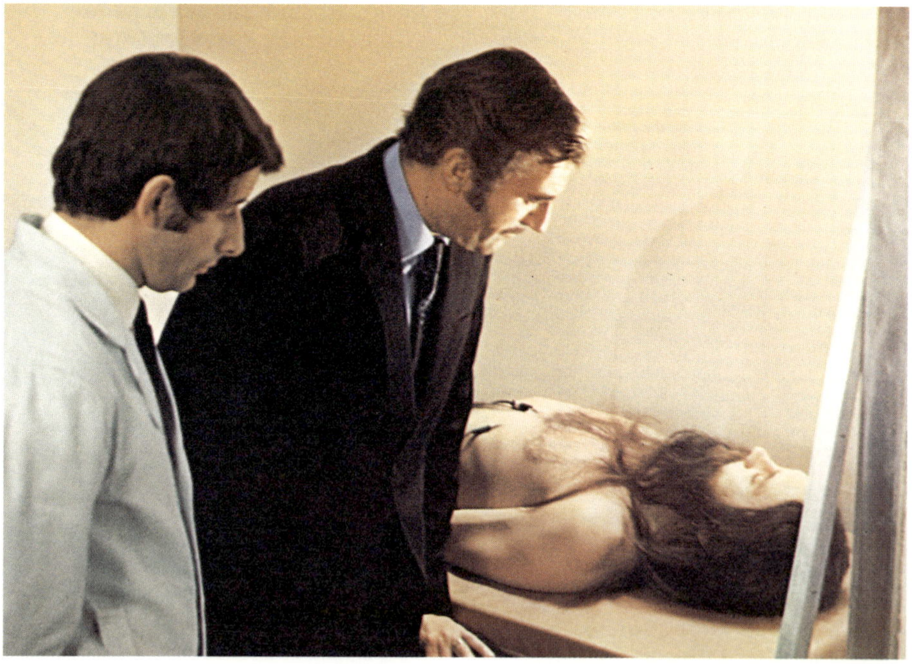

***Above:** The Man Who Thought Life.*
***Right:** The Mind of Mr. Soames.*

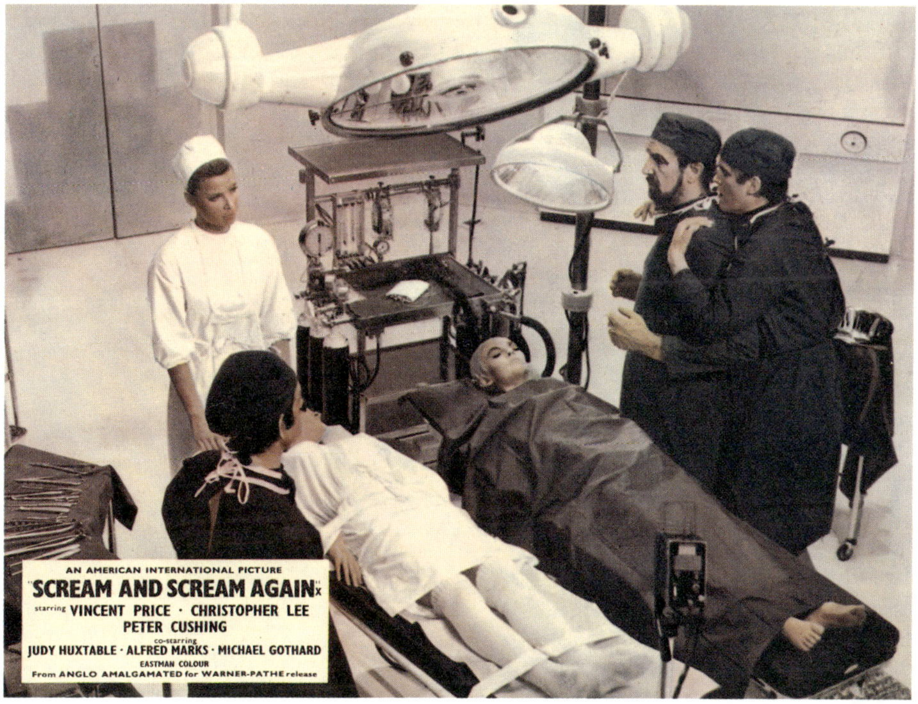

be seen to be believed. They sure must have loved multi-monster movies in Mexico.
Sequels: SANTO CONTRA LOS CAZADORES DE CABEZAS (qv; 1969) and LOS CAMPEONES JUSTICIEROS (1970)

SCREAM AND SCREAM AGAIN

UK, 1969. Dir: Gordon Hessler. With: Vincent Price, Christopher Lee, Peter Cushing, Judy Huxtable, Alfred Marks, Michael Gothard. American International/Amicus. Colour.

A cult classic of the science fiction/horror genre, which benefits from a clever and amusing performance by Marks as harassed police superintendent Bellaver, investigating a series of savage murders where each of the bodies has been sucked dry of blood. Christopher Wicking's confused screenplay, based on Peter Saxon's novel *The Disorientated Man*, finally leads to a plot by Price's Dr Browning to create a new race of superbeings. The three horror stars are grievously wasted (particularly Cushing, who shares no scenes with the other two and is killed off early on). "But what of the dream?" asks Price. "There is only nightmare," replies Lee.

SEXY PROBITISSIMO

(aka SUPER SEXY INTERDIT. USA: FORBIDDEN FEMININITY)
Italy, 1963. Dir: Marcello Martinelli. With: Karmela, Lilli de Saigon, Monique, Joan Clair, Diana West, Poppy Scott. Gino Mordini Produzioni Cinematografiche/Atlantis Films/Olympic International. Colour.

Nudie musical with cabaret sketches that include the Frankenstein Monster pursuing the doctor's beautiful assistant, Martians, cavemen, an astronaut and a victim of Count Dracula. The director supplies the commentary. The American version includes new footage.

SILENT NIGHT, LONELY NIGHT

USA, 1969. Dir: Daniel Petrie. With: Lloyd Bridges, Shirley Jones, Carrie Snodgress, Robert Lipton, Cloris Leachman, Lynn Carlin. Universal. Colour.

TV movie based on the play by Robert Anderson. A chance Christmas meeting at a New England inn turns into romance for lonely middle-agers Bridges and Jones. With a young Jeff Bridges and clips from *Bride of Frankenstein* (1935).

SUPERARGO VS. THE ROBOTS

(Orig: IL RE DEI CRIMINALI/ SUPERDRAGO E I GIGANTI SENZA VOLTO/SUPERAGO EL GIGANTE. USA: aka DEVILMAN STORY. UK: THE DEVIL'S MAN)
Italy/Spain, 1966 (1969). Dir: Paul Maxwell (Paolo Binachini). With: Ken Wood (Giovanni Cianfriglia), Guy Madison, Liz Barrett (Luisa Baratto), Aldo Sambrell, Alan Collins (Luciano Picozzi), Diana Lorys. GV-SEC Film/Izaro/Lion International. Colour.
Sequel to *Superargo vs. Diabolicus* (1966). Bulletproof wrestling hero Superargo (Wood) aids a scientist's daughter (Barrett) in finding her kidnapped father. He is being held captive in North Africa by silver-helmeted villain Devilman (Sambrell), who is planning to have a mechanical superbrain transplanted into his head.

SWEET CHARITY

USA, 1969. Dir: Bob Fosse. With: Shirley MacLaine, John McMartin, Ricardo Montalban, Sammy Davis Jr, Chita Rivera, Stubby Kaye. Universal. Colour.
Fosse made his début as a film director with this energetic musical about a prostitute with a heart of gold. Adapted from the Broadway show written by Neil Simon, which in turn was based on Federico Fellini's *Nights of Cabiria* (1957). Includes the songs 'Big Spender', 'If They Could See Me Now' and 'Rhythm of Life', plus clips from *Frankenstein* (1931).

EL TESTAMENTO DEL FRANKENSTEIN

Spain, 1964. Dir: José Luis Madrid. With: Gerard Landry, George Vallis.
A descendant of Frankenstein (Landry) creates yet another Monster (Vallis).

THEY SAVED HITLER'S BRAIN

(aka MADMEN OF MANDORAS)
USA, 1963. Dir: David Bradley. With: Audrey Caire, Walter Stocker, Carlos Rivas, John Holland, Dani Lynn, Nestor Paiva. Sans/Crown International. B&W.
Filmed on an almost nothing budget, with some sequences apparently shot in Mexico or the Philippines and an impressive car crash lifted from *Thunder Road* (1958). The incoherent plot has an American secret agent taking his wife to Mandoras to stop a group of Nazis from wiping out the world's population with a secret toxic gas. When the only scientist with an antidote is kidnapped along with his daughter, it turns out that Hitler's head (kept alive in a glass container but unable to do much more than raise its eyebrows) is behind the whole silly plot! Director Bradley made his début in 1941 directing a teenage Charlton Heston in an amateur version of *Peer Gynt*.

IL TUNNEL SOTTO IL MONDO

Italy, 1968. Dir: Luigi Cozzi. With: Alberto Moro, Bruno Salviero, Anna Mantovani, Lello Maraniello, Gretel Fehr, Isabell Karllson. Idea Film. Colour.
Based on the short science fiction story 'The Tunnel Under the World' by Frederik Pohl. A man discovers an entire town

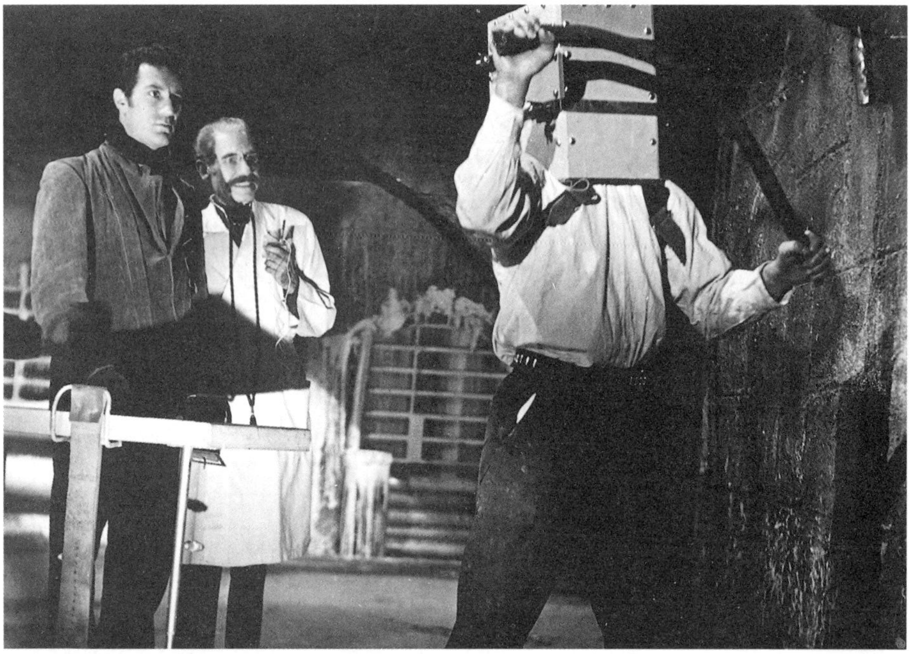

Above left: *Orlak, El Infierno de Frankenstein. (FJA).*
Below left: *Santo y Blue Demon vs. los Monstruos. (FJA).*

Above: Seconds.

being electronically controlled by a giant corporation. Pietro Rosati appears as an alien vampire. This apparently includes footage from Cozzi's *Isabell, A Dream* (1968), featuring Frankenstein's Monster, Dracula and the Mummy (actors wearing Don Post masks), and (Abbott and Costello) *Meet Frankenstein* (1948).

LA VENGANZA DE LAS MUJERES VAMPIRO

(aka SANTO EN LA VENGANZA DE LAS MUJERES VAMPIRO/SANTO Y LA MALDICION DE LAS VAMPIRAS) Mexico, 1969. Dir: Federico Curiel. With: Santo (Rodolfo Guzmán Huerta or Eric del Castillo), Norma Lazareno, Gina Romand, Aldo Monti, Victor Junco, Patricia Ferrer. Cinematografica Flama/Peliculas Latinoamericanas. Colour.

Despite the title, this is not really a sequel to *Samson vs. the Vampire Women* (1961), but an uncredited remake of *Atacan Las Brujas* (1964). Using the blood of a night-club dancer, mad Dr Brancor (Junco) revives the undead Countess Mayra (Romand), who believes that Santo, the silver masked wrestler, is the descendant of the man who staked her vampire ancestors. The doctor also creates the Frankenstein Monster-like Razos (Nathaniel Leon) from spare cadavers.

Sequel: SANTO CONTRA LOS JINETES DEL TERROR (1970)

VENGEANCE

(aka EIN TOTER SUCHT SEINEN MORDER. USA: THE BRAIN) UK/West Germany, 1962. Dir: Freddie Francis. With: Anne Heywood, Peter Van Eyck, Cecil Parker, Bernard Lee, Maxine Audley, Jeremy Spenser. British Lion/C.C.C. B&W.

This third version of Curt Siodmak's novel *Donovan's Brain* marked the horror directing début of cinematographer Francis. This time the science fiction plot is combined with a murder mystery. When a private plane belonging to powerful tycoon Max Holt crashes on the Sussex Downs, his still-living brain is kept alive by Dr Peter Corrie (Van Eyck) and his colleague Frank Shears (Lee). However, the disembodied brain soon begins to exert a strange hypnotic influence over Corrie. With a nice twist ending and solid support from British character actors Miles Malleson, Jack MacGowran, George A. Cooper and John Junkin.

WAR OF THE GARGANTUAS

(Orig: FURANKENSHUTAIN NO KAIJU — SANDA TAI GAILAH) Japan/USA, 1966 (1970). Dir: Inoshiro Honda. With: Russ Tamblyn, Kumi Mizuno, Kenji Sahara, Kipp Hamilton, Jun Tazaki. Toho/American International Pictures. Colour.

Intended as a sequel to *Frankenstein Conquers the World* (1964), all references to the earlier film were deleted during shooting by the American producer. It features a friendly (brown) giant Frankenstein Monster and his evil (green) brother battling each other in the middle of Eiji Tsuburaya's miniature Tokyo. Includes shots of a giant octopus attacking a ship, cut from the 1964 film. This was apparently based (uncredited) on one of Willis O'Brien's yeti stories.

WAY...WAY OUT

USA, 1966. Dir: Gordon Douglas. With: Jerry Lewis, Connie Stevens, Robert Morley, Dennis Weaver, Brian Keith, Dick Shawn, Anita Ekberg. Twentieth Century-Fox. Colour.

Dire science fiction comedy in which Lewis travels to the Moon with Stevens. Includes clips from *Frankenstein* (1931).

YELLOW SUBMARINE

UK, 1968. Dir: George Dunning. With: The Beatles (John Lennon, Paul McCartney, George Harrison, Ringo Starr). Voices: John Clive, Geoffrey Hughes. Apple Films/King Features/Subafilms/United Artists. Colour.

Cartoon musical fantasy based around fourteen songs performed by The Beatles. The Fab Four escape a grey Liverpool and travel to Pepperland to save their alter-egos, Sergeant Pepper's Lonely Hearts Club Band, from the music-hating Blue Meanies. With brief glimpses of the Frankenstein Monster and King Kong, voices by Paul Angelus, Dick Emery and Lance Percival, and a contrived live-action epilogue featuring the boys themselves.

the

It seemed that with the death of Boris Karloff, any dignity Mary Shelley's twisted creation may still have retained also passed away. Even Hammer Films, who had won the Queen's Award to Industry in 1968, began to lose direction, relying on sex and violence to boost its flagging output.

With **The Horror of Frankenstein (1970)**, *director Jimmy Sangster (b 1924) basically remade his original script for* **The Curse of Frankenstein (1957)** *as a comedy, replacing Peter Cushing with the younger Ralph Bates (1940-1991) and casting Dave Prowse as the Monster. The same year, Cushing himself appeared very briefly as the Baron (along with Christopher Lee's Dracula) in another comedy,* **One More Time (1970)**. *The actor returned to the role he had made his own with* **Frankenstein and the Monster from Hell (1973)**, *which again featured Prowse as the Monster and marked the triumphant return of director Terence Fisher one last time.*

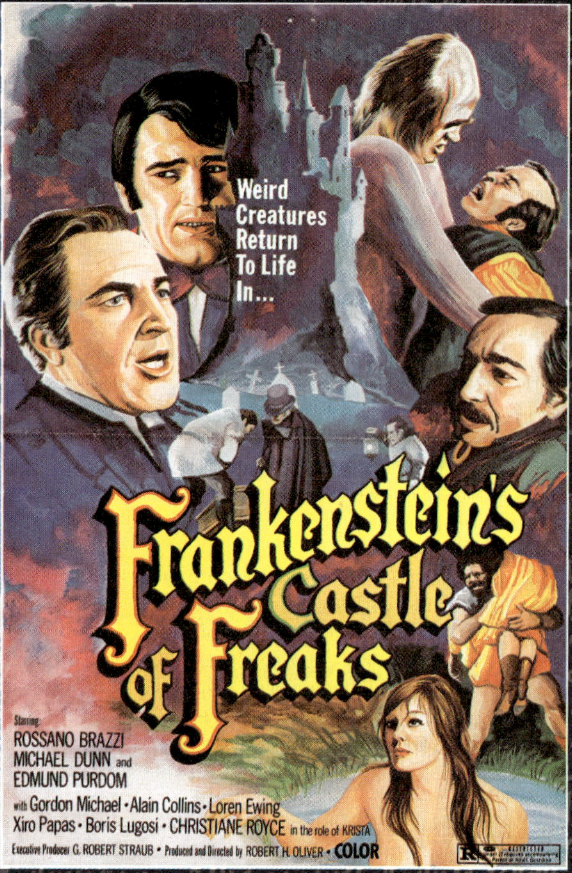

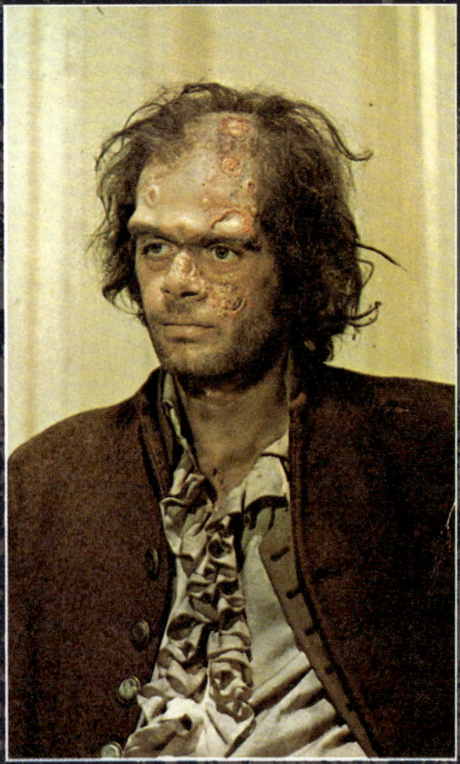
Frankenstein: The True Story.

Hammer wasn't the only studio experimenting with greater sexual freedom; Sara Bay made love to her own creation in **Lady Frankenstein (1971)**, *while poor old Dennis Price (1915-1973) found himself surrounded by plenty of nudity and incomprehensible plots in director Jesus Franco's* **Dracula Prisoner of Frankenstein (1972)** *and its sequel* **The Erotic Rites of Frankenstein (1972)**. *The actor also turned up as Professor Van Helsing in the musical/comedy* **Son of Dracula (1973)**, *pitted against Freddie Jones' evil Baron Frankenstein.*

Dracula vs. Frankenstein (1970) *was another mess that*

1970s

marked the end for two veteran performers. An ailing J. Carrol Naish (1900-1973) and Lon Chaney Jr (in a non-speaking role due to his throat cancer) were reunited from **House of Frankenstein (1944)** *for this cheap exploitation feature. Of similar quality was the blaxploitation* **Blackenstein (1972)** *and* **Frankenstein's Castle of Freaks (1973)**, *the latter featuring Rossano Brazzi as Count Frankenstein.*

There were still some serious attempts to adapt Mary Shelley's classic, as **Pastel de Sangre (1971)**, **Victor Frankenstein (1976)**, *and the television movies* **Frankenstein (1973)** *and* **Frankenstein: The True Story (1973)** *proved; but other films, like* **Dr. Frankenstein on Campus (1970)**, **Frankenstein '80 (1972)** *and* **Flesh for Frankenstein (1973)**, *were content to rework the original story with gratuitous gore and nudity where required.*

It was therefore something of a surprise that the best Frankenstein movie of the decade was a comedy — Mel Brooks' beautifully recreated tribute to the Universal series, **Young Frankenstein (1974)**. *"The look and feel is German Expressionism," explained the director. "It's a salute to James Whale and the wonderful directors of the past, and that beautiful black and white look..." Unfortunately, it was followed by two very inferior spoofs,* **Frankenstein — Italian Style (1975)** *and the Spanish* **Sevimli Frankestayn (1975)**.

At least **The Rocky Horror Picture Show (1975)** *was content to satirise the horror genre with exhilarating songs and a memorable cast of bizarre characters, which resulted in it achieving something of a cult status.*

By the end of the 1970s the bubble had finally burst and the third and most successful horror cycle was over. Hammer and American International were gone, while most of the great stars and directors were either dead or retired. Before things got better, there was still worse to come...

Young Frankenstein.

ALLEGRO NON TROPPO

Italy, 1976. Dir: Bruno Bozzetto. Voices: Maurizio Nichetti, Nestor Gavay, Maurizio Micheli, Maria Luisa Giozannina. Bruno Bozzetto Films. Colour/B&W.

Feature length cartoon parody of Walt Disney's *Fantasia* (1940), with live-action framing sequences in black and white. A hunchbacked character called Frankenstein enters a castle dungeon to create an ending for the film.

THE AMAZING TRANSPLANT

USA, 1970 (1971). Dir: Louis Silverman and Dawn Whitman (Doris Wishman). With: Juan Fernandez, Linda Southern, Larry Hunter, Kim Pope. Jerand/Mostest Productions. Colour.

Softcore sex comedy in which virgin Arthur Baron (Fernandez) receives a penis transplant from his dying friend Felix. Unfortunately, a side effect involves Arthur's new organ becoming excited whenever he sees a woman wearing gold ear-rings and he turns into a killer. Filmed in New York, this was released the same year as two other penis transplant movies.

ASYLUM

(USA: aka HOUSE OF CRAZIES)
UK, 1972. Dir: Roy Ward Baker. With: Peter Cushing, Britt Ekland, Herbert Lom, Patrick Magee, Barry Morse, Barbara Parkins. Amicus/Harbor. Colour.

All-star episodic horror thriller, scripted by Robert Bloch and based on his own short stories. When Dr Martin (Robert Powell) arrives to take up a new post at a remote private asylum, he must first discover the identity of the now-insane head of the institution, Dr Starr. 'Frozen Fear' is fun as Sylvia Syms' neatly-wrapped severed limbs take voodoo revenge on her husband Richard Todd and his lover Parkins; Cushing adds dignity to 'The Weird Tailor', trying to bring his dead son back to life with a magic suit; Britt Ekland and Charlotte Rampling share a psychological secret in 'Lucy Comes to Stay'; however, 'Mannikins of Horror' fails to overcome the low budget, as Lom's homicidal homunculi are revealed as clumsy-looking toys filled with human eviscera. With a nice shock ending and solid support from James Villiers and Geoffrey Bayldon.

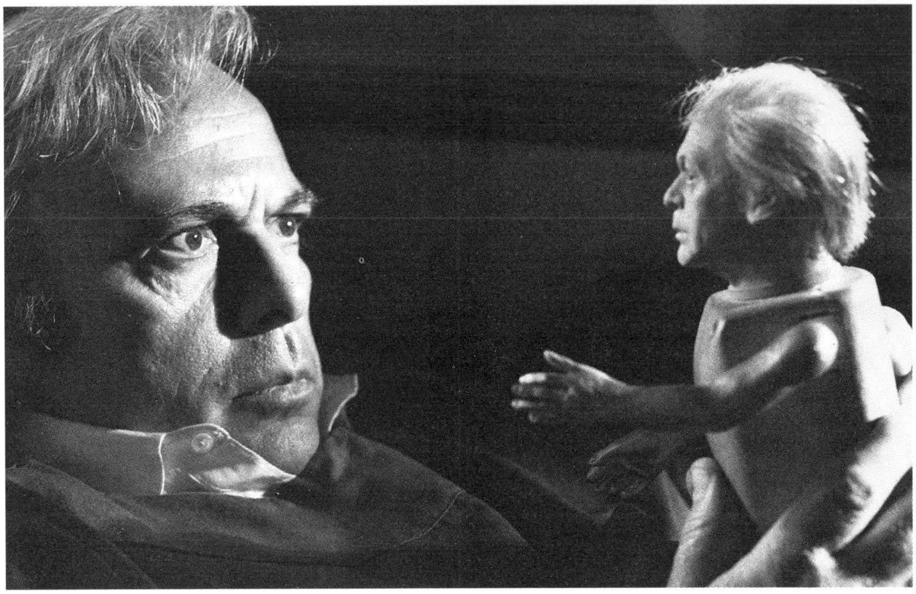

BEAST OF BLOOD

(USA: aka BEAST OF THE DEAD. UK: BLOOD DEVILS)
Philippines/USA, 1970. Dir: Eddie Romero. With: John Ashley, Celeste Yarnall, Alfonso Carvajal, Liza Belmonte, Eddie Garcia, Bruno Punzalan. Hemisphere Pictures. Colour.

Sequel to *The Mad Doctor of Blood Island* (1969). Ashley's hero returns to the Pacific island and discovers that the mad Dr Lorca (Garcia) is still alive and attempting to transplant the severed head of the green-blooded monster onto a new body. In the end, the doctor is killed by the headless creature. When originally released in America, audiences were given sick bags.

LAS BESTIAS DEL TERROR

(aka SANTO CONTRA LAS BESTIAS DEL TERROR)
Mexico, 1972. Dir: Alfredo B. Crevenna. With: Santo (Rodolfo Guzman Huerta or Eric del Castillo), Elsa Cardenas, Antonio de Hud, Victor Junco, Alma Ferrari. Colour.

When another mad scientist brings the dead back to life, Santo the silver masked wrestler takes on the beasts of terror.
Sequel: SANTO CONTRA LA MAGIA NEGRA (1972)

BLACKENSTEIN

(aka BLACK FRANKENSTEIN)
USA, 1972. Dir: William A. (Al) Levey. With: John Hart, Ivory Stone, Liz Renay, Roosevelt Jackson,

Top: *Asylum.*
Above: *The Boys from Brazil.*

Andrea King, Nick Bolin. Exclusive International. Colour.

Feeble attempt to cash-in on the blaxploitation market of the early 1970s. The white Dr Stein (Hart) experiments on a black Vietnam war veteran (Joe DeSue), using an experimental DNA formula to attach new limbs to his body. But a jealous lab assistant swaps the formula, resulting in a crazed monster with a square afro who kills women and eats their intestines. In the end the creature is torn apart by LA police dogs. The laboratory equipment was originally created by Ken Strickfaden for Universal's *Frankenstein* (1931). A sequel announced in 1976, *Black Frankenstein Meets the White Werewolf*, was thankfully never made.

BLOOD OF GHASTLY HORROR

(aka PSYCHO-A-GO-GO/THE FIEND WITH THE ELECTRONIC BRAIN/ MAN WITH THE SYNTHETIC BRAIN)
USA, 1972. Dir: Al Adamson. With: John Carradine, Kent Taylor, Tommy Kirk, Regina Carrol, Roy Morton, Tracey Robbins. TAL/ Independent-International. Colour.
Okay, pay attention: producer/director Adamson originally made this in 1965 as *Psycho-a-Go-Go*, with Morton as a killer with an electronic control device in his head. New scenes were added in 1969 and it was released as *The Fiend with the Electronic Brain*. More scenes were added in 1972 and the title changed again (it later turned up on American TV and in the UK as *Man With the Synthetic Brain*). Whatever the title, it is still an incomprehensible mess. Carradine plays the mad Dr Vanard, experimenting with human guinea pigs. Taylor is another mad scientist out to revenge his son's death using a disfiguring serum and a green-tinged monster. And ex-Disney star Kirk appears as a befuddled police detective who throws up when he discovers a severed head in a box. With Regina Carrol (Mrs Al Adamson). Filmed in 'Chill-O-Rama'.

THE BOYS FROM BRAZIL

Portugal/USA/UK/Austria, 1978. Dir: Franklin J. Schaffner. With: Gregory Peck, Laurence Olivier, James Mason, Lilli Palmer, Uta Hagen, Denholm Elliott. ITC/ Producer Circle. Colour.
Slow adaptation of Ira Levin's novel about war criminal Dr Joseph Mengele (Peck) using genetic experiments to create clones of Adolf Hitler throughout the world. Olivier plays his elderly Nazi hunter, Ezra Lieberman, with a distracting silly voice, while Mason is simply wasted. With Steve Guttenberg, Michael Gough, Linda Hayden, Bruno Ganz, Walter Gotell and John Dehner. The longer American version has a different ending from the print originally released in Britain.

BRACULA — THE TERROR OF THE LIVING DEAD!

(Orig: LA ORGIA DE LOS MUERTOS/ LA ORGIA DEI MORTI. USA: aka RETURN OF THE ZOMBIES/BEYOND THE LIVING DEAD. USA/UK: aka THE HANGING WOMAN)
Spain/Italy, 1972 (1974). Dir: John Davidson (José Luis Merino). With: Stan Cooper (Stelvio Rosi), Vickie Nesbitt (Dianik Zurakowska), Marcella Wright (Maria Pia Conte), Catherine Gilbert, Gerald (Gerard) Tichy, Carl Mansion (Mancini). Preodimex/Petruka Films/ International Artists. Colour.
Set in the nineteenth century Carpathians, the mad Dr Leon (Tichy) harnesses 'nebula electricity' in his experiments to bring the dead back to life through capsules implanted in their brains. In the end, the doctor's mental control fails and he is strangled by his blind creations. Eleventh billed Paul Nash (Paul Naschy aka Jacinto Molina) plays Igor, a necrophiliac grave-digger who is decapitated by hero Cooper after being revived as a zombie.

BRAIN OF BLOOD

(USA: aka THE BRAIN/THE UNDYING BRAIN/THE CREATURE'S REVENGE)
USA/Philippines, 1971. Dir: Al Adamson. With: Grant Williams, Kent Taylor, John Bloom, Regina Carrol, Vicki Volante, Angelo Rossitto. Phil-Am Enterprises/ Hemisphere Pictures. Colour.
As if Eddie Romero's series of Filipino *Blood Island* movies weren't bad enough, the producers hired Al Adamson to make his own contribution to the mad doctor

Above right: *The Brood.*
Below right: *Capulina contra los Monstruos.*

genre. The result is predictably terrible. Taylor stars as Dr Lloyd Trent, whose experiments with brain transplanting result in Gor (Bloom), an ugly pinhead monster. Meanwhile, Dorro (Rossitto), his sadistic dwarf assistant, torments the women they keep chained in the cellar for their blood. With Zandor Vorkov (Roger Engell) and guest star Reed Hadley as the Amir. It was also released in Canada under the title *Brain Damage*.

THE BROOD

Canada, 1979. Dir: David Cronenberg. With: Oliver Reed, Samantha Eggar, Art Hindle, Nula Fitzgerald, Henry Beckman, Susan Hogan. Mutual Productions/Elgin International. Colour.

One of Cronenberg's most underrated films. In the Somafree experimental clinic, the enigmatic Dr Raglan (a surprisingly restrained Reed) convinces his patients to externalise the shape of their rage. This results in neurotic patient Nola Carveth (Eggar) giving multiple birth to deformed homicidal children who do her subconscious bidding (like clubbing a schoolteacher to death in front of her young class). The bloody killings are handled with style and the twist ending is genuinely unexpected.

CAPULINA CONTRA LOS MONSTRUOS

Mexico, 1972. Dir: René Cardona. With: Gasper Henaine 'Capulina', Gloriella, Hector Andremar. Estudios America/Panorama Films/Azteca Films. Colour.

More humour from the moustachioed comedian Capulina as he meets the Frankenstein Monster, a vampire and a werewolf. Don't they ever get tired of this plot in Mexico?

CARDIAC ARREST

USA, 1978 (1979). Dir: Murray Mintz. With: Garry Goodrow, Mike Chan, Maxwell Gail, Susan O'Connell, Ray Reinhardt, Robert A. Behling. Murriku Production Partners/Independent Network Inc/Film Ventures International. Colour.

Low budget thriller in which San Francisco cop Clancy Higgins (Goodrow) investigates a series of bizarre killings where the hearts of the victims are removed. His unorthodox methods eventually uncover a black market in human organ transplants. With an early appearance by Fred Ward as a murderous ambulance driver.

CHABELO Y PEPITO VS. LOS MONSTRUOS

(aka CHABELO Y PEPITO CONTRA LOS MONSTRUOS)

Mexico, 1973. Dir: José Estrada. With: Chabelo (Xavier Lopez), Pepito (Martin Ramos), Silvia Pasquel. Alameda Films. Colour.

Yet another Mexican multi-monster marathon. This features the comedy team of Pepito and Chabelo confronting a Karloffian Frankenstein Monster, Dracula, a werewolf, Mr Hyde, the Mummy, a gorilla and the Creature from the Black Lagoon.

THE CLONE MASTER

USA, 1978. Dir: Don Medford. With: Art Hindle, Robyn Douglas, Ed Lauter, Ralph Bellamy, John Van Dreelen, Mario Roccuzzo. Paramount. Colour.

TV pilot movie in which biochemist Hindle clones himself thirteen times and sends the telepathic duplicates out to battle evil. It never became a series.

THE CLONES

(UK: CLONES)

USA, 1973. Dir: Paul Hunt and Lamar Card. With: Michael Greene, Otis Young, Gregory Sierra, Susan Hunt, Stanley Adams, Alex Nicol. Hunt-Card Productions/Filmmakers

International. Colour.
Low budget science fiction thriller in which research scientist Greene escapes from a secret government laboratory only to discover he's been cloned by Adams, who plans to rule the world. With veterans Bruce Bennett, Angelo Rossitto and John Barrymore Jr. Filmed under the title *Dead Man Running.*

THE CLONES OF BRUCE LEE

(Orig: SHEN-WEI SAN MENG-LUNG) Hong Kong/Thailand, circa 1979 (1980). Dir: Joseph Kong (Chiang Hung). With: Lu Hsiao-Lung, Kuo Shih-Chih, Chu Lung, Yang Szu, Tsai I-Ming, Chiang Tao. Wei Ling/ Jay Jay/Newport/Media Home Entertainment. Colour.
Following the death of Bruce Lee, the mad Professor Lucas creates three crime busting clones of the martial arts star (Dragon Lee, Bruce Le, Bruce Lai). They battle the 'bronze men', an army of drugged zombies who are defeated when they are forced to eat poisonous grass(!) This also includes a death ray.

THE CLONING OF CLIFFORD SWIMMER

USA, 1974. Dir: Lela Swift. With: Peter Haskell, Lance Kerwin, Sheree North, Sharon Farrell. Lefferts. Colour.
Made-for-TV movie in which a scientist creates a clone.

COMA

USA, 1978. Dir: Michael Crichton. With: Geneviève Bujold, Michael Douglas, Elizabeth Ashley, Rip Torn, Richard Widmark, Lois Chiles. Metro-Goldwyn-Mayer. Colour.
Writer/director Crichton's entertaining adaptation of Robin Cook's best-selling medical horror novel. When one of her close friends unexpectedly suffers irreparable brain damage after a routine operation, Dr Susan Wheeler (a sympathetic Bujold) finds her life and sanity threatened as she uncovers a plot to sell body parts to the menacing Jefferson Institute. With Tom Selleck in a small role. Music by Jerry Goldsmith.

Left: *Chabelo y Pepito vs. los Monstruos.*
Below: *Coma.*

COMPUTERCIDE

(Orig: THE FINAL EYE) USA, 1977 (1982). Dir: Robert Michael Lewis. With: Joseph Cortase, Tom Clancy, Susan George, David Huddleston, Donald Pleasence, Linda Gillin. Paramount/ Culzean. Colour.
Made-for-TV pilot movie which sat on the shelf for five years. Set in the mid-1990s, the world's last private eye (Cortase) searches for a missing scientist and uncovers a utopian community and a cloning conspiracy.

CRIMSON

(Orig: LAS RATAS NO DUERMEN DE NOCHE/L'HOMME A LA TETE COUPEE OU LE VIOL ET L'ENFER) Spain/France, 1973 (1974). Dir: John

Fortune (Juan Fortuny). With: Paul Naschy (Jacinto Molina), Richard Palmer, Carlos Otero, Oliver Mathot, Silvia Solar, Victor Israel. Producciones Mezquiriz/Eurocine-Europrodis. Colour.
Crime thriller in which Naschy's injured gangster has the brain of decapitated rival 'El Sadico' transplanted into his head by Palmer's professor. Pretty soon the two criminal minds are vying for the same body. An unofficial remake of *Black Friday* (1940), the original Spanish title translates as *Rats Don't Sleep at Night*. The French version, released in 1976, apparently includes softcore inserts.

CRY UNCLE!

USA, 1971. Dir: John G. Avildsen. With: Allen Garfield, Madeleine de la Roux, Devin Goldenberg, David Kirk, Sean Walsh, Nancy Salmon. Crest Films. Colour.
Tasteless private eye spoof that includes clips from *Bride of Frankenstein* (1935).

THE DARKER SIDE OF TERROR

USA, 1979. Dir: Gus Trikonis. With: Robert Forster, Adrienne Barbeau, Ray Milland, John Lehne, David Sheiner, Denise du Barry. Banner Associates. Colour.
TV movie in which Professor Paul Corwin creates a homicidal clone of himself. Forster does okay playing both roles, but Barbeau is totally wasted as his wife. The enigmatic ending never reveals whether it is the scientist or his double who survives.

Above: Death Race 2000.

THE DEAD DON'T DIE

USA, 1974. Dir: Curtis Harrington. With: George Hamilton, Linda Cristal, Joan Blondell, Ralph Meeker, James McEachin, Ray Milland. Douglas S. Cramer Co. Colour.
Wonderfully enjoyable TV movie, scripted by Robert Bloch and based on his pulp horror/detective story. Special guest star Milland plays the master villain who is bringing the dead back to life in 1930s Chicago in an attempt to rule the world. The film may have a poverty row look, but Harrington's direction is atmospheric, there's an impressive zombie attack in a graveyard and the dream B-movie cast includes genre veterans Reggie Nalder (as a revived corpse), Milton Parsons and Yvette Vickers.

DEATH RACE 2000

USA, 1975. Dir: Paul Bartel. With: David Carradine, Simone Griffeth, Sylvester Stallone, Mary Woronov, Roberta Collins, Martin Kove. New World Pictures. Colour.
Enjoyable futuristic road movie, co-scripted by Robert Thom and Charles B. Griffith (based on an original story, 'The Racer', by Ib Melchior) and produced by Roger Corman. In Mr President's fascist United Provinces of America, five teams enter the twentieth Annual Transcont-inental Road Race from New York to New Los Angeles, scoring points for the quickest time and each person they hit and kill along the route. Carradine stars as masked champion racer 'Frankenstein', who has supposedly been rebuilt after surviving repeated crashes in his car, The Monster. However, a pre-stardom Stallone steals the film as his rival, the manic Machine Gun Joe Viterbo. Featuring comic book characters and mayhem, with cameos by Joyce Jameson, director Bartel as a doctor and John Landis as a mechanic. Lewis Teague and Charles B. Griffith directed the second units. Some scenes were later reused in *Hollywood Boulevard* (1976).

DEATH SMILES ON A MURDERER

(Orig: LA MORTE HA SORRISO ALL'ASSASSINO)
Italy, 1972. Dir: Aristide Massaccesi. With: Ewa Aulin, Klaus Kinski, Angela Bo, Sergio Doria, Attilio Dottesio, Giacomo Rossi Stuart. Dany Film/Avco Embassy. Colour.
Confusing Italian horror thriller set in turn-of-the-century Germany. Dr Sturges (Kinski) attempts to reanimate the dead using an ancient Inca formula. With a hunchback, several razor killings and Aulin (*Candy* [1968]) as a decomposing corpse.

DEVIL KISS

(Orig: LA CARESSE DE SATAN. USA: aka THE PERVERSE KISS OF SATAN)
France/Spain, 1973 (1977). Dir: Georges Gigo. With: Sylvia Solar (Genevieve Couzain), Oliver Mathews (Mathot), José Ruiz Lifante, Victor Israel, Daniel Martin, Evelyn Scott. Home Cinema Corporation. Colour.
The usual blend of sex and horror as a vengeful clairvoyant (Solar), the mad Professor Gruber (Mathot) and their midget assistant use cellular regeneration to revive a car accident victim as an ugly-looking monster.

DOCTOR GORE

(aka THE BODY SHOP)
USA, 1975. Dir: Pat Patterson. With: J.G. Patterson, Jenny D(r)iggers, Roy Mehaffey, Don Brandon. Video Communications/Paragon Video Productions. Colour.
Tormented by the death of his wife, a crazy paediatrician murders young girls in an attempt to construct the 'perfect' woman. The video release includes an introduction by Herschell Gordon Lewis.

DRACULA PRISONER OF FRANKENSTEIN

(Orig: DRACULA CONTRA FRANKENSTEIN/DRACULA CONTRA EL DOCTOR FRANKENSTEIN/ DRACULA PRISONNIER DE FRANKENSTEIN. USA/UK: THE SCREAMING DEAD)
Spain/France/Liechtenstein/ Portugal, 1972. Dir: Jess (Jesús) Franco. With: Denis (Dennis) Price, Howard Vernon (Mario Lippert), Mary Francis (Paca Gabaldon), Albert (Alberto) Dalbes, Genevieve Deloir, Josiane Gibert. Fenix Films/ Prodif Ets/CFFP/Interfilm. Colour.
The first of three films by Franco, loosely connected by many of the same characters and actors. Dr Frankenstein (a sick-looking Price, dubbed by a younger voice) and his mute servant Morpho (Luis Barboo) revive a green-faced Dracula (Vernon) so that together with his vampire brides they can create an undead army to conquer the world. Fernando Bilbao plays a Karloff-like Frankenstein Monster, and Dr Seward (Dalbes), a gypsy witch and a mangy werewolf (Brandy) are also involved. This was supposedly a homage to director James Whale! More tedious ineptitude from director Franco and another nail in the coffin of Dennis Price's career.
Sequel: THE EROTIC RITES OF FRANKENSTEIN (qv; 1972)

DRACULA VS. FRANKENSTEIN

(aka BLOOD OF FRANKENSTEIN/ THEY'RE COMING TO GET YOU/ REVENGE OF DRACULA)
USA, 1970. Dir: Al Adamson. With: J. Carrol Naish, Lon Chaney, Zandor Vorkov (Roger Engell), Anthony Eisley, Regina Carrol, Greydon Clark. Independent-International Pictures. Colour.
Feeble, seventy year-old, wheelchair-bound veteran Naish (*House of Frankenstein* [1944], etc) came out of retirement to play the last Dr Frankenstein, experimenting with blood in an attempt to cure his crippled legs. He is aided by such side-show horrors as monster axe murderer Groton the Mad Zombie (a mute, pathetic-looking Chaney Jr) and Grazbo the dwarf (Angelo Rossitto). Russ Tamblyn (as a biker) and Jim Davis are special guest stars. Forrest J Ackerman was the technical consultant and plays Dr Beaumont, who is crushed to death by a puffy Frankenstein Monster (John Bloom). Vorkov's hammy Dracula has a ring that zaps people — including ageing hippy hero Eisley. The electronic equipment was originally created by Ken Strickfaden for *Bride of Frankenstein* (1935). This was another mess from director Al Adamson, who shot it over a couple of years (originally as *The Blood Seekers* in 1969). It marked a tragic end to the careers of both Naish and Chaney Jr.

DR. FRANKENSTEIN ON CAMPUS

(Orig: FLICK. UK: FRANKENSTEIN ON CAMPUS)
Canada, 1970. Dir: Gil Taylor. With: Robin Ward, Kathleen Sawyer, Austin Willis, Sean Sullivan, Ty Haller, Tony Moffat-Lynch. Astral Films/Agincourt. Colour.
Possibly filmed as early as 1967. With the help of a mysterious professor (Sullivan), Viktor Frankenstein IV (Ward) creates lethal mind-control tablets which he uses to revenge himself on those students who tormented him. In the end, Viktor is revealed to be an artificial creature.

Below: *Dracula Prisoner of Frankenstein.*

Top: *Everything You Always Wanted to Know About Sex* *But Were Afraid to Ask.*

EMBRYO

(USA: aka CREATED TO KILL) USA, 1975. Dir: Ralph Nelson. With: Rock Hudson, Barbara Carrera, Diane Ladd, Roddy McDowall, Anne Schedeen, John Elerick. Sandy Howard Productions/Astral Bellevue Pathe. Colour.

Hudson gives a strong performance as Dr Paul Holliston, a misguided scientist who creates a serum which can speed up the growth of a three-month-old foetus. After ten days, the result is the beautiful but homicidal Victoria (Carrera). Director Nelson returns to some of the themes he previously explored in *Charly* (1968), but this time he allows the material to degenerate into melodrama. With a fun but pointless cameo by McDowall and a climax in which Carrera transforms into an old hag (make-up effects created by, among others, Dan Striepeke and John Chambers). Featuring Dr Joyce Brothers as herself.

THE EROTIC RITES OF FRANKENSTEIN

(Orig: LES EXPERIENCES EROTIQUES DE FRANKENSTEIN/LA MALDICION DE FRANKENSTEIN. UK: aka THE CURSE OF FRANKENSTEIN) France/Spain/Portugal, 1972. Dir: Jess (Jesús) Franco. With: Denis (Dennis) Price, Howard Vernon (Mario Lippert), Anne Libert (Josiane Gibert), Britt Nichols (Brit Nicols), Albert (Alberto) Dalbes, Luis Barboo. Comtoir Français du Film Production/Fenix-Film. Colour.

Jesús Franco's equally incomprehensible sequel to *Dracula Prisoner of Frankenstein* (1972). An ill-looking Dennis Price returns briefly as Dr Frankestein (*sic*), giving his silver-skinned creation (Fred Harrison aka Fernando Bilbao) the ability to speak before being killed by blind birdwoman Melissa (Libert) and her servant Caronte (Barboo). She takes the Monster back to her living dead master, Count Cagliostro (Vernon), who uses his mental powers to enslave Frankestein's daughter Vera (Beatrice [Beatriz] Savon) and forces her to create a female creature which he can mate with the Monster to propagate a new master race. With Britt Nichols as Abigail/Madame Orloff. Franco's attempts to recreate the Hammer style fail miserably, although this mess is occasionally punctuated by flashes of wild imagination. Lina Romay makes her film début as Esmeralda, but only in the Spanish version, and director Franco turns up as Frankenstein's assistant Morpho.

Sequel: LA FILLE DE DRACULA (1972)

EL ESPIRITU DE LA COLMENA

(aka THE SPIRIT OF THE BEEHIVE) Spain, 1973. Dir: Victor Erice. With: Fernando Fernan Gomez, Teresa Gimpera, Ana Torrent, Isabel Telleria, Miguel Picazo, José Villasante. Elias Querejeta P.C. Colour.

Delightful childhood fantasy. In 1940, the Universal *Frankenstein* (*El Dr. Frankenstein, Autor del Monstruo* [1931]) is shown in a small Castillian village. After the screening, young Ana (Torrent) believes her sister Isabel (Telleria) when the latter tells her the Monster is a real spirit. When she becomes lost in the woods, Ana imagines that the Karloffian Frankenstein Monster (Villasante) is coming for her.

EVERY HOME SHOULD HAVE ONE

(USA: THINK DIRTY) UK, 1970. Dir: Jim Clark. With: Marty Feldman, Judy Cornwell,

Shelly Berman, Julie Ege, Patrick Cargill, Jack Watson. Example Productions/British Lion. Colour.
Dated comedy which marked pop-eyed comedian Feldman's first starring role. As a daydreaming advertising executive who is obsessed with sex, he imagines himself as a vampire battling the Frankenstein Monster, a hedonistic Pan and a cartoon Superman pitted against Batman (Dinsdale Landen) in one of several sequences created by the Richard Williams Studio.

EVERYTHING YOU ALWAYS WANTED TO KNOW ABOUT SEX* *BUT WERE AFRAID TO ASK

USA, 1972. Dir: Woody Allen. With: Woody Allen, John Carradine, Lou Jacobi, Louise Lasser, Anthony Quayle, Tony Randall. United Artists/Brodsky-Gould Productions. Colour.
Episodic comedy from writer, director and star Allen, loosely based on a serious sex manual by Dr David Reuben. The best two of the seven sketches involve Allen playing a court jester trying to use an aphrodisiac on the Queen (Lynn Redgrave) and a reluctant sperm causing consternation to his controllers (Randall and a wasted Burt Reynolds). Gene Wilder turns up as a doctor who falls in love with a sheep, and veteran John Carradine plays over-the-top mad scientist Dr Bernardo who creates a giant siliconised breast which escapes and terrorises the countryside.

FLEISCH

(USA: SPARE PARTS)
West Germany/USA, 1979. Dir: Rainer Erler. With: Jutta Speidel, Wolf Roth, Herbert Herrmann, Charlotte Kerr, Christoph Lindbert, Bob Cunningham. Pentagramma Productions. Colour.
Muddled thriller, written, produced and directed by Erler, based on his own novel. It owes much to *Coma* (1978) as American trucker Roth and Speidel's weak heroine investigate a mysterious group who kidnap healthy victims and sell their body parts to the highest bidder. The fact that the people behind the plot are never revealed is just one of the film's many implausibilities.

FLESH FOR FRANKENSTEIN

(Orig: IL MOSTRO E IN TAVOLA... BARONE FRANKENSTEIN/CARNE PER FRANKENSTEIN/CHAIR POUR FRANKENSTEIN. USA: aka ANDY WARHOL'S FRANKENSTEIN/ FRANKENSTEIN)
Italy/France, 1973. Dir: Paul Morrissey (and Antonio Margheriti). With: Joe Dallesandro, Monique Van Vooren, Udo Kier, Arno Juerging (Jürging), Dalila di Lazzaro, Srdjan Zelenovic. Pagnia Cinematografica Champion/EMI. Colour.
From the same writer/director(s) as *Blood for Dracula* (1973), this adaptation of the Mary Shelley novel has little to recommend it. Kier's Baron Frankenstein spends most of the film explaining how brilliant he is and trying to create the 'Serbian ideal' of a super-race by mating his male and female monsters (Carlo Mancini and Srdjan Zelenovic), until his entrails end up impaled on a pole. Juerging plays his assistant Otto, while Dallesandro's Brooklyn-accented shepherd seems totally out of place amongst the incestuous sex, gratuitous gore and black humour. Most of the characters end up either strangled or decapitated as Frankenstein's two children begin work on their own creation. Originally released in 3-D Spacevision, with uneven results.
Remake: FRANKENSTEIN: THE TRUE STORY (qv; 1973)

FOLLOW ME

(USA: THE PUBLIC EYE)
UK, 1971 (1972). Dir: Carol Reed. With: Mia Farrow, Topol, Michael Jayston, Margaret Rawlings, Annette Crosbie, Dudley Foster. Universal/Rank. Colour.
Romantic comedy scripted by Peter Shaffer and based on his play *The Public Eye*. Topol plays Julian Cristoforou, an eccentric private detective who falls in love with the woman he is following (played by Farrow). Includes a fake double bill (*Werewolves from Mars/Bloodsuckers from Venus*) with clips from Hammer's *The Evil of Frankenstein* (1964) and *Frankenstein Created Woman* (1966).

FRANKENSTEIN

USA, 1973. Dir: Glenn Jordan. With: Robert Foxworth, Susan Strasberg, Heidi Vaughn, Bo Svenson, John Karlen, Philip Bourneuf. Dan Curtis Productions. Colour.
Miserable TV movie adaptation of Mary Shelley's novel, shot on video and originally shown in two parts on ABC Wide World of Entertainment. Foxworth overacts as Victor Frankenstein and he's not helped by a lacklustre supporting cast, dire script, awful music score and unimaginative direction. Only Svenson (billed as The Giant) gives a reasonable performance as the sympathetic creature. With Rosella Olson as the Monster's bride. Yet another version of the story we could have done without. Low on horror, high on angst.
Remake: FLESH FOR FRANKENSTEIN (qv; 1973)

Below: Flesh for Frankenstein.

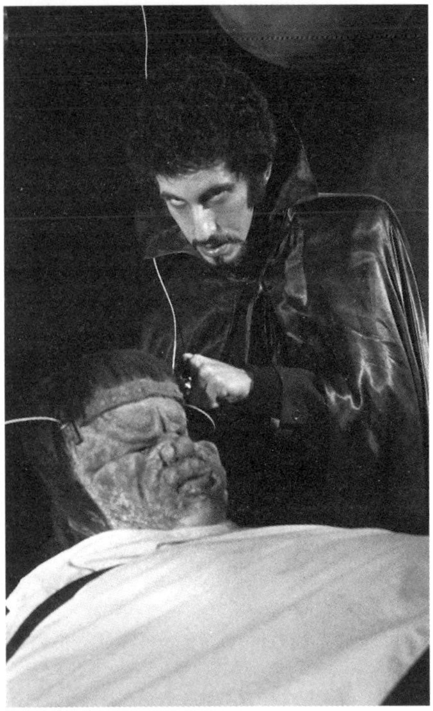

FRANKENSTEIN AND THE MONSTER FROM HELL

UK, 1973 (1974). Dir: Terence Fisher. With: Peter Cushing, Shane Briant, Madeline Smith, John Stratton, Bernard Lee, Clifford Mollison. Hammer Films. Colour.

The sixth and last in Hammer's Frankenstein series marks a return to form for the studio. Despite the low budget, obvious care was taken with the casting, design and photography. Making a superb entrance, Cushing returns as the obsessed Baron Frankenstein (aka Dr Victor), his hands horribly burned, who is helped by Dr Simon Helder (Briant) to create a new Monster (Dave Prowse in an unconvincing body suit) from the lunatic inhabitants of Carlsbad's asylum for the criminally insane. The script by John Elder (Anthony Hinds) works on several levels and this is a fitting end to both the series and the career of director Fisher (who died in 1980). With Patrick Troughton as a bodysnatcher.

FRANKENSTEIN '80

(Orig: MOSAICO)
Italy/West Germany, 1972. Dir: Mario Mancini. With: John Richardson, Gordon Mitchell, Renato Romano, Xiro Papas, Dalila Parker, Bob Fiz. M.G.D. Film Productions/MPI. Colour.

An ugly-looking film in which reporter Karl (Richardson) discovers that Dr Otto Frankenstein (Mitchell) has created a sex-mad Monster he calls Mosaic (Papas). The creature goes on the rampage, ripping off women's blouses and killing its creator, before a built-in self-destruct mechanism causes its brain to collapse after forty-eight hours. With some gory scalpel murders and actual footage of transplant surgery.

FRANKENSTEIN — ITALIAN STYLE

(Orig: FRANKENSTEIN ALL'ITALIANA/PRENDIMI, STRAZIAMI, CHE BRUCIO DI PASSIONE)
Italy, 1975. Dir: Armando Crispino. With: Aldo Maccione, Jenny Tann, Ninetto Davoli, Gianrico Tedeschi, Anna Mazzemauro, Lorenzo Guerrieri. Euro International/RPA. Colour.

Comedy sexploitation version of *Young Frankenstein* (1974). Professor Frankenstein (Tedeschi) creates a well-endowed Monster (Maccione) that ends up servicing his assistant Igor (Davoli), wife (Tann) and servant (Mazzemauro) before the scientist transplants his creation's penis onto himself.
Remake: SEVIMLİ FRANKESTAYN (qv; 1975)

FRANKENSTEIN OF SUNNYBROOK FARM

USA, 1971. Dir: William Rotsler.

Underground short in which two nudists watch the psychedelic film of the title.

FRANKENSTEIN'S CASTLE OF FREAKS

(Orig: IL CASTELLO DELLA PAURA. USA: aka HOUSE OF FREAKS)
Italy, 1973. Dir: Robert H. Oliver. With: Rossano Brazzi, Michael Dunn, Edmund Purdom, Christiane Royce, Gordon Mitchell, Alan (Alain) Collins (Luciano Pigozzi). Classic Film International/ Cinerama. Colour.

Sleazy sex/horror film featuring *South Pacific* (1958) star Brazzi (sounding like a cross between Chico Marx and Bela Lugosi) as Count Frankenstein. He brings caveman Goliath (Loren Ewing) back from the dead with his electric accumulator and gives him the brain of a young girl. With poor Michael Dunn as Genz the Evil Dwarf, Gordon Mitchell as Igor and an actor named Boris Lugosi(!) playing Ook, the Neanderthal man.

Above: *El Espiritu de la Colmena.*
Above left: *Dracula vs. Frankenstein. (FJA).*

FRANKENSTEIN: THE TRUE STORY

UK, 1973. Dir: Jack Smight. With: James Mason, Leonard Whiting, David McCallum, Jane Seymour, Nicola Pagett, Michael Sarrazin. Universal. Colour.

Impressive three-hour adaptation by Christopher Isherwood and Don Bachardy, first shown as part of TV's NBC World Premiere Movie and given a cinema release in Britain in a shortened version. The original splits neatly into two parts: the first stays fairly faithful to the original novel, with Whiting's Victor Frankenstein creating a sympathetic creature (Sarrazin) whose body slowly begins to decay. However, the second half is an outlandish sequel, with Mason's power-mad mesmerist, Dr Polidori, controlling Prima, a homicidal female monster (Seymour). The all-star cast includes McCallum as Frankenstein's mentor Henry Clerval, plus Michael Wilding, Clarissa Kaye, Agnes Moorehead, Margaret Leighton, Ralph Richardson, John Gielgud and Tom Baker.
Remake: VICTOR FRANKENSTEIN (qv; 1976)

THE GOLDEN VOYAGE OF SINBAD

UK/Spain, 1973. Dir: Gordon Hessler. With: John Philip Law, Caroline Munro, Tom Baker, Douglas Wilmer, Martin Shaw, Grégoire Aslan. Columbia. Colour.

Probably the best of Charles H. Schneer and Ray Harryhausen's Arabian Nights adventures. Screenwriter Brian Clemens (TV's *The Avengers*) and director Hessler bring a darker than usual touch to this juvenile fantasy. After acquiring two-thirds of a magical amulet, Sinbad (a likeable Law) and his crew must beat the evil magician Koura (Baker) to the lost continent of Lemuria. Harryhausen's superb stop-motion set-pieces (filmed in Dynarama) include a ship's figurehead coming to life; a sword fight with a many-armed statue of Kali; the climactic confrontation between a centaur and a gryphon; and, best of all, Koura's creation of a miniature flying homunculus. With Munro's busty slave girl in a bizarre dream sequence, an unbilled Robert Shaw as the Oracle and a brief homage to the 1940 *The Thief of Bagdad*. Music by Miklos Rozsa.

Sequel: SINBAD AND THE EYE OF THE TIGER (1977)

GOLEM

Poland, 1979. Dir: Piotr Szulkin. With: Marek Walczewski, Krystyna Janda, Joanna Zolkowska, Krzysztof Majchrzak, Mariusz Dmochowski, Wieslaw Drzewica. Zespoly Filmowe/Perspekty. Colour.

Set in a post-apocalyptic society where all humans are controlled by technology except for outsider Pernat (Walczewski). While administrator Holtrum (Dmochowski) experiments with the creation of artificial life, Pernat gradually becomes identified with a Golem-like creature which is his double.

Sequel: WOJNA SWIATOW — NASTEPNE STULECIE (1981)

THE GROUNDSTAR CONSPIRACY

Canada, 1972. Dir: Lamont Johnson. With: George Peppard, Michael Sarrazin, Christine Belford, Cliff Potts, James Olson, Tim O'Connor. Universal/Hal Roach International. Colour.

Based on the novel *The Alien* by L.P. Davies. An explosion at the top secret headquarters of an American space research project involves tough security agent Tuxan (Peppard) in a sabotage plot. Sarrazin gives a sympathetic performance as amnesiac John Welles, whose body is rebuilt after the explosion. The twist ending comes as a real surprise.

HALLOWEEN WITH THE ADDAMS FAMILY

(Orig: HALLOWEEN WITH THE NEW ADDAMS FAMILY)

USA, 1977. Dir: Dennis Steinmetz. With: John Astin, Carolyn Jones, Jackie Coogan, Ted Cassidy, Lisa Loring, Vito Scotti. Charles Fries/NBC-TV. Colour.

Disappointing revival of the hit 1960s series, based on Charles Addams' cartoons. Original cast members Astin, Jones, Coogan and Cassidy (as the Frankenstein Monster-like butler Lurch) are reunited in a story which also features Suzanne Krazna as Countess Dracula and Felix Silla as Cousin Itt. Shot on video, it was originally shown as a special, then reissued as a TV movie in 1980.

***Above left:** The Erotic Rites of Frankenstein.*
***Below:** Flesh for Frankenstein.*

Other Monsters

Although Boris Karloff (1887-1969) is the actor most often associated with the role of Frankenstein's Monster, over the years numerous other performers have played the creature stitched together from human cadavers.

Even before Karloff essayed the part, American silent actor Charles Stanton Ogle (1865-1940) portrayed the misshapen monstrosity in the first film adaptation of *Frankenstein* (1910). English-born actor Percy Darrell Standing played the artificially-created 'Brute Man' in *Life Without Soul* (1915), while no prints apparently survive of Italian actor Umberto Guarracino's performance as *Il Mostro di Frankenstein* (1920).

An uncredited actor appeared as the Monster in the novelty Technicolor short *Two Hearts in Wax Time* (1935), and Frankenstein's creation was lampooned by the Ritz Brothers in the musical comedies *Sing, Baby, Sing* and *One in a Million* (both 1936).

Although he vowed never to play the part again after *Son of Frankenstein* (1939), Karloff did don Jack Pierce's distinctive make-up one more time in 1940 for an all-star charity baseball game at Los Angeles' Gilmore Stadium. He also appeared on television in Ben Lane's make-up for the Monster in the 1962 *Route 66* episode, 'Lizard's Leg and Owlet's Wing'.

The next actor to portray the character was Ed Payson, who was made up by Jack Kevan to resemble Karloff's appearance in *Son of Frankenstein* for the 3-D novelty short *Third Dimensional Murder* (1940). Universal's madcap comedy *Hellzapoppin'* (1941) featured a gag cameo by actor-stuntman Dale Van Sickel (1906-1976) in the classic make-up, but the first actor to step into Karloff's weighted boots in the regular series was Lon Chaney Jr (1906-1973) in *The Ghost of Frankenstein* (1942).

"It took four hours to make me up," complained the actor. "Then they led me to the set. They dug a hole in the cliff and put me in. They stuck a straw in my mouth and covered me up with cement. It took till twelve o'clock to get me sealed in. Then everybody went to lunch!"

When it proved impractical for Chaney Jr to play both title roles in *Frankenstein Meets the Wolf Man* (1943), a humbled Bela Lugosi (1882-1956) was hired for the role he had so vociferously rejected in 1931. However, the actor, who turned sixty during filming, was obviously too old and frail to portray the Monster.

Lugosi's fourth wife Lillian recalled that her husband, "...had to be at the

Right: *The Ghost of Frankenstein.*
Below: *House of Frankenstein.*

studio at five in the morning. The headpiece weighed five pounds; those boots together weighed over twenty pounds; the whole schmeer took like four hours to get on. They had a special chair on the set for the Monster to sit in."

Quickly realising they had made a mistake, Universal also hired forty-one year-old, six-foot-four stuntman Edwin (Eddie) Parker (1900-1960), who had already doubled for Chaney Jr in the previous film. It was Parker who performed the more demanding scenes, while Lugosi was featured in the close-ups.

The next actor to play the Monster didn't need a stunt double. Forty-four year-old Glenn Strange (1899-1973) was a boxer, wrestler, rodeo performer and stuntman/bit player. On *House of Frankenstein* (1944), the six-foot-four Strange was coached in the part by Karloff himself. He later paid tribute to the star:

"I'd never have been the Monster I was if it hadn't been for Boris Karloff. He had finished his scenes and could have gone home, but he stayed on and worked with me. He showed me how to make the Monster's moves properly and how to do the walk that makes the Monster so frightening."

"He wasn't as lucky as I was," said Karloff about Strange's performance. "I got the cream of it, being the first. I know I wished him lots of luck...hoping it would do as much for him as it did for me."

Strange recreated the role the following year in *House of Dracula* and again in *Meet Frankenstein* (1948). When a stunt went wrong during the latter film, the actor broke his foot and Chaney Jr donned Bud Westmore's and Jack Kevan's make-up to throw a stunt girl through a window. Strange finally completed his scenes with his foot in a cast. Both actors subsequently portrayed the Universal Monster in different episodes of television's *The Colgate Comedy Hour* with Abbott and Costello.

Many actors have played Frankenstein's creation since. Another uncredited performer donned the Universal make-up for *Abbott and Costello Meet Dr. Jekyll and Mr. Hyde* (1953). Gary Conway (b 1938) appeared as a horribly scarred creation in both *I Was a Teenage Frankenstein* (1957) and *How to Make a Monster* (1958), while Harry Wilson was the male actor who wore the lipstick as *Frankenstein's Daughter* in 1958.

Above right: *The Curse of Frankenstein.*
Below: *Frankenstein Meets the Wolf Man.*

Thirty-five year-old Christopher Lee (b 1922) made his horror début as the Creature in Hammer's *The Curse of Frankenstein* (1957), but when the series continued with Peter Cushing's Baron, his creations were played by Michael Gwynn (1916-1976) in *The Revenge of Frankenstein* (1958), Australian wrestler Kiwi Kingston in *The Evil of Frankenstein* (1964), twenty-one year-old Austrian Susan Denberg in *Frankenstein Created Woman* (1966) and Freddie Jones (b 1927) in *Frankenstein Must Be Destroyed* (1969).

British Heavyweight weightlifting champion Dave Prowse (b 1935) first portrayed the Monster in a gag appearance in the James Bond spoof *Casino Royale* (1967). He recreated the role in Hammer's *The Horror of Frankenstein* (1970), but was completely unrecognisable as Peter Cushing's creation in *Frankenstein and the Monster from Hell* (1973). Four years later the two actors were reunited in *Star Wars*, when Prowse's evil Darth Vader served Cushing's Grand Moff Tarkin.

But no matter which performer is beneath the prosthetics, Boris Karloff perhaps summed it up best when he said: "Anybody who can take that make-up every morning deserves respect." However, in later years the actor also quipped: "With all that make-up on it's impossible for anyone to tell it isn't me. Every time they make another Frankenstein picture, I get all the fan mail. The other fellow gets the cheque."

L'HOMME AU CERVEAU GREFFE

France/Italy/West Germany, 1972. Dir: Jacques Doniol-Valcroze. With: Mathieu Carrière, Jean-Pierre Aumont, Nicoletta Machiavelli, Michel Duchaussoy, Marianne Eggerickx, Martine Sarcey. Parc Film/Mag Bodard/Marianne Productions/UGC/Mars Produzione/ Paramount Orion Film. Colour.

The brain of a dying surgeon (Aumont) is transplanted into the body of a young racing driver (Carrière). Problems occur when the recipient body's girlfriend turns out to be the surgeon's daughter (Machiavelli).

HORRIFYING EXPERIMENTS OF S.S. LAST DAYS

(aka THE BEAST IN HEAT/NAZI HOLOCAUST)
Italy, 1976. Dir: Ivan Katansky. With: Macha Magall, John Braun, Kim Gatti, Sal Boris. Eterna Films. Colour.

Banned in Britain as a video nasty. An evil female Nazi scientist (Magall) creates a monstrous apeman throwback (Boris), which attacks women as part of a genetic research experiment. Pretty tasteless stuff.

HORROR HOSPITAL

(USA: aka COMPUTER KILLERS)
UK, 1973. Dir: Antony Balch. With: Michael Gough, Robin Askwith, Vanessa Shaw, Ellen Pollock, Skip Martin, Dennis Price. Noteworthy Films. Colour.

Amateurish horror movie co-scripted and directed by independent distributor Balch, a former collaborator with William S. Burroughs. A songwriter (Askwith) and a young girl (the awful Vanessa Shaw) stay at a health hotel run by the horribly disfigured Dr Storm (Gough), who is experimenting with brain operations and electronically-controlled zombies. With Skip Martin as Frederick, a rebellious dwarf, and guest star Price as Mr Pollack, a camp travel agent for Hairy Holidays. Produced by Richard Gordon and released as *Frankenstein's Horror-Klinik* in Germany and *La Griffe de Frankenstein* in France.

THE HORROR OF FRANKENSTEIN

UK, 1970. Dir: Jimmy Sangster. With: Ralph Bates, Kate O'Mara, Veronica Carlson, Dennis Price, Graham James, Bernard Archard. Hammer Films. Colour.

Co-scripted, produced and directed by Sangster, this ill-advised comedy remake of *The Curse of Frankenstein* (1957) has nothing to do with Hammer's series starring Peter Cushing. Bates is a totally unsympathetic Victor Frankenstein who creates a Monster (David Prowse) that is a mindless killer. With Price as a fawning graverobber who gets his wife (Joan Rice) to do all the digging and Jon Finch as a police inspector.

Remake: LADY FRANKENSTEIN (qv; 1971)

THE HORROR SHOW

USA, 1979. Dir: Richard Schickel. With: Anthony Perkins, Boris Karloff, Bela Lugosi, Charles Laughton, Claude Rains, Lon Chaney Sr. Universal. Colour/B&W.

Made-for-TV documentary celebrating 'sixty magical years of movie monsters' from Universal studios. Hosted by Perkins and including clips of all the above plus Lon Chaney Jr, Vincent Price, Christopher Lee, Bette Davis, John Barrymore, Janet

***Above left and below:** Frankenstein and the Monster from Hell.*

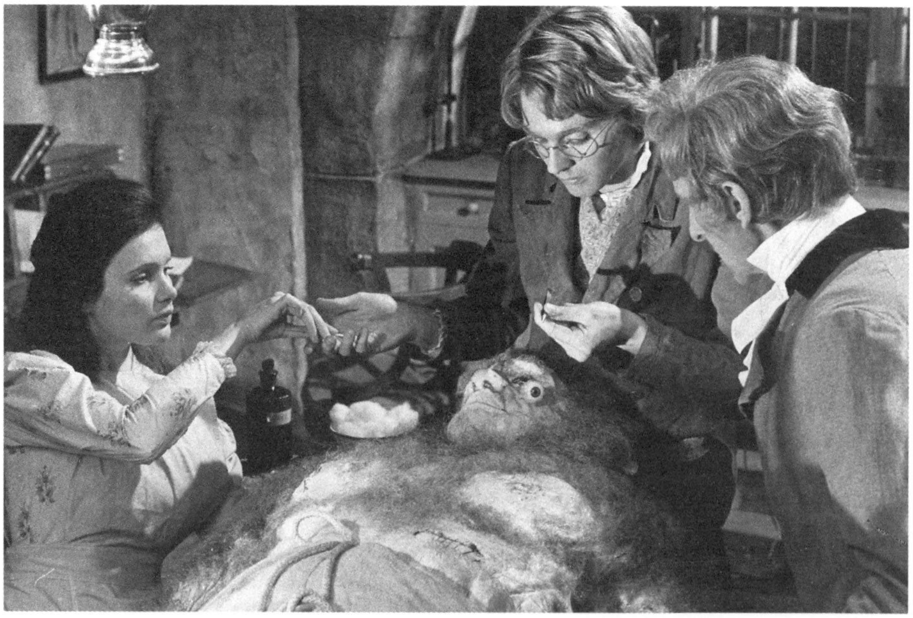

Leigh, Lee Remick, Robert Shaw, Charlton Heston and many more from Universal's Frankenstein series, *Dracula* (1930), *Psycho* (1960), *The Incredible Shrinking Man* (1957), *The Birds* (1963), etc. Produced, written and directed by Schickel.

HOUSE OF THE LIVING DEAD

(Orig: SKADUWEES OOR BRUGPLAAS. USA: DOCTOR MANIAC)
South Africa, 1973. Dir: Ray Austin. With: Mark Burns, Shirley Ann Field, David Oxley, Margaret Inglis, Dia Sydow, Lynne Maree. Associated Film Producers/Worldwide. Colour.
Nineteenth century mad scientist Burns experiments on his family. In the end he is driven to his death by the stolen souls of his victims when they escape their containers.

THE HUNCHBACK OF THE MORGUE

(Orig: EL JOROBADO DE LA MORGUE. USA: aka THE RUE MORGUE MASSACRES)
Spain, 1972. Dir: Javier Aguirre. With: Paul Naschy (Jacinto Molina), Rossana Yanni, Vic Winner (Victor Alcazar), Alberto Dalbes, Maria Perschy, Manuel De Blas. Eva Film. Colour.
Naschy (who also wrote the script under his real name) stars as Gotho the hunchback who loves a dying girl. He steals her body and keeps it in an underground torture chamber where it is attacked by rats (in one scene, real rats are apparently set on fire and the actor suffered rodent bites). A mad scientist (Dalbes) promises to restore life to the girl in return for bodies to feed the monster he has created. In the end almost everyone ends up dead, with Gotho falling into a vat of acid. Despite plenty of gratuitous gore and nudity, this is actually one of Naschy's better films.

THE INCREDIBLE 2-HEADED TRANSPLANT

USA, 1970. Dir: Anthony N. Lanza. With: Bruce Dern, Pat Priest, Casey Kasem, Albert Cole, John Bloom, Berry Kroeger. American International Pictures. Colour.

Left: *Horror Hospital.*
Below: *The Horror of Frankenstein. (FJA).*

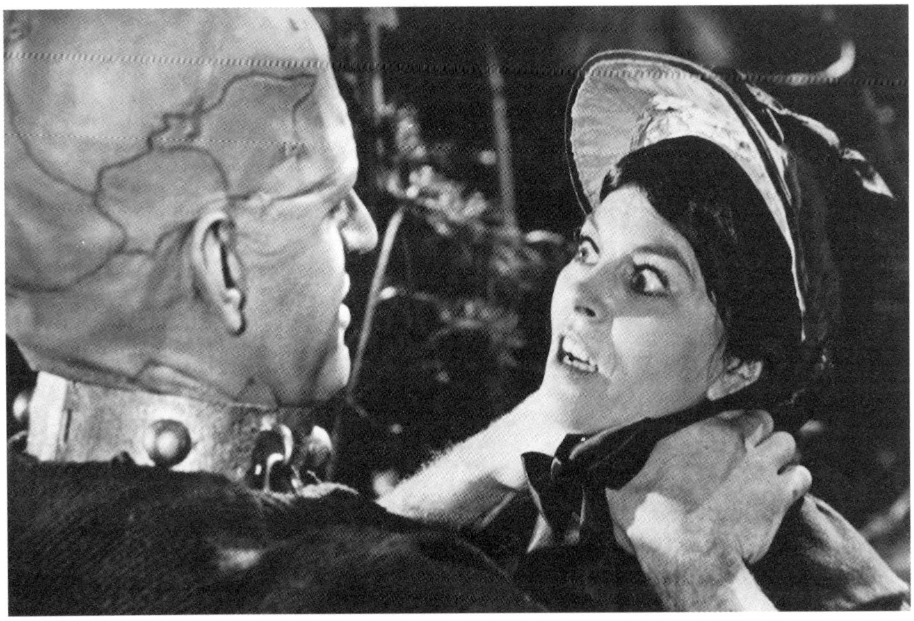

Sleazy, low budget horror movie in which Dern's mad scientist grafts the head of a drooling psycho killer on to the body of a retarded handyman (Bloom, the Monster in *Dracula vs. Frankenstein* [1970]). With Pat Priest from TV's *The Munsters*, TV music host Kasem (wearing a selection of terrible shirts), TV horror host Seymour (Larry Vincent) as a gardener and veteran Kroeger as Dern's assistant. The two-headed effect is rarely convincing. Directed by the one-time editor of Ray Dennis Steckler movies.

IN SEARCH OF DRACULA

(Orig: PA JAKT EFTER DRACULA. UK: aka IN SEARCH OF THE REAL DRACULA)
Transylvania/Sweden, 1971. Dir: Calvin Floyd (and Tony Forsberg). With: Christopher Lee. Aspeckt Films. Colour.
Travelogue-type documentary about vampires, made for Swedish TV and based on the book of the same title by Raymond T. McNally and Radu Florescu. Narrator Christopher Lee looks at the historic facts, the folklore, the literature and finally the films. He also appears as himself, Vlad Tepes and Count Dracula (in scenes shot especially for the film). The longer theatrical version apparently includes material from Florescu's book *In Search of Frankenstein*, plus clips from *Dracula vs. Frankenstein* (1970).

THE INTERVIEW

USA, 1973. Dir: Richard Beymer.
Underground short featuring clips from *House of Dracula* (1945).

LA INVASION DE LOS MUERTOS

(aka BLUE DEMON Y ZOVEK EL LA INVASION DE LOS MUERTOS)
Mexico, 1972. Dir: René Cardona. With: Blue Demon (Alejandro Cruz), Crista Linder, Zovek, Jorge Mistral, Cesar Silva, Luis Mariscal. Azteca. Colour
This time masked Mexican wrestler Blue Demon and escape artist Professor Zovek take on Dracula (Silva), a zombie (Mariscal) and the Frankenstein Monster (Tarzan Moreno) when a radioactive meteorite falls to Earth and revives the dead.
Sequel: VUELVEN LOS CAMPEONES JUSTICIEROS (1972)

KISS MEETS THE PHANTOM

(aka KISS MEETS THE PHANTOM OF THE PARK/ATTACK OF THE PHANTOMS)
USA, 1978. Dir: Gordon Hessler. With: KISS (Gene Simmons, Peter Criss, Ace Frehley, Paul Stanley), Anthony Zerbe, Deborah Ryan. Hanna-Barbera/KISS-Aucoin Productions/Avco Embassy Pictures. Colour.
TV movie set in a financially floundering amusement park. When the members of glam rock group KISS are hired to boost admissions, they end up battling robot figures of the Frankenstein Monster, Dracula, the Wolf Man, the Mummy and other creatures created by vengeful mechanical wizard Abner Devereaux (Zerbe) in his House of Horrors. With Brion James in a supporting role and the band performing 'Rock and Roll All Night', 'Love Gun' and 'Black Diamond'.

LADY FRANKENSTEIN

(Orig: LA FIGLIA DI FRANKENSTEIN) Italy, 1971 (1972). Dir: Mel Well(e)s (Ernst von Theumer). With: Joseph Cotten, Sara Bay (Rosalba Neri), Mickey Hargitay, Paul Müller, Paul Whiteman, Herbert Fux. Condor International/New World Pictures. Colour.
'Only the Monster she made could satisfy her strange desires!' enticed the ads. This crude reworking of Mary Shelley's original has Bay's Tanya Frankenstein creating a laughable creature (who walks around as if drilling on a parade ground) to battle her father's disfigured Monster. Poor old Joseph Cotten is completely wasted in a cameo as Baron Frankenstein, and you know you're in trouble when the best performance in the film comes from Hargitay as a police captain. During the climax, Bay is strangled by her creation as she makes love to it! The director played Gravis Mushnik in Roger Corman's *The Little Shop of Horrors* (1960).
Remake: FRANKENSTEIN (qv; 1973)

LISZTOMANIA

UK, 1975. Dir: Ken Russell. With: Roger Daltrey, Sara Kestelman, Paul Nicholas, Fiona Lewis, Veronica Quilligan, Nell Campbell. Goodtimes Enterprises/Warner Bros. Colour.
Highly fantastic version of the life of composer Franz Liszt (Daltrey). Includes a vampire-like Richard Wagner (Nicholas), who rises from the grave as a murderous Frankenstein/Hitler Monster, and cameos by Ringo Starr as the Pope, John Justin, Rick Wakeman, Oliver Reed and Georgina Hale.

THE LUCIFER COMPLEX

USA, 1979. Dir: David L. Hewitt and Kenneth Hartford. With: Robert Vaughn, Merrie Lynn Ross, Keenan Wynn, Aldo Ray, William Lanning, Ross Durfee. Vista/Gold Key. Colour.
Co-writer/co-director Hewitt proves that he's learned nothing about film-making since *The Wizard of Mars* back in 1965. After an interminable discourse on the futility of war, a near-future viewer of a video time capsule watches as toupeed secret agent Vaughn (still trying to relive his *The Man from U.N.C.L.E.* days) tries to stop Fourth Reich Nazis Wynn and Ray, under the command of an aged Führer, from creating an army of clones to conquer the world. In the end he fails. Originally shot in 1976 with the futuristic wraparound sequences added later, this is so inept that there's even a shot of the clapperboard edited into a fight sequence!

THE MAD BAKER.

USA, 1972. Dir: Ted Petok. Regency/Crunch Bird Studios. Colour.
Ten minute cartoon spoof in which a Frankenstein Monster made of chocolate cake terrorises the countryside until it is finally trapped in a windmill.

THE MUTATIONS

(USA: aka THE FREAKMAKER)
UK, 1973. Dir: Jack Cardiff. With: Donald Pleasence, Tom Baker, Brad Harris, Julie Ege, Michael Dunn, Jill Haworth. Getty Picture Corporation/Columbia. Colour.
Sleazy horror thriller in which Pleasence's mad German scientist Dr Nolter attempts to create a new race of creatures by combining human and plant life. Future Doctor Who Baker plays Lynch, the dis-

***Below:** Frankenstein – Italian Style.*

Above: Frankenstein: The True Story.

figured owner of a carnival sideshow who displays the deformed victims. With always reliable dwarf actor Michael Dunn in his last role (he died the same year), a walking Venus flytrap monster (Scott Anthony) and a number of real circus freaks. The daft plot is helped by the excellent photography of Paul Beeson and cinematographer-turned-director Cardiff, and some remarkable time-lapse sequences created by Ken Middleton.

NECROPOLIS

Italy, 1970. Dir: Franco Borcani. With: Viva Auder, Tina Aumont, Carmelo Bene, Pierre Clementi, B. Corazzari, Paul Jabara. Cosmoseion/Q Productions. Colour.

Art movie which purports to be a 'statement about life'. Includes the Frankenstein Monster, Countess Elizabeth Bathory (here called Mathory), Satan, King Kong, Attila the Hun, Montezuma, the Minotaur and other characters.

THE NINTH CONFIGURATION

(aka TWINKLE, TWINKLE, KILLER KANE)

USA, 1979. Dir: William Peter Blatty. With: Stacy Keach, Scott Wilson, Jason Miller, Ed Flanders, Neville Brand, George DiCenzo. ITC Film Distributors. Colour.

Author Blatty (*The Exorcist*) brings his bizarre novel *Twinkle, Twinkle, Killer Kane* to the screen as writer/producer/director. The result is a fascinating failure. Keach gives a strong performance as Colonel Hudson Kane, the new head psychiatrist at a Gothic castle full of disturbed soldiers. He turns out to be crazier than everyone else. Some wonderful moments sit side-by-side with pretentious rubbish. Attempts to create a horror atmosphere (a man in a Frankenstein Monster mask, pictures of Bela Lugosi, the supernatural ending) don't really work, but the impressive cast includes Moses Gunn, Robert Loggia, Joe Spinell, Tom Atkins and Richard Lynch. This exists in various versions, ranging in length from 99 to 140 minutes.

ODIO A MI CUERPO

(aka I HATE MY BODY)

Spain/Switzerland, 1974. Dir: Leon Klimovsky. With: Alexandra Bastedo, Byron Mabe, Narciso Ibañez Menta, Gemma Cuervo, Manuolo Zarzo, Eva León. Galaxia Films/Andre Kuhn. Colour.

Misogynistic exploitation movie in which the brain of a male engineer is transplanted into the body of a woman (Bastedo).

ONE-ARMED BANDIT

Sweden, 1974. Dir: Peter Kruse. Svenska. Colour.

Cartoon short in which gamblers are swallowed by Frankenstein fruit machines.

ONE MORE TIME

UK, 1970. Dir: Jerry Lewis. With: Peter Lawford, Sammy Davis Jr, Esther Anderson, Maggie Wright, Leslie Sands, John Wood. Chrislaw/Tracemark/United Artists. Colour.

Unfunny comedy sequel to *Salt and Pepper* (1968), which also starred executive producers Lawford and Davis Jr as Soho

O LUCKY MAN!

UK, 1973. Dir: Lindsay Anderson. With: Malcolm McDowell, Ralph Richardson, Rachel Roberts, Arthur Lowe, Helen Mirren, Mona Washbourne. Memorial/Sam/Warner Bros. Colour.

As optimistic coffee salesman Mick Travis (McDowell, repeating his role from Anderson's *If...* [1968] with more than a nod to Stanley Kubrick's *A Clockwork Orange* [1971]) travels around the north of England, he is plunged into a series of bizarre and satirical encounters. As a research volunteer in a private medical clinic, he discovers the mad Dr Millar (the wonderful Graham Crowden) is transplanting human heads onto animal bodies (creating an horrific pig-boy monster). Many of the cast appear in more than one role, and the director turns up as himself. With Dandy Nichols, Peter Jeffrey, producer Michael Medwin, Edward Judd, Brian Glover and many others. Music by Alan Price.

Sequel: BRITANNIA HOSPITAL (qv; 1982)

nightclub owners who can't stay out of trouble. An unbilled Peter Cushing and Christopher Lee turn up very briefly as Baron Frankenstein and Dracula respectively. This is the only film Lewis directed which he hasn't starred in. He shouldn't have bothered.

PANE VY JSTE VDOVA

Czechoslovakia, 1971. Dir: Vaclav Vorlicek. With: Iva Janzurova, Olga Shoberova (Olinka Berova), Jiri Sovak, Jiri Hrzan, Jan Libieck, Eduard Cupak. Studio Barrandov. B&W.

Gory black comedy about limb and brain transplants. Janzurova portrays Mrs Stub, an artificially-created person, plus two other characters.

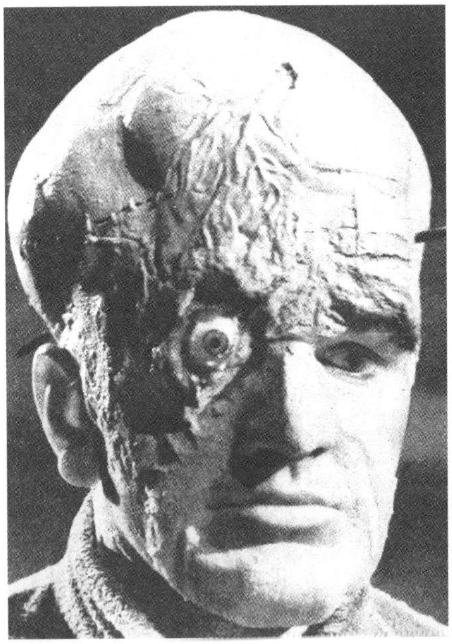

PARTS — THE CLONUS HORROR

(aka THE CLONUS HORROR) USA, 1979. Dir: Robert S. Fiveson. With: Tim Donnelly, Dick Sargent, Keenan Wynn, Paulette Breen, Peter Graves, David Hooks. Group 1 Films. Colour.

Renegade clone Donnelly tries to expose a political conspiracy involving duplicates of powerful people in this low budget science fiction thriller.

PASTEL DE SANGRE

Spain, 1971. Dir: José Maria Vallés, Emilio Martinez Lázaro, Francisco Bellmunt and Jaime Chávarri. With: Marta May, Charo López, Marisa Paredes, Romy, Julián Ugarte, Carlos Otero. P.C. Teide. Colour.

The title translates as *Blood Pie.* Four-part horror movie with episodes about medieval witchcraft ('Tarota'), the creation of a beautiful Frankenstein Monster ('Victor Frankenstein'), Romans versus Celtic vampires ('Terror Entre Cristianos') and a ghostly chiller ('The Dance').

PERCY

UK, 1971. Dir: Ralph Thomas. With: Hywel Bennett, Elke Sommer, Britt Ekland, Denholm Elliott, Cyd Hayman, Janet Key. Anglo-EMI/ Welbeck. Colour.

Comedy from the director of the Carry On films, based on the novel by Raymond Hitchcock. Edwin Anthony (Bennett) receives the first penis transplant from Elliott's doctor and sets out to discover its previous owner. Music by The Kinks. Vincent Price turned up in the limp sequel! **Sequel: PERCY'S PROGRESS (1974).**

Below Left: *Lady Frankenstein. (FJA).*
Below right: *The Mutations.*

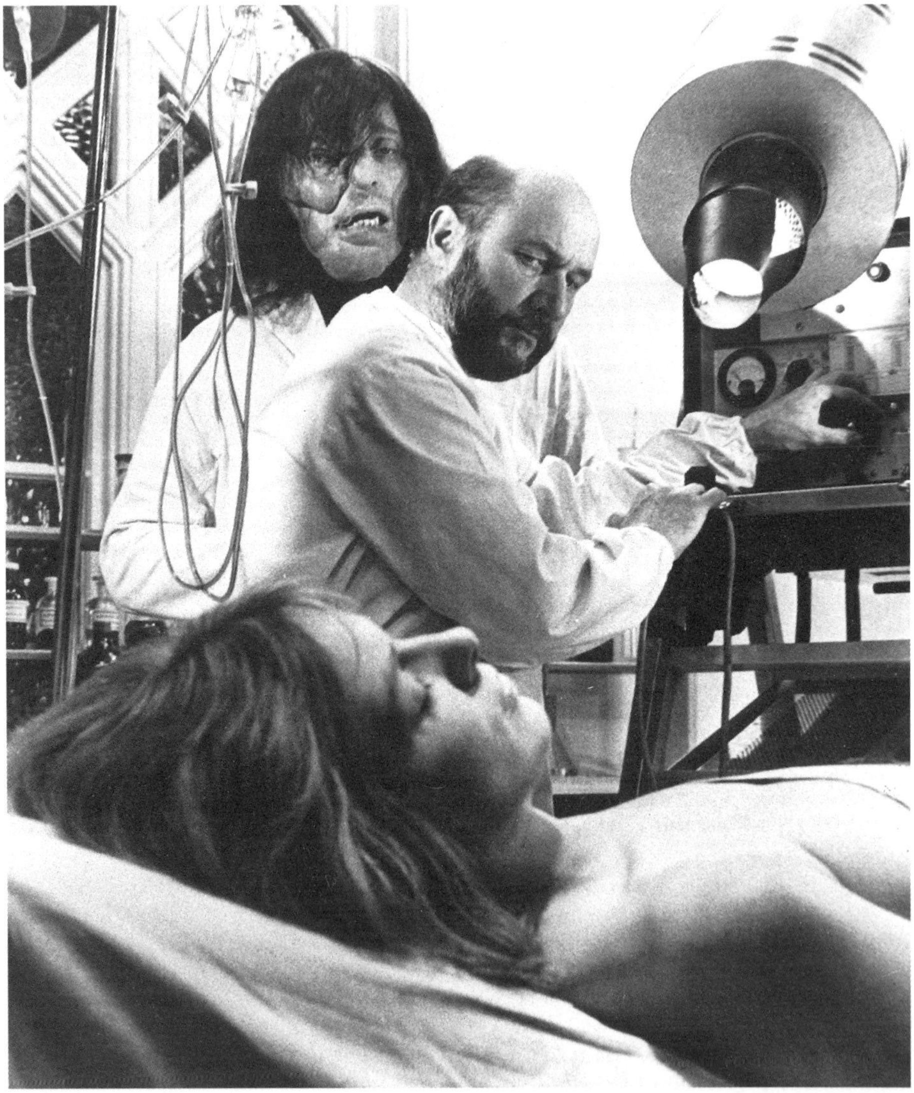

PHANTOM OF THE PARADISE

USA, 1974. Dir: Brian De Palma. With: Paul Williams, William Finley, Jessica Harper, George Memmoli, Harold Oblong, Archie Hahn. Twentieth-Century Fox. Colour.

De Palma's inventive musical reworking of classic horror themes. Winslow Leach (Finley) has his rock opera version of the Faust legend stolen by ageless music impresario Swan (Williams), who has sold his own soul to the Devil. When Swan decides to open his showcase rock palace, the Paradise, with Winslow's opera, the crazed and disfigured composer seeks revenge. Combines elements of *The Phantom of the Opera, The Picture of Dorian Gray, Psycho, The Cabinet of Dr. Caligari* and *The Manchurian Candidate* with a *Frankenstein* musical number in which outrageous rock star Beef (Gerrit Graham) is assembled from body parts before being electrocuted by the masked Phantom. With great pastiche songs by Williams and an impressive screen début by Harper (*Suspiria* [1976], etc). All references to Swan Song Records had to be optically removed when Led Zeppelin's company sued.

RENDEZVOUS

USA, 1973. Dir: Cortlandt B. Hull. Troc Film Corporation. B&W.

Five minute underground short which uses a montage of clips from Universal's *Frankenstein* (1931), *Bride of Frankenstein* (1935), *Son of Frankenstein* (1939), *House of Frankenstein* (1944) and *House of Dracula* (1945), amongst others, set to the music of Frank Sinatra's 'Strangers in the Night'.

Sequel: REVENGE OF RENDEZVOUS (qv; 1975)

THE RESURRECTION OF ZACHARY WHEELER

USA, 1971. Dir: Robert Wynn. With: Leslie Nielsen, Bradford Dillman, James Daly, Angie Dickinson, Jack Carter, Lee Giroux. Vidtronics/Gold Key Entertainments. Colour.

Reporter Nielsen discovers a secret research installation in New Mexico where Daly's sinister scientist is keeping politically important people alive by a DNA cloning process. Dillman's playboy senator is resurrected using organs taken from scientifically-created zombies called somas. This low budget science fiction thriller was shot on video and then transferred to film.

Above right: *Phantom of the Paradise.*
Below: *The Mutations.*

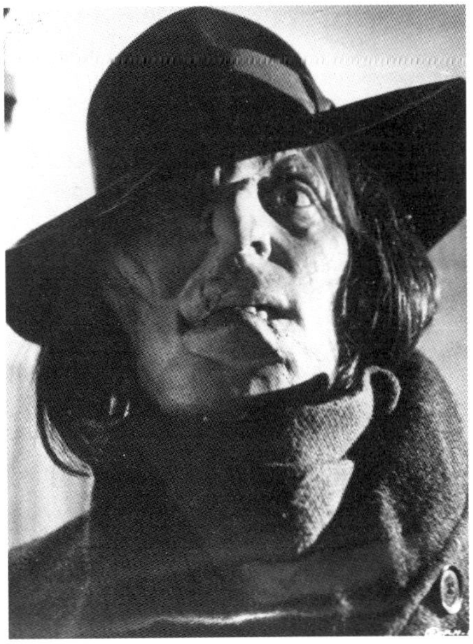

THE RETURN OF THE PINK PANTHER

UK, 1975. Dir: Blake Edwards. With: Peter Sellers, Christopher Plummer, Catherine Schell, Herbert Lom, Burt Kwouk, Peter Arne. ITC Jewel Productions/Pimlico Films/United Artists. Colour.

The fourth Pink Panther film and the third to star Sellers as the bumbling Inspector Clouseau. Not the best in the series, with the plot's elaborate jewel heist lost beneath the slapstick comedy, but the cartoon title sequence (animated by the Richard Williams Studio) includes the Pink Panther imitating the Frankenstein Monster.

Sequel: THE PINK PANTHER STRIKES AGAIN (1976)

REVENGE OF RENDEZVOUS

USA, 1975. Dir: Cortlandt B. Hull. Troc Film Corporation. B&W.

Five minute underground short, which uses a montage of clips from *Bride of Frankenstein* (1935), *Son of Frankenstein* (1939), *House of Frankenstein* (1944), *House of Dracula* (1945) and *Young Frankenstein* (1974) set to the music of Frank Sinatra's 'Watch What Happens'. A follow-up to the same director's *Rendezvous* (1973).

THE ROCKY HORROR PICTURE SHOW

UK, 1975. Dir: Jim Sharman. With: Tim Curry, Susan Sarandon, Barry Bostwick, Richard O'Brien, Patricia Quinn, Little Nell (Nell Campbell). Twentieth Century-Fox. Colour.

Based on O'Brien's long-running stage musical, this originally flopped at the box-office before becoming a surprise cult hit. Director Sharman doesn't try to open up the film version too much and wisely allows the bizarre sets, offbeat characters and great pastiche rock 'n' roll songs to carry the movie. When their car breaks down during a storm, newlyweds Brad and Janet Majors (Bostwick and Sarandon) seek help at a nearby spooky mansion. They soon discover they've stumbled on the annual convention of aliens from the planet Transylvania, and sweet transvestite Dr Frank N. Furter (an outrageous Curry) is about to reveal his latest creation: blond, blue-eyed Rocky (Peter Hinwood). Great support from O'Brien as the rebellious butler Riff Raff (a handyman), plus Meatloaf as the doomed Eddie and Charles Gray as the deadpan narrator. It was reissued with various re-edited endings. A sequel first announced in 1979 (*Rocky Horror II/The Rocky Horror Show Again*) still remains unmade. "Let's do the Time Warp again!"

Sequel: SHOCK TREATMENT (1981)

SANTO CONTRA LA HIJA DE FRANKENSTEIN

(aka LA HIJA DE FRANKENSTEIN)
Mexico, 1971 (1972). Dir: Miguel M. Delgado. With: Santo (Rodolfo Guzman Huerta or Eric del Castillo), Gina Romand, Anel, Roberto Canedo, Carlos Agosti, Sonia Fuentes. Cinematografica Calderon/ Azteca Films. Colour.

Frankenstein's daughter (Romand) uses the blood of her female victims to remain young. She creates a Frankenstein-type monster called Ursus and tries to obtain the 'powerful' blood of Santo, the silver masked hero. In the end, Santo wrestles Frankenstein's apeman to the death and teams up with the acid-scarred Ursus to defeat the mad offspring's plans.

Sequel: SANTO CONTRA LOS ASESINOS DE OTROS MUNDOS (1971)

Below: The Rocky Horror Picture Show.

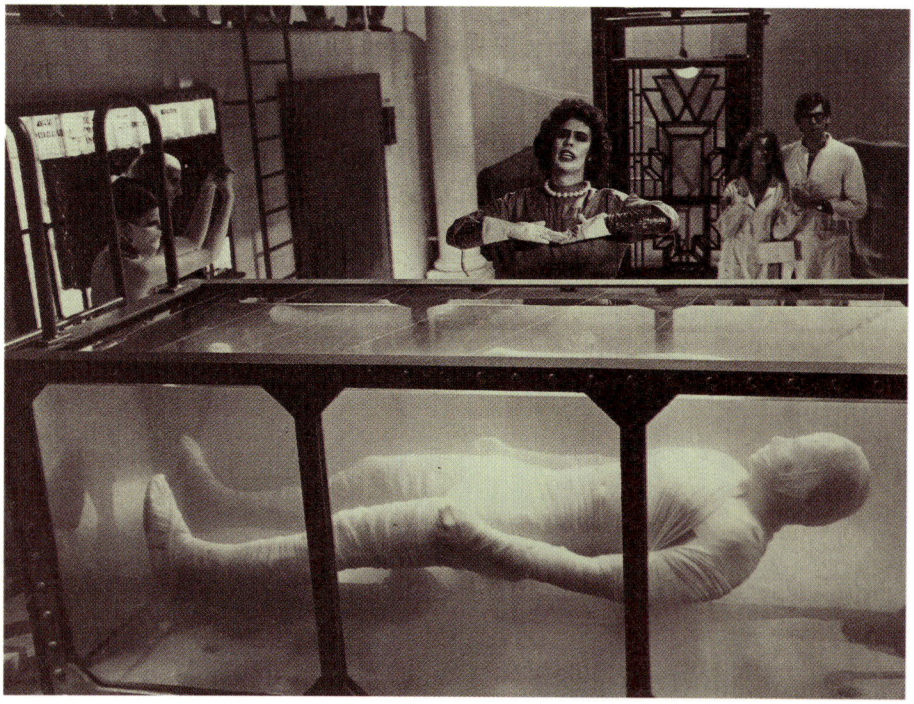

SANTO Y BLUE DEMON CONTRA EL DR. FRANKENSTEIN

Mexico, 1970. Dir: Miguel M. Delgado. With: Santo (Rudolfo Guzman Huerta or Eric del Castillo), Blue Demon (Alejandro Cruz), Sasha Montenegro, Jorge Russek, Ivonne Govea. Cinematografica Calderon. Colour.

The two masked wrestling heroes battle male and female monsters created by Dr Frankenstein.

Sequels: SANTO Y MANTEQUILLA NAPOLES EN LA VENGANZA DE LA LLORONA (1974) and SANTO Y BLUE DEMON EN EL MISTERIO DE LAS BERMUDAS (1978)

SCREAM OF THE DEMON LOVER

(Orig: IVANNA. USA: aka BLOOD CASTLE)
Italy/Spain, 1970 (1971). Dir: J. (José) L. (Luis) Merino. With: Erna Schurer, Charles Quinney, Agostina Belli, Cristiana Galloni, Antonio Gimenez Escribano, Mariano Vidal Molina. Prodimex Films/Hispaner Films/New World Pictures. Colour.

Nineteenth century horror drama in which a beautiful biochemist (Schurer) arrives at Dalmar Castle, where the local Baron Janos (Quinney) is trying to reanimate the charred remains of his brother Igor. He needn't have bothered, as his horribly-scarred sibling is running around the village killing off the local women. Merino's direction includes some imaginative touches, and Belli gives a stand-out performance as Olga, the evil housekeeper.

THE SECRET OF DR. CHALMERS

(Orig: TRASPLANTE DE UN CEREBRO/IL SEGRETO DEL DR. CHALMERS/L'UOMO CHE VISSE DUE VOLTE)
Spain/Italy, 1970. Dir: Juan Logar. With: Eduardo Fajardo, Simón Andreu, Silvia Dionisio, José Guardiola, Frank Wolff, Nuria Torray. Filmardis/Roma. Colour.

The brain of a rebellious young man is transplanted into the body of a conservative middle-aged judge, who eventually goes mad. Obvious symbolism from writer/producer/director Logar.

SEVIMLI FRANKESTAYN

Turkey, 1975. Dir: Nejat Saydem. With: Savas Basar, Bulent Kayabas, Meral Orhonsay, Sevda Karaca, Yuksel Gozen, Mualla Firat. Acar Films. Colour.

Comedy spoof that apparently owes much to *Young Frankenstein* (1974).

THE SEXUAL LIFE OF FRANKENSTEIN

France, 1970. Dir: Harry Novack. Colour.

Sex film.

SHANKS

USA/Canada, 1974. Dir: William Castle (and Marcel Marceau and Jack Hill). With: Marcel Marceau, Philippe Clay, Tsilla Chelton, Cindy Eilbacher, Helena Kallianiotes, Larry Bishop. Paramount. Colour.

The last film to be directed by 'Showman of Shock' Castle, who died in 1977. French mime Marceau plays mute puppeteer Malcolm Shanks who uses the electrical invention of wrinkled scientist Old Walker (also played by Marceau) to bring the dead back to life. A strange, uneven film in which it's never clear whether the revived corpses are merely imagined by Shanks. With minimal dialogue, old-fashioned title cards, a gang of bikers, an unhealthy relationship between the puppeteer and a young girl (Eilbacher) and Castle making his usual cameo appearance as a grocer. Alex North's terrible music score was nominated for an Academy Award.

SKOLOVANJE

Yugoslavia, 1970. Dir: Zlatko Bourek and Zlatko Sacer. Zabred. Colour.

Nine minute cartoon which apparently includes an appearance by the Frankenstein Monster. The title translates as *Schooling*.

THE SNOOP SISTERS: A BLACK DAY FOR BLUEBEARD

USA, 1973 (1974). With: Helen Hayes, Mildred Natwick, Lou Antonio, Bert Convey, Vincent Price, Roddy McDowall. Universal. Colour.

TV movie segment of The NBC Tuesday Mystery Movie featuring veterans Hayes and Natwick as spinster sleuths Ernesta and Gwendolyn Snoop. Price gives a delightful performance as old-time horror film star Michael Bastian, who is accused of murdering his wife at a comeback film festival held in his honour. With McDowall in the cast, it's not difficult to guess the identity of the real killer. With scenes from an imaginary Bastian movie, *Gravely Yours* (incorporating clips from *Bride of Frankenstein* [1935]).

I SOGNI DEL SIGNOR ROSSI

Italy, 1978. Dir: Bruno Bozetto. Colour.

Cartoon short in which the Frankenstein Monster appears in the dreams of Mr Rossi.

SON OF DRACULA

(aka YOUNG DRACULA)

UK, 1973 (1974). Dir: Freddie Francis. With: Harry Nilsson, Ringo Starr, Rosanna Lee, Freddie Jones, Dennis Price, Skip Martin. Apple Films/Cinemation Industries. Colour.

Filmed under the title *Count Downe*, this is a musical horror film in which Harry Nilsson plays the son of Dracula. Producer Ringo is Merlin the Magician, with Freddie Jones as Baron Frankenstein, who controls the monstrous inhabitants of the Netherworld. Dennis Price (who died the same year) turns up as Van Helsing. With rock stars Peter Frampton, Keith Moon and John Bonham. No wonder director Francis went back to being a cinematographer on such movies as *The Elephant Man* (1980) and *Dune* (1984).

THE STEPFORD WIVES

USA, 1974. Dir: Bryan Forbes. With: Katharine Ross, Paula Prentiss, Peter Masterson, Nanette Newman, Tina Louise, Patrick O'Neal. Columbia/Polomar. Colour.

Based on the novel by Ira Levin, actor Forbes' American début as a director is a skilful science fiction thriller which keeps the audience guessing until the powerful climax. Something is 'wrong' with the women of the Connecticut town of Stepford — over night they become too perfect.

Bottom: Santo Contra la Hija de Frankenstein.

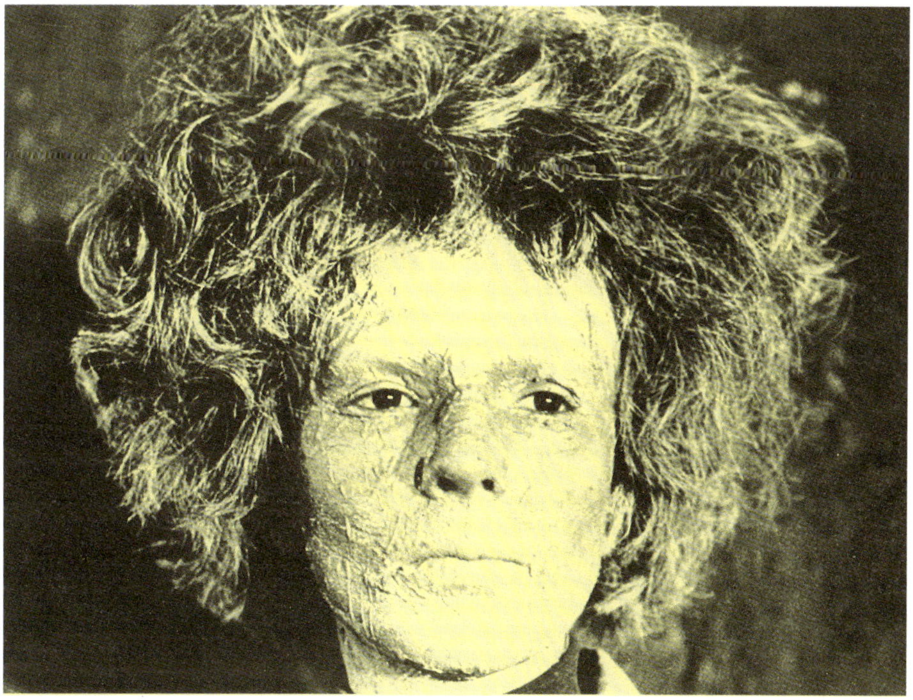

In the end, housewife Joanna (Ross) confronts a blank-eyed, well-endowed duplicate of herself created by ex-Disneyland employee Dale Coba (O'Neal). Dick Smith was responsible for the make-up effects.
Sequel: THE REVENGE OF THE STEPFORD WIVES (qv; 1980)

SUMMER OF SECRETS

Australia, 1976. Dir: Jim Sharman. With: Arthur Dignam, Rufus Collins, Nell Campbell, Kate Fitzpatrick, Andrew Sharp. Secret Picture Productions. Colour.
From the director of *The Rocky Horror Picture Show* (1975). Dignam plays a mad scientist living on an island who uses revolutionary brain surgery to revive his dead wife (Fitzpatrick). Not a big hit.

THE THING WITH TWO HEADS

USA, 1972. Dir: Lee Frost. With: Ray Milland, 'Rosey' (Roosevelt) Grier, Don Marshall, Roger Perry, Chelsea Brown, Kathy Bauman. Saber/ American International. Colour.
From the producer and co-writer of *The Incredible 2-Headed Transplant* (1970) comes another variation on the theme, with veteran Milland playing a grouchy, bigoted scientist whose head is grafted onto the body of black pro football star 'Rosey' Grier (an effect created by, amongst others, Dan Striepeke and Pete Peterson). Director Frost, obviously realising how silly the idea is, makes the most of some witty dialogue and a chase sequence in which fourteen police cars are wrecked. With cameos by screenwriters Frost and Wes Bishop, and Rick Baker playing a two-headed gorilla.

Above: *Santo Contra la Hija de Frankenstein. (FJA).*
Below left: *The Thing With Two Heads.*
Below right: *Young Frankenstein. (FJA).*

TRANSPLANT

(Orig: TRASPLANTE A LA ITALIANA)
Italy/Spain, 1970 (1971). Dir: Steno (Stefano Vanzina). With: Carlo Giuffre, Fernando Bilbao, Renato Rascel, Roberto Camardiel, Rafael Alonso, Vicente Roca. Rizzoli-Dia/ Cinemation. Colour.
An old man seeks a penis transplant from a well-endowed donor so that he can please his young wife. One of three films using the same theme released in 1971.

VICTOR FRANKENSTEIN

(USA: aka TERROR OF FRANKENSTEIN)
Sweden/Ireland, 1976. Dir: Calvin Floyd. With: Leon Vitali, Per Oscarsson, Nicholas Clay, Stacey Dorning, Jan Ohlsson, Olof Bergström. Aspekt Film. Colour.
Numbingly faithful adaptation of 'the classic by Mary Shelly' (*sic*), with Vitali as the doomed Victor Frankenstein. Despite a botched creation sequence, Oscarsson's articulate Monster is a tragic and truly disturbing creation with its death-like pallor and childish rage. Co-written, produced and directed by Floyd, this includes footage of the actual killing of a cow.
Remake: MYSTERY! FRANKENSTEIN — LEGEND OF TERROR (qv; 1981)

WARUM BELLT HERR BOBIKOW?

West Germany/Italy, 1976. Dir: Alberto Lattuada. With: Max von Sydow, Eleonora Giorgi, Mario Adorf, Cochi Ponzoni, Vadim Glowna, Rena Niehaus. Colour.
Science fiction comedy, based on the novel by Michael Bulgakov. After receiving various transplants involving human

YOUNG FRANKENSTEIN

USA, 1974. Dir: Mel Brooks. With: Gene Wilder, Peter Boyle, Marty Feldman, Cloris Leachman, Teri Garr, Kenneth Mars. Twentieth Century-Fox/Gruskoff-Venture Films/Crossbow Productions/Jouer. B&W.

A wonderful parody of the heyday of Universal's Frankenstein series, beautifully recreated in black and white and hilariously scripted by star Wilder and director Brooks (reunited from *Blazing Saddles* [1974]). Wilder plays eccentric brain surgeon Dr Frederick Frankenstein ("that's *Frahnkensteen*"), who travels to Transylvania to receive a family legacy. With the help of Feldman's Igor ("Hump? What hump?") and Garr's beautiful laboratory assistant Inga, he soon begins building his own Monster (Boyle in make-up created by William Tuttle) with which to astound the medical profession. With Mars as the one-armed Inspector Kemp, Madeline Kahn as Elizabeth, Gene Hackman playing a blind hermit and Kenneth Strickfaden's original laboratory equipment from the 1931 *Frankenstein*. Worth catching for the 'Puttin' on the Ritz' routine alone. Apparently, John Carradine's narration was deleted before release.

Remake: FRANKENSTEIN — ITALIAN STYLE (qv; 1975)

organs, a dog is transformed into the troublesome Mr Bobikow.

THE WEREWOLF OF WASHINGTON

USA, 1973. Dir: Milton Moses Ginsberg. With: Dean Stockwell, Biff Maguire, Clifton James, Jane House, Michael Dunn, Beeson Carroll. Millco. Colour.

This low budget horror comedy begins well, with Presidential aide Jack Whittier (Stockwell) bitten by a werewolf in a middle European country straight out of the old Universal films, but it never really lives up to its promise of a wolfman loose in the White House. In one scene, the lycanthrope encounters a dormant Frankenstein Monster in the secret laboratory of Dunn's sinister dwarf scientist, Dr Kiss. Writer/director Ginsberg's attempts at social commentary — particularly the Watergate scandal — never really work.

THE WHIZ KID AND THE CARNIVAL CAPER

USA, 1976. Dir: Tom Letch. With: Jack Kruschen, John Colicos, Jaclyn Smith, Dick Bakalyan, Eric Shea, John Lupton. Walt Disney Productions. Colour.

TV movie shown in two parts on *The Wonderful World of Disney*. Boy inventor Alvin Fernald (Shea) attends a carnival where a man claiming to be Dr Frankenstein is exhibiting his robot monster. Alvin creates his own 'Whangdoogle Monster' which helps foil a bank robbery before exploding.

WONDER WOMEN

(USA: aka THE DEADLY AND THE BEAUTIFUL)

USA/Philippines, 1973. Dir: Robert O'Neil. With: Nancy Kwan, Ross Hagen, Maria de Aragon, Roberta Collins, Sid Haig, Vic Diaz. Central/General Film Corporation. Colour.

'Kung fu girls on the rampage..!' promised the ads. Producer/star Hagen plays Lloyds insurance investigator Mike Harber. He arrives on the volcanic island fortress of evil dragon lady Dr Tsu (Kwan), whose army of women kidnap the world's top athletes to use their organs in transplant experiments. In the end, the doctor's monstrous failures seek revenge. Filmed under the titles *Women of Transplant Island* and *The Terrible Transplants of Dr Tsu*.

ZE ZIVOTA DETI

Czechoslovakia, 1977. Dir: Milos Macourek. Kratky. Colour.

Nine minute cartoon in which a child's toy is transformed into a Golem that goes on a destructive rampage.

Below: *Young Frankenstein. (FJA).*

the

With the end of the old studio system and the growth of the home entertainment industry, a new breed of independent film producer began churning out product aimed primarily at video, television and the youth market.

Donald Pleasence played Victor Jr in the Mexican-made comedy **Frankenstein's Great-Aunt Tillie (1983)**, *David Muir was the titular scientist in* **Dr. Hackenstein (1987)** *and Mark Blankfield portrayed Dr Bob Frankenstein in* **Frankenstein General Hospital (1988)**. *Fred Gwynne donned the Universal Monster make-up one last time for the TV movie* **The Munsters' Revenge (1981)** *and Frankenstein's creature (Peter Buntic) was demythologised as an accident victim in* **Transylvania 6-5000 (1985)**. *It's difficult to tell if Jerry Warren intended* **Frankenstein Island (1981)** *to be serious or not; his veteran cast — including John Carradine as Dr Frankenstein — certainly had no idea.*

At least Fred Dekker exuberantly paid tribute to the old Universal series with his children's film **The Monster Squad (1987)**, *and twenty-five year-old wunderkind Tim Burton showed even more respect for the saga in his short pastiche* **Frankenweenie (1984)**.

As for more serious examinations, the TV movie **Doctor Franken (1980)** *tried to update Mary Shelley's novel, as did the French film* **Frankenstein 90 (1984)**, *while yet another traditional TV version of* **Frankenstein (1984)** *added nothing new to the many adaptations. Stuart Gordon's splatter-packed* **Re-**

Re-Animator.

1980s

Animator (1985) *was much more fun, but had about as much in common with H.P. Lovecraft's original story as most adaptations of* **Frankenstein** *had with Shelley's book. If the sequel,* **Bride of Re-Animator (1989)**, *was something of a disappointment, at least it owed part of its inspiration to Universal's* **Bride of Frankenstein (1935)**, *as did Franc Roddam's* **The Bride (1985)**, *which worked as both a sequel and a remake to James Whale's classic.*

Spanish film star Paul Naschy (b 1936) added Frankenstein's creation to his repertoire in both **Buenas Noches, Senor Monstruo (1982)** *and* **Howl of the Devil (1988)**, *and the Monster also turned up in* **Dracula tan Exarchia (1983)**, **Mixed Up (1985)**, **Who is Afraid of Dracula (1985)** *and* **Waxwork (1988)**.

170 years after first writing **Frankenstein; or, The Modern Prometheus**, *the story of how Mary Shelley and her friends spent their summer on the shores of Lake Geneva was turned into not just one, but three movies.*

Gothic.

The Bride.

These ranged from Ken Russell's ludicrously histrionic **Gothic (1986)** *to the more sedate, if less interesting,* **Haunted Summer (1988)** *and* **Rowing with the Wind (1988)**.

Unfortunately, film-makers had twisted and debased Shelley's original creature to such an extent that it is doubtful whether even the author would have recognised her own creation any longer. A similar depreciation had afflicted that other horror staple, the vampire, and it was a revival of Bram Stoker's immortal Count that would lead to a similar resurgence of interest in Frankenstein and his Monster...

BEVERLY HILLS BODY$NATCHERS

USA, 1989. Dir: Jon Mostow. With: Vic Tayback, Frank Gorshin, Rodney Eastman, Warren Selko, Art Metrano, Seth Jaffe. Busybody Productions/Hess-Kallberg Associates/McGuffin Productions/ Shapiro Glickenhaus Entertainment. Colour.

Teen comedy in which brothers Freddie and Vincent (Eastman and Selko) start work in a Mafia-run funeral home and discover that a greedy mortician (Tayback) and a crazy doctor (Gorshin) have invented a serum for bringing the dead back to life for profit. It's not nearly as funny as it should be.

Top: The Bride.
Above: Bride of Re-Animator.

BLOOD RELATIONS

Canada, 1988. Dir: Graeme Campbell. With: Jan Rubes, Lydie Denier, Kevin Hicks, Lynne Adams, Ray Walston, Stephen Saylor. SC Entertainment. Colour.

Erotic black comedy, scripted by actor Saylor, in which the scheming Denier is trapped in a house with Rubes, Hicks and Walston, three generations of lascivious men from the wealthy Wells family. She discovers they survive by transplanting their brains into younger bodies, and they are looking for a receptacle for a female mind...

B.O.R.N.

USA, 1988. Dir: Ross Hagen. With: Ross Hagen, Hoke Howell, P.J. Soles, William Smith, Russ Tamblyn, Clint Howard. The Movie Outfit/Prism Entertainment. Colour.

When rancher Hagen's step-daughters are kidnapped and the rest of his family brutally murdered, he teams up with a retired cop buddy (Howell) to track down an organisation dealing in black market organ transplants. With such villains as Smith's sinister Dr Farley, Tamblyn's crazy killer, Howard's creepy orderly and Soles' bouffant-haired dragon lady, be prepared for a sleazy slice of low budget exploitation. Most of the stars were also involved in various production capacities. In case you were wondering, the video box explains that the title stands for Body Organ Replacement Network.

BRAIN DEAD

USA, 1989. Dir: Adam Simon. With: Bill Pullman, Bill Paxton, Bud Cort, Patricia Charbonneau, Nicholas Pryor, George Kennedy. Concorde/ New Horizons. Colour.

Roger Corman dusted off *Paranoia*, an unproduced 1963 screenplay by the late Charles Beaumont, and gave it to director Simon and ex-wife producer Julie Corman. The result is an offbeat, low budget horror thriller in which Pullman's brain-loving scientist starts out by investigating colleague Cort's madness and ends up crazier than everyone else thanks to corporate villains Paxton and Kennedy. The film's second half is an extended schizophrenic nightmare in which reality and fantasy merge.

BRAINWAVES

USA, 1982. Dir: Ulli Lommel. With: Keir Dullea, Suzanna Love, Vera Miles, Tony Curtis, Percy Rodrigues, Paul Willson. Cinamerica. Colour.

Written, produced, photographed and directed by one-time Fassbinder associate Lommel. When housewife Kaylie Bedford (Love, aka Mrs Lommel) undergoes a revolutionary brain operation, she starts to 'see' the brain patterns of the murdered donor and so becomes a target for the killer. Curtis gives a strangely erratic performance as Dr Clavius, the inventor of the process. Routine stalk 'n' slash thrills.

THE BRIDE

France/UK, 1985. Dir: Franc Roddam. With: Sting, Jennifer

Beals, Geraldine Page, Clancy Brown, Anthony Higgins, David Rappaport. Columbia. Colour.
Romantic fable which, after a superb creation sequence, almost picks up where *Bride of Frankenstein* (1935) ended. Although overlong and slow in places, this remains an impressive version of Mary Shelley's classic, thanks to the stunning photography, atmospheric French locations, beautiful set design and strong casting: Sting's Charles Frankenstein grows more monstrous as Brown's sympathetic creature becomes more human, thanks to the guidance of a friendly dwarf (Rappaport). The supporting cast includes Page as a housekeeper, Alexei Sayle and Phil Daniels as comic villains, Quentin Crisp as the Baron's assistant, plus Veruschka, Ken Campbell and Guy Rolfe. Only Beals disappoints as the Monster's mate.

BRIDE OF RE-ANIMATOR

(UK: RE-ANIMATOR 2)
USA, 1989 (1990). Dir: Brian Yuzna. With: Bruce Abbott, Claude Earl Jones, Fabiana Udenio, David Gale, Kathleen Kinmont, Jeffrey Combs. Wildstreet. Colour.
Disappointing B-movie sequel to Stuart Gordon's inventive *Re-Animator* (1985). Directed by the producer of the earlier film, it picks up where the original left off, with Herbert West and Dan Cain (Combs and Abbott) back at Miskatonic University using spare body parts to create life instead of trying to reanimate it. Returning from the first film, Gale as the still-living decapitated head of Dr Hill (now with added bat wings!) is wasted. However, the creation of the Bride (Kinmont) almost recaptures the magic of James Whale's 1935 classic and Screaming Mad George's special effects are impressive, if predictable. This doesn't have much to do with H.P. Lovecraft's original novella. It was heavily cut by the censor in Britain.

BRITANNIA HOSPITAL

UK, 1982. Dir: Lindsay Anderson. With: Leonard Rossiter, Graham Crowden, Joan Plowright, Jill Bennett, Marsha Hunt, Malcolm McDowell. EMI Films. Colour.
This dark satire caused an outcry in Britain when first released. Director Anderson concludes the loose trilogy he began with *If...* (1968) and *O Lucky Man!* (1973), set in an anarchic near-future during street riots and a visit by the Queen Mother to a run-down hospital. Crowden's delightfully mad Professor Millar and his assistant (Bennett) are secretly creating a patchwork monster with the head of TV reporter Mick Travis (McDowell, recreating his role from the previous two films) and enough gore to rival *Re-Animator* (1985). In the end, Millar reveals his Genesis project — a giant living brain. The impressive supporting cast includes Mark Hamill from *Star Wars* (1977), Robin Askwith, Peter Jeffrey, Fulton Mackay, Dandy Nichols, Vivian Pickles, Valentine Dyall, Roland Culver and guest appearances by Alan Bates and Arthur Lowe (in one of his last roles). A bitter attack on British politics and the collapse of the National Health Service, this was a box-office flop. Music by Alan Price.

***Above:** Lindsay Anderson and cast behind-the-scenes, Britannia Hospital.*
***Left:** Bride of Re-Animator.*

BUENAS NOCHES, SENOR MONSTRUO

Spain, 1982. Dir: Antonio Mercero. With: Regaliz, Paul Naschy (Jacinto Molina), Luis Escobar, Fernando Bilbao. Frade. Colour.
Musical comedy for children, with Naschy as a werewolf (not Waldemar Daninsky), the Frankenstein Monster,

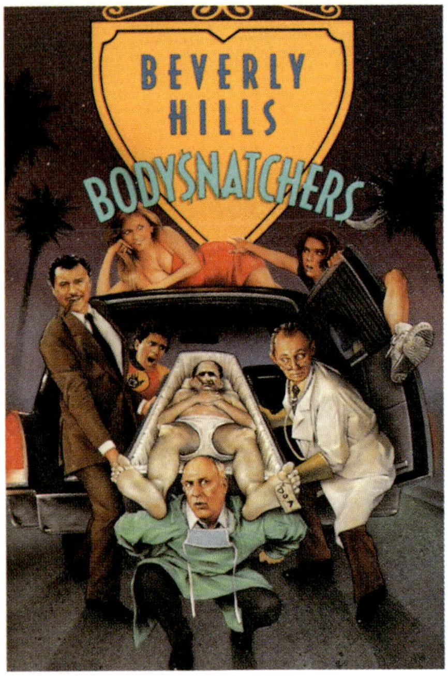

Count Dracula and Quasimodo. The title translates as *Good Evening, Mr Monster.*

CHILLER

USA, 1985. Dir: Wes Craven. With: Michael Beck, Beatrice Straight, Laura Johnson, Dick O'Neill, Alan Fudge, Craig Richard Nelson. Polar Films/J.D. Feigelson. Colour.

TV movie from Craven, the creator of *A Nightmare on Elm Street* (1984). Beck plays Miles Creighton, a young man accidentally released from cryogenic suspension after ten years and possessed by a murderous supernatural force. Good support from Straight as Miles' disbelieving mother and Paul Sorvino as a Reverend whose suspicions nearly get him killed. Make-up effects created by Stan Winston.

CITY OF WOMEN

(Orig: LA CITTA DELLE DONNE/LA CITE DES FEMMES)
Italy/France, 1980. Dir: Federico Fellini. With: Marcello Mastroianni, Anna Prucnal, Bernice Stegers, Iole Silvani, Donatella Damiani, Ettore Manni. Opera Film Produzione/Gaumont. Colour.

In one of Fellini's lesser films, Snaporaz (Mastroianni) goes on a dream-quest where he encounters various fantasy women, including one wearing a Frankenstein Monster mask.

COMING SOON

USA, 1982 (1983). Dir: John Landis. With: Jamie Lee Curtis. Universal. Colour/B&W.

Hour-long compilation of classic Universal trailers, including those for the studio's entire Frankenstein series and Hammer's *The Evil of Frankenstein* (1964). Scripted and co-produced by Mick Garris and hosted by scream queen Curtis on the Universal backlot.

CREATOR

USA, 1985. Dir: Ivan Passer. With: Peter O'Toole, Mariel Hemingway, Vincent Spano, Virginia Madsen, David Ogden Stiers, John Dehner. Universal/Kings Road Productions. Colour.

Offbeat blend of comedy and drama as O'Toole's crazy scientist attempts to recreate his long-dead wife from her preserved cells and revive Madsen from a coma. Based on a novel by Jeremy Leven. With veteran Jeff Corey.

D.A.R.Y.L.

USA/UK, 1985. Dir: Simon Wincer. With: Mary Beth Hurt, Michael McKean, Kathryn Walker, Colleen Camp, Josef Sommer, Barret Oliver. Paramount. Colour.

Likeable juvenile science fiction adventure. Oliver plays the ten year-old titular character who is in reality an escaped experiment — Data Analyzing Robot Youth Lifeform — an organic body with a super-computer for a brain. He becomes a

DAY OF THE DEAD

USA, 1985. Dir: George A. Romero. With: Lori Cardille, Terry Alexander, Joe Pilato, Richard Liberty, Howard Sherman, Jarlath Conroy. Laurel/UFDC. Colour.

Writer/director Romero's third *Dead* movie (following *Night of the Living Dead* [1968] and *Dawn of the Dead* [1978]). A small group of survivors — both military and scientific — hold out beneath ground while flesh-eating zombies control the world above. While the others fight amongst themselves, Liberty's insane Dr Logan (called 'Frankenstein' by the other characters) experiments on the brains of the living dead in an attempt to control them. Budget cuts at the last minute prevented this from concluding the series. However, it is filled with strong performances (particularly Cardille's tough heroine), improved zombie make-up and gore effects by Tom Savini, a great music score by John Harrison and some nice offbeat humour.

***Right:** The Bride.*

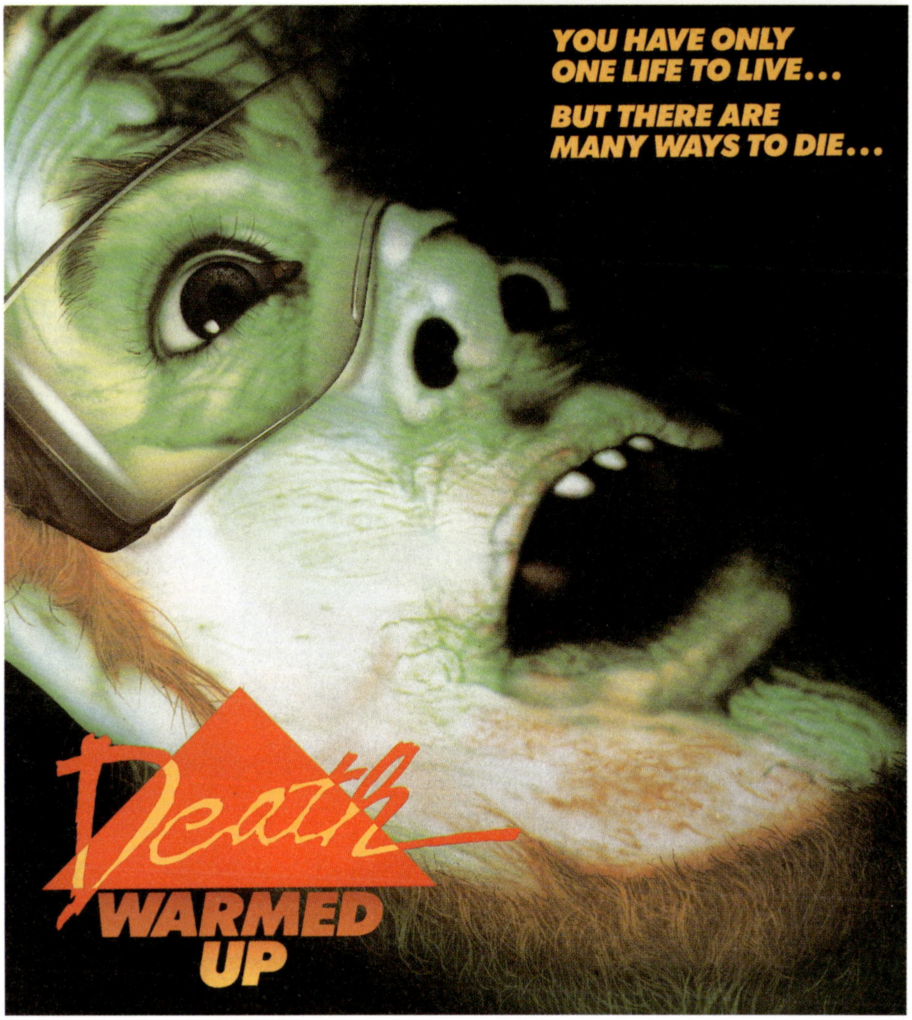

foster child and makes friends in the community, but his scientist creators want him back and the military try to terminate him. The best scenes involve Daryl using his superhuman powers to win a baseball game and an exciting climax in which he escapes in a futuristic jet fighter. Undemanding family entertainment. Music by Marvin Hamlisch.

DEAD & BURIED

USA, 1981. Dir: Gary A. Sherman. With: James Farentino, Melody Anderson, Jack Albertson, Dennis Redfield, Nancy Locke Hauser, Lisa Blount. Avco Embassy. Colour.

In his last role, Albertson plays a mad mortician who revives the dead (make-up effects by Stan Winston and Bill Muns) in the small New England town of Potter's Bluff. Farentino is the perplexed local sheriff. From the director of *Death Line* (1972) and scripted by Ronald Shusett and Dan O'Bannon, the creators of *Alien* (1979).

DEAD HEAT

USA, 1988. Dir: Mark Goldblatt. With: Treat Williams, Joe Piscopo, Darren McGavin, Lindsay Frost, Vincent Price, Keye Luke. New World Pictures. Colour.

Underrated horror/action thriller. Williams and comedian Piscopo play a pair of tough Los Angeles cops investigating a series of zombie heists. They uncover a plot by Price's sinister scientist to create a rich man's resurrection machine. In an enjoyable plot twist, Williams is killed and his coroner girlfriend (Clare Kirkconnell) uses the machine to allow him twelve hours to track down his killers as his revived body begins to fall apart. Editor-turned-director Goldblatt gives the film a high budget gloss and includes some exciting action sequences, while cameos from genre villains McGavin, Price and Luke add to the fun.

DEADLY FRIEND

USA, 1986. Dir: Wes Craven. With: Matthew Laborteaux, Kristy Swanson, Michael Sharrett, Anne Twomey, Anne Ramsey, Richard Marcus. Warner Bros. Colour.

Neat little horror thriller, scripted by Bruce Joel Rubin and based on Diana Henstell's novel *Friend*. When budding mad scientist Paul Conway (the likeable Laborteaux) moves into a new neighbourhood with his friendly robot, he falls in love with the girl next door (Swanson). However, when she is killed in an accident, he implants the robot's brain into her skull and she returns to a form of semi-life — only now she's a homicidal zombie bent on revenge. The teenage cast work well, particularly Swanson as the confused corpse, and it ends with a nice *frisson* as Paul decides that if at first you don't succeed...

DEATH WARMED UP

New Zealand, 1984. Dir: David Blyth. With: Michael Hurst, Margaret Umbers, David Letch, William Upjohn, Norelle Scott, Gary Day. Tucker Production Company/ New Zealand Film Commission. Colour.

Sub-Cronenberg tale of illegal brain operations and mutant zombies created by the demented Dr Archer Howell (Day), who menaces two teenage couples on a remote island. Unfortunately, Blyth's film is all style and no substance, and the thin script remains standard mad scientist stuff with more gore and black humour than usual. Letch stands out as Spider, the leader of the punk zombies, and Bruno Lawrence plays hunchback Tex Monroe, whose brain explodes. Winner of the Grand Prix at the 1984 International Festival of Fantasy and Science Fiction Films in Paris.

DOCTOR FRANKEN

USA, 1980. Dir: Marvin J. Chomsky and Jeff Lieberman. With: Robert Vaughn, Robert Perault, David Selby, Teri Garr, Josef Sommer, Cynthia Harris. NBC. Colour.

TV movie pilot filmed in 1979 as *The Franken Project*, 'suggested' by Mary Shelley's novel. Vaughn plays Dr Arno Franken, a direct descendant of the legendary Dr Frankenstein, who works as a New York surgeon and builds a creature (Perault) out of spare organs. Despite an open ending, the ugly photography and downbeat story ensured this never became a regular series.

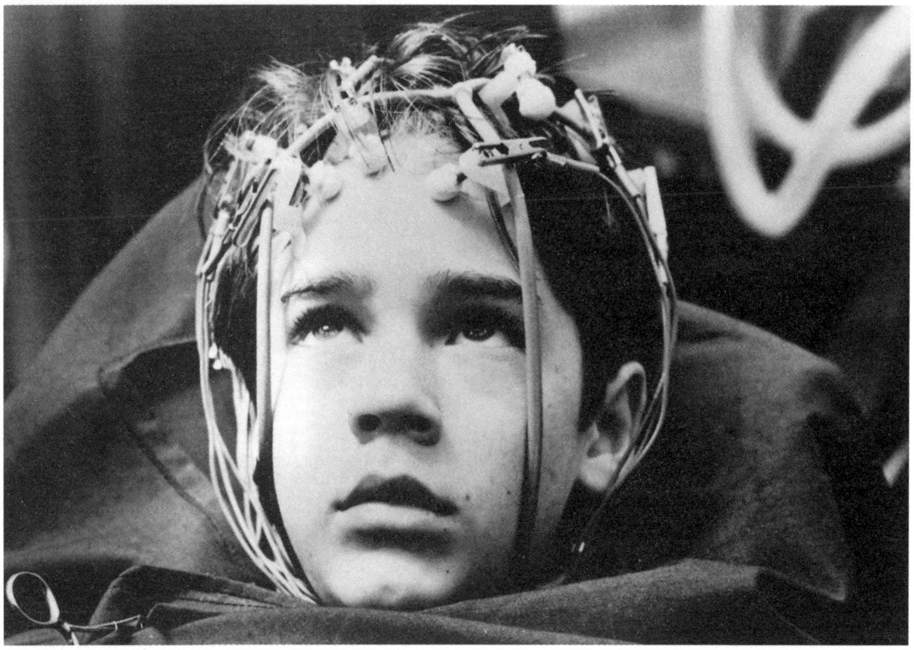

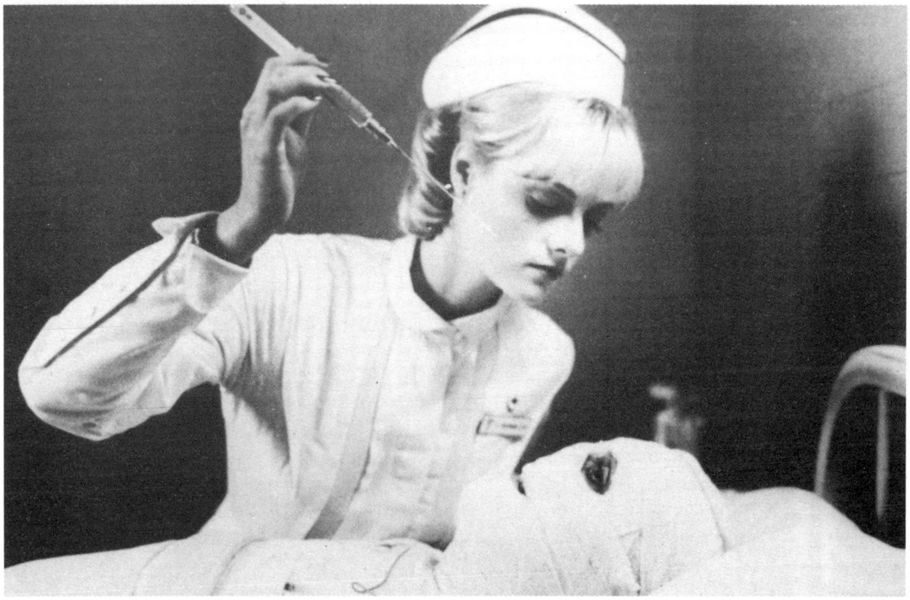

Top: *D.A.R.Y.L.*
Above: *Dead & Buried.*

DRACULA TAN EXARCHIA

Greece, 1983. Dir: Nikos Zervos. With: Kostas Soumas, Yannis Panousis, Vangelis Contronis. Allagi Films. Colour.

Set in Athens, Dracula and his servant dig up the bodies of famous musicians to construct, Frankenstein-like, a superhuman rock star. The last half of the film consists of the creature's performance.

DR. HACKENSTEIN

USA, 1987. Dir: Richard Clark. With: David Muir, Stacey Travis, Catherine Davis Cox, Dyanne DiRosario, John Alexis, William Schreiner. Marketing Media/Vista Street Films. Colour.

Gory, direct-to-video horror comedy. In 1912, Dr Elliott Hackenstein (Muir) keeps the head of his decapitated wife (Sylvia Lee Baker) alive. When three young women accidentally run their car off the road, they take refuge in his house over night and each just happens to have the parts he needs to complete his experiments and create a new body for his wife. With cameo appearances by Phyllis Diller and the husband and wife team of Logan and Anne Ramsey (in one of her last performances), who turn up as comic graverobbers.

DR. PENETRATION

USA, 1986. With: Stacey Donovan, Taija Rae, Melissa Melendez, Brittany Stryker, Sheri St. Clair, Lois Ayres. Wet Video. Colour.

Hardcore spoof of both *The Rocky Horror Picture Show* (1975) and *Dr. Strangelove or: How I Learned to Stop Worrying and Love the Bomb* (1963). The eponymous doctor experiments with the help of lovely assistant Igor and Barbara the Lobster Woman.

FLESH FOR FRANKENSTEIN

USA, circa 1980s With: Dana Lynn, Nikki Knight, Ebony Ayes. Colour.

Hardcore horror feature in which Dana Lynn plays the immortal, man-hungry, man-made, man-handler created from the body parts of hookers.

FRANKENSTEIN

UK, 1984. Dir: Victor Gialanella. With: Robert Powell, Carrie Fisher, David Warner, John Gielgud, Terence Alexander, Susan Wooldridge. Yorkshire Television. Colour.

Another TV movie version (shot on video), adapted by Gialanella from his stage play. This adds nothing to previous adaptations and, although Warner gives his scarred creature (complete with cropped hair) an air of pathos, most of the performances are disappointing (especially Wooldridge). With Powell as Victor Frankenstein, Gielgud as the blind hermit De Lacey, Fisher (doing a passable English accent) as Elizabeth and Edward Judd giving the film's best performance as a graverobber axed to death by the Monster. Almost everyone ends up dead at the finish. Mary Shelley isn't even credited!

Remake: FRANKENSTEIN 90 (qv; 1984)

FRANKENSTEIN GENERAL HOSPITAL

USA, 1988. Dir: Deborah Roberts. With: Mark Blankfield, Leslie Jordan, Jonathan Farwell, Kathy Shower, Hamilton Mitchell, Irwin Keyes. New Star Entertainment. Colour.

Silly *Young Frankenstein*-type spoof. Dr Bob Frankenstein (Blankfield doing a Gene Wilder impersonation), the great-great-grandson of the original, creates a new Monster (Keyes) in his monochromatic laboratory beneath General Hospital. With a few laughs, some mild nudity, a photo of Colin Clive, *Studs* TV presenter Mark DeCarlo and a cameo by singer Bobby 'Boris' Pickett.

FRANKENSTEIN ISLAND

USA/Mexico, 1981. Dir: Jerry Warren. With: Robert Clarke, Steve Brodie, Cameron Mitchell, Robert Christopher, Tain Bodkin, Patrick O'Neil. Chriswar/Jerry Warren. Colour.

Several B-movie stars turn up in the worst film of their careers, produced and directed by legendary low budget veteran Warren. It's difficult to decide if this is meant to be funny or not. Clarke heads a group of balloonists who crash on a mysterious island populated by bikini-clad warrior women descended from aliens! Frankenstein's great-great-granddaughter, Sheila, is also around trying to keep her ancient husband alive by experimenting on captives, while the Karloffian Monster escapes from beneath the sea. It all turns out to have been a dream...or was it? With a wasted Mitchell playing a Poe-quoting sailor, Brodie as a yo-ho-ho pirate and Andrew Duggan in a brief cameo as a navy officer. Scenes of John Carradine's ghost of Dr Frankenstein talking rubbish were obviously filmed earlier.

FRANKENSTEIN, LA VERITABLE HISTOIRE

France, circa 1981 Dir: Roland Portiche.

Experimental short which is apparently a homage to James Whale's *Frankenstein* (1931).

FRANKENSTEIN 90

France, 1984. Dir: Alain Jessua. With: Jean Rochefort, Eddy Mitchell, Fiona Gelin, Herma Vos, Ged Marlon, Serge Marquand. A.J. Films/TF 1 Films/AMLF. Colour.

Contemporary reworking of Mary Shelley's *Frankenstein* which mixes horror and humour. Cybernetics genius Victor Frankenstein (Rochefort) equips his Monster with a micro-processor for a brain. But when the scientist creates a sexy mate from the bodies of murdered disco dancers, the ugly creature (Mitchell) prefers the doctor's gentle girlfriend Elizabeth (Gelin).

Remake: FRANKENSTEIN (qv; 1992)

FRANKENSTEIN'S GREAT-AUNT TILLIE

Mexico, 1983 (1985). Dir: Myron J. Gold. With: Donald Pleasence, Yvonne Furneaux, June Wilkinson, Aldo Ray, Zsa Zsa Gabor, Rod Colbin, Chandler Garrison. Tillie Productions. Colour.

Comedy set in the Transylvanian town of Mucklefugger, written, produced and directed by Gold. When the town council plan to repossess the Frankenstein family mansion for non-payment of taxes, Pleasence's Victor Jr, his buxom compan-

ion (Wilkinson) and his youthful-looking 109 year-old great-aunt (Furneaux) arrive to search for the family fortune and become involved with women's emancipation. With a green-faced Monster who looks like Herman Munster. Filmed in English.

FRANKENWEENIE

USA, 1984. Dir: Tim Burton. With: Shelley Duvall, Daniel Stern, Barret Oliver, Joseph Maher, Roz Braverman, Paul Bartel. Walt Disney Productions. B&W.

A follow-up to his equally offbeat *Vincent* (1982), twenty-five year-old Burton designed and directed this twenty-seven minute short, using stylised sets and black and white photography to faithfully pay homage to James Whale's original (even Kenneth Strickfaden's electrical apparatus was dusted off for use again). This time the Frankensteins are a contemporary middle class family whose dog Sparky is accidentally killed by a car. Inspired by his science teacher (a nice cameo by Bartel) and experiments with a dead frog, their ten year-old son Victor (Oliver) digs up his canine pet and uses electricity to bring it back to life in his bedroom laboratory — with problematical results. Never quite as amusing nor as inventive as it might have been, this remains a beautifully crafted, one-joke idea.

***Above and left:** Deadly Friend.*

Other Frankensteins

The screen's first Dr Frankenstein was played by silent actor Augustus Phillips in the 1910 Edison Film Company production of *Frankenstein*. The character's name was changed to Dr William Frawley when William A. Cohill essayed the role in *Life Without Soul* (1915), and in 1920 producer Luciano Albertini starred as the creator of *Il Mostro di Frankenstein*, an apparently lost Italian version.

Tragic British actor Colin Clive (1900-1937) starred as Henry Frankenstein (the Christian name was first changed from the novel's Victor in Peggy Webling's 1927 stage adaptation) in both Universal's *Frankenstein* (1931) and *Bride of Frankenstein* (1935). However, by the time the studio began filming its second sequel, *Son of Frankenstein* (1939), the alcoholic Clive had been dead for two years. The actor was still represented by a full-length portrait in the film and the titular role went to South African-born (Phillip St John) Basil Rathbone (1892-1967) who, as Baron Wolf von Frankenstein, returned with his family to the ancestral castle to continue his father's experiments. With the help of the broken-necked shepherd Ygor (Bela Lugosi), Wolf reanimated the Monster (Boris Karloff), but eventually sent it plummeting into a boiling sulphur pit.

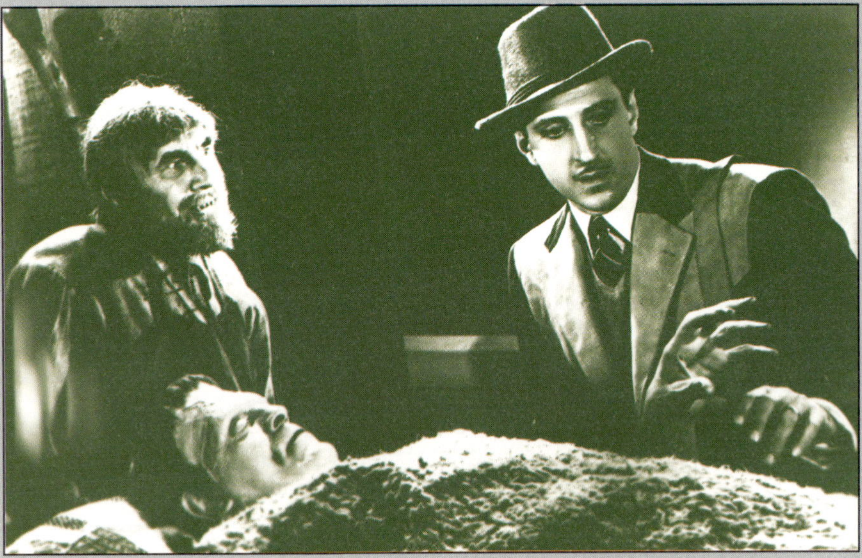

Above: *Son of Frankenstein.*
Below left: *The Ghost of Frankenstein.*

Sir Cedric (Webster) Hardwicke (1893-1964), who had been knighted in 1934 for his outstanding performances on the London stage, portrayed not only *The Ghost of Frankenstein* in 1942, but also Ludwig, the second son of Frankenstein, who was tricked by Dr Bohmer (Lionel Atwill) into transplanting the brain of Ygor (Lugosi) into the Monster (Lon Chaney Jr). As Baroness Elsa Frankenstein, Hungarian-born actress-singer Ilona Massey (Ilona Hajmassy, 1910-1974) attempted to restore the family honour by artificially draining off the energies of both the Monster (Lugosi) and Lawrence Talbot (Chaney Jr) in *Frankenstein Meets the Wolf Man* (1943).

It didn't work, and having apparently exhausted the family tree, Universal next cast Boris Karloff (1887-1969) as Dr Gustav Niemann, the brother of the original Frankenstein's assistant, in *House of Frankenstein* (1944). With Daniel the homicidal hunchback (J. Carrol Naish), he not only reanimated the Monster (Glenn Strange), but also the Wolf Man (Chaney Jr) and Count Dracula (John Carradine). The following year, Onslow Stevens (Onslow Ford Stevenson, 1902-1977) repeated the mistake in *House of Dracula*. As Dr Franz Edelmann, he attempted to cure the monsters of their various afflictions, apparently succeeding with Talbot's Wolf Man (Chaney Jr), despite being turned into a vampire by an unrepentant Dracula (Carradine).

It obviously wasn't a permanent condition, because by *Meet Frankenstein* (1948) Larry Talbot (Chaney Jr) was once again reverting to his bestial nature, while Yugoslavian actress Lenore Aubert (b 1913) played Dr Sandra Mornay who, with the help of Count Dracula (Lugosi), wanted to transplant the brain of baggage clerk Wilbur Grey (Lou Costello) into the Monster (Strange).

Whit Bissell (1914-1981) starred as a contemporary Dr Frankenstein, reanimating car crash victims in *I Was a Teenage Frankenstein* (1957), while Karloff portrayed another modern ancestor, the crippled Baron Victor, as well as the revealed face of the Monster in *Frankenstein 1970* (1958). The same year, Donald Murphy appeared as Oliver Frank, the grandson of you-know-who and creator of the eponymous female creature in *Frankenstein's Daughter*.

Confusingly, it was Frankenstein's *granddaughter* who Narda Onyx played in *Jesse James Meets Frankenstein's Daughter* (1965). Sara Bay was Tanya Frankenstein, competing with her famous father (Joseph Cotten, 1905-1994) in *Lady Frankenstein* (1971), and Gina Romand appeared in much the same role in *Santo contra la Hija de Frankenstein* (1971).

Veteran J. Carrol Naish (1900-1973) ended his career at a low point playing a wheelchair-bound Dr Frankenstein in *Dracula vs. Frankenstein* (1970). Another sick-looking Dr Frankenstein was played by Dennis Price (Dennistoun Franklyn John Rose-Price, 1915-1973) in Jesus Franco's *Dracula Prisoner of Frankenstein* (1972) and its equally incomprehensible sequel, *The Erotic Rites of Frankenstein* (1972). Udo Kier (b 1944) was the sex-crazed Baron Frankenstein in *Flesh for Frankenstein* (1973), while Italian-born Rossano Brazzi (b 1916) must have been desperate to consider appearing as Count Frankenstein in *Frankenstein's Castle of Freaks* (1973). Gene Wilder (Jerry Silberman, b 1934) did his best to disguise his birthright as Dr Frederick *Frahnkensteen* in Mel Brooks' inspired comedy *Young Frankenstein* (1974).

As Baron Victor Frankenstein, Peter Cushing (b 1913) dominated Hammer Films' Frankenstein series, which lasted from 1957 until 1973. The only exception was the studio's 1970 production *The Horror of Frankenstein*, when Ralph Bates (1940-1991) took over the role in Jimmy Sangster's ill-advised comedy.

John Carradine (Richmond Reed Carradine, 1906-1988) made a brief appearance as the doctor in *Frankenstein Island* (1981), Donald Pleasence (b 1919) was Victor Jr in *Frankenstein's Great-Aunt Tillie* (1983), and rock star Sting's (Gordon Summers, b 1951) Charles Frankenstein created a mate for the Monster (Clancy Brown) in *The Bride* (1985).

Television Frankenstein's have included John Newland, Anton Diffring, Ian Holm, Robert Foxworth, Leonard Whiting, Robert Powell, Patrick Bergin, and even Viveca Lindfors as *Frankenstein's Auntie* (1986).

Raul Julia's (b 1940) Dr Frankenstein co-existed with his creation and creator in Roger Corman's *Frankenstein Unbound* (1990), and Kenneth Branagh (b 1960) both directed and played the obsessed creator of life in *Mary Shelley's Frankenstein* (1994).

It would appear that so long as there are monsters to be made, there will always be those who are willing to delve into secrets Man Was Never Meant to Know...

***Below:** I Was a Teenage Frankenstein.*
***Bottom:** Frankenstein's Daughter. (FJA).*

THE FUNHOUSE

USA, 1981. Dir: Tobe Hooper. With: Cooper Huckabee, Miles Chapin, Largo Woodruff, Sylvia Miles, William Finley, Kevin Conway. Universal. Colour.

Disappointing horror thriller from director Hooper (*The Texas Chain Saw Massacre* [1974], etc). It begins promisingly with a *Psycho* (1960) in-joke and the build up to a Ray Bradbury-ish carnival and freak show, but soon degenerates when a group of dislikable teenagers are trapped in a funhouse with a mutated monster (created by Rick Baker and Craig Reardon) and its murderous father (Conway). The mutant (played by mime Wayne Doba) dresses up as Universal's Frankenstein Monster. It is left to a brief cameo by William Finley as Marco the Magnificent and newcomer Elizabeth Berridge to brighten an otherwise dull film. With a clip from *Bride of Frankenstein* (1935). The American cable TV version apparently includes restored footage.

GEEK MAGGOT BINGO

USA, 1983. Dir: Nick Zedd. With: Robert Andrews, Brenda Bergman, Richard Hell, Donna Death, (John) Zacherle, Bob Martin. Weirdo Films/Penetration. Colour.

Zedd follows up his directing début on *They Eat Scum* (1979) with this horror spoof featuring a mad doctor Frankenberry (Andrews), Bruno Zeus as a hunchback, a female vampire (Death), some nudity and a two-headed Formaldehyde Man (created by Ed French). Shot in 16mm on obviously cardboard sets. TV horror host Zacherley is shown sleeping during the breaks.

Above: Death Warmed Up.
Below: The Funhouse.

GOTHIC

UK, 1986. Dir: Ken Russell. With: Gabriel Byrne, Julian Sands, Natasha Richardson, Myriam Cyr, Timothy Spall, Alec Mango. Virgin Vision. Colour.

During the late 1960s, Paul McCartney announced that he was going to play Percy Shelley in a movie musical based on the occurrences at the Villa Diodati in June 1816. It probably wouldn't have been as bad as this ludicrously overwrought retelling of the events that led to Mary Shelley writing *Frankenstein*. During a crazed night, Lord Byron (Byrne), Percy Bysshe Shelley (Sands), Mary (Richardson), her half-sister Claire (Cyr) and the blood-obsessed Dr John Polidori (Spall) tell ghost stories, indulge in drink, drugs and debauchery, and wander around the Swiss villa encountering a half-glimpsed Monster (a composite of their 'worst fears') conjured up by sex, a seance and their subconscious. Russell directs the historic histrionics at full throttle, piling each stupidity upon the next, and he's not helped by Stephen Volk's unintentionally hilarious script or the terrible performances. At least Cyr and Spall bring a pantomime exuberance to their roles. Music by Thomas Dolby.

GRAMPA'S MONSTER MOVIES

USA, 1988. Dir: Peter Zasuly. With: Al Lewis. Voices: Kieth Williams. Amvest Video. Colour/B&W.

Disappointing video compilation of Universal trailers, hosted by Lewis (as the vampiric Grampa from TV's *The Munsters* [1964-66]). Includes material from all the studio's Frankenstein movies, amongst many others, but few surprises.

HAUNTED SUMMER

USA, 1988. Dir: Ivan Passer. With: Philip Anglim, Laura Dern, Alice Krige, Eric Stoltz, Alex Winter.

Cannon Films. Colour.
Based on the novel by Anne Edwards, this was originally announced in 1986 with John Huston directing. It is one of two versions released in the same year based on the events of June 1816 which led up to Mary Godwin/Shelley (Krige) writing *Frankenstein*. Also enjoying a stay at the Villa Diodati are Lord Byron (Anglim), Claire Clairmont (Dern), Percy Shelley (Stoltz) and Dr Polidori (Winter). Music by Christopher Young.

THE HENDERSON MONSTER

USA, 1980. Dir: Waris Hussein. With: Jason Miller, Christine Lahti, Stephen Collins, David Spielberg, Nehemiah Persoff, Larry Gates. Titus Productions. Colour.
Dull TV movie about egotistical scientist Thomas Henderson (Miller) who, through his experiments with recombinant DNA, creates a controversial new bacterium in his university laboratory. A combination of *Frankenstein* allegory and soap opera.

HORRIBLE HORROR

USA, 1986. Dir: David Bergman. With: Zacherley (John Zacherle). Movietime Inc/Bergman-Harris. Colour/B&W.
Value-for-money video collection of trailers, out-takes and genre clips, presented by manic 1950s TV horror host Zacherley from his movie dungeon. Includes rare clips of Karloff and Lugosi, and excerpts from the Hammer TV pilot *Tales of Frankenstein* (1958), plus, most interesting of all, several out-takes from (Abbott and Costello) *Meet Frankenstein* (1948).

THE HOUSE BY THE CEMETERY

(Orig: QUELLA VILLA ACCANTO AL CIMITERO/FREUDSTEIN) Italy/USA, 1982. Dir: Lucio Fulci. With: Katherine MacColl, Paolo Malco, Dagmar Lassander, Ania Pieroni, Giovanni Frezza, Silvia Collatina. Fulvia. Colour.
Over-the-top Gothic horrors from director Fulci. Following the death of the previous occupant, a researcher, his wife and their young son move into a haunted house. Still alive in the cellar is a radical turn-of-the-century doctor, Freudstein (Giovanni de Nava), his decaying flesh kept alive by the transplanted bodies of his victims. The murders are particularly nasty and the atmospheric story is muddled by a subplot involving the ghost of a young girl.

HOWL OF THE DEVIL

(Orig: EL AULLIDO DEL DIABLO) Spain, 1988. Dir: Paul Naschy (Jacinto Molina). With: Paul Naschy (Jacinto Molina), Caroline Munro, Howard Vernon (Mario Lippert), Sergio Molina, Fernando Hilbelck. Lorion. Colour.
Naschy not only writes and directs, but also plays ten classic horror roles as a crazy actor. These include the Frankenstein Monster, a vampire, Fu Manchu, Mr Hyde, the Phantom of the Opera, Quasimodo, the Devil, his zombie twin and, of course, a werewolf. A blend of horror nostalgia and explicit gore, with Vernon turning up as a sinister manservant. This was Naschy's first film shot in English.

THE IMMORTALIZER

USA, 1989 (1990). Dir: Joel Bender. With: Ron Kay, Chris Crone, Melody Patterson, Clarke Lindsley, Bekki Armstrong. RCA/Columbia. Colour.
The insane Dr Devine (Ray) transplants young brains into ageing bodies in his private laboratory. Meanwhile, the left-over corpses are disposed of by two derelict assistants who feed them to a pit full of ugly cannibal mutants. When another evil doctor turns up, the nurse (Patterson, from TV's *F Troop!*) wants them both. In the end, her brain is transplanted into a new (naked) body. A direct-to-video mess.

KAIBUTSU KUN, KAIBUTSU KANDO ENO SHOTAI

Japan, 1981. Dir: Hiroshi Fukutomi. Voices: Masako Nozawa, Katsue Miwa, Taroh Sagami, Kaneta Kimotsuki, Takuzoh Kamiyama, Dai Kanai. Sin-ei Doga/Toho International. Colour.
Feature-length cartoon based on the

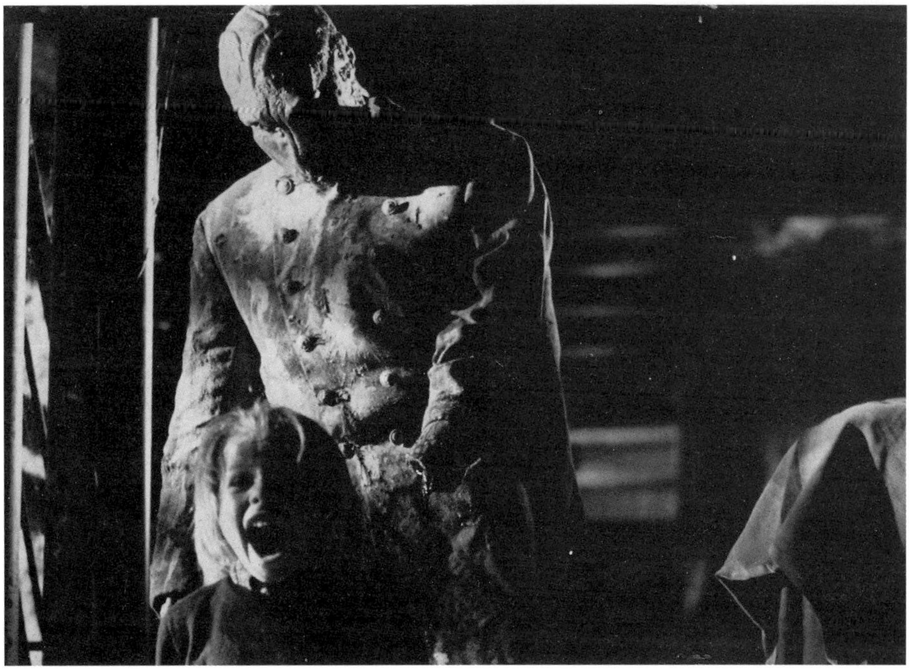

Above right: *Gothic.*
Below right: *The House by the Cemetery.*

THE MAN WITH TWO BRAINS

USA, 1983. Dir: Carl Reiner. With: Steve Martin, Kathleen Turner, David Warner, Paul Benedict, Richard Brestoff, James Cromwell. Aspen/Warner Bros. Colour.

Often hilarious comedy, loosely based on *Donovan's Brain* (a clip from the 1953 movie turns up on TV). Brain surgeon Dr Michael Hfuhruhurr (Martin) marries scum-queen Dolores (Turner) but falls in love with one of Dr Neceffiter's (Warner) collection of brains in jars (voiced by Sissy Spacek). The gags vary between the obvious and the just plain silly, but there's some wonderful dialogue and a happy ending. With Merv Griffin in an unbilled cameo as an Argento-like elevator killer, and Jeffrey Combs.

Kaibutsu Kun comic strip by Fujio Fujiko. The Monster Prince Kaibutsu Kun and his monster friends Furanken, Dorakyura and Ohkami-Otoko travel to the Monster Land, where they battle a huge Golem and other bizarre creatures to obtain the magical ingredients that will save their human friend Hiroshi, who has been turned to stone.

THE KINDRED

USA, 1986. Dir: Jeffrey Obrow and Stephen Carpenter. With: David Allen Brooks, Amanda Pays, Talia Balsam, Kim Hunter, Rod Steiger, Timothy Gibbs. F/M Entertainment. Colour.

This ludicrous horror thriller has no less than five scriptwriters credited (including Joseph Stefano). Mad scientist Steiger (in an ill-fitting hair piece) steals bodies for his research and keeps the failed experiments locked in the basement. However, it soon turns out that his one-time colleague (a frail-looking Hunter) has progressed further with her genetic research, and her son and his friends discover a giant tentacled mutation which is very, very hungry. The terrible Amanda Pays turns into a fish.

LIVSFARLIG FILM

Sweden, 1987. Dir: Suzanne Osten. With: Etienne Glaser, Stina Ekblad, Henrik Holmborg, Lena T. Hansson, Agneta Ekmanner, Helge Skoog. Sandrew/SVT-1/Film Teknik. Colour.

Comedy set in the near future in which famous horror film director Emil Frankenstein (Glaser) searches for his missing daughter (a star of vampire films) and discovers political refugees hiding in the studio. He decides to make a film about them, but is eventually decapitated. The title translates as *Lethal Film*.

MIAMI HORROR

(aka MIAMI GOLEM)

Italy/USA, 1985 (1987). Dir: Martin Herbert (Alberto Martino). With:

David Warbeck, Laura Trotter, Lawrence Loddi, John Ireland. Panther/Twin Tower Enterprises. Colour.
A scientist experimenting with bacteria from space creates a mutant baby monster (here called a Golem). Warbeck plays a TV reporter investigating the case, Trotter is the psychic who helps him and veteran Ireland is the leader of the gang who kidnap the creature. Filmed in Florida.

MIXED UP

Hong Kong, 1985. Dir: Henry S. Chen. Colour.
A teens-in-peril horror comedy featuring a vampire and a Frankenstein-like creature. During the climax, the two monsters battle it out on a yacht.

MONKEY SHINES

(aka MONKEY SHINES AN EXPERIMENT IN FEAR)
USA, 1988. Dir: George A. Romero. With: Jason Beghe, John Pankow, Kate McNeil, Joyce Van Patten, Christine Forrest (Romero), Stephen Root. Orion. Colour.
Filmed under the title *Ella* and not released in Britain for nearly two years, this adaptation of Michael Stewart's novel is one of director Romero's most accomplished movies to date. Beghe is convincing as the crippled athlete Allan Mann whose capuchin monkey companion Ella (played by Boo) develops a telepathic link with her master and a psychotic hatred of anyone who upsets the embittered paraplegic. Pretty soon people are being burned to death in their beds or electrocuted in the bath. This is because the drug-addicted Dr Fisher (the excellent Pankow) has been injecting the monkey with human brain cells to raise its intelligence. Only during the prerequisite thunderstorm climax (apparently subject to studio interference) does Romero allow the film to topple over into cliché. Make-up effects by Tom Savini.

THE MONSTER SQUAD

USA, 1987. Dir: Fred Dekker. With: Andre Gower, Robby Kiger, Stephen Macht, Duncan Regehr, Tom Noonan, Brent Chalem. Taft Entertainment/Keith Barrish. Colour.
From writer/director Dekker (*Night of the Creeps* [1986]) and co-writer Shane Black comes a delightful horror comedy for children that echoes the Universal series of the 1940s. Dracula (an impressive Regehr) is in a small American town to recover an amulet of evil. Only a group of kids, known as The Monster Squad, recognise the danger, and despite the intervention of Van Helsing (Jack Gwillim), the Count teams up with the Frankenstein Monster (Noonan), a wolfman, gill man and mummy to create havoc. Great special effects, non-stop action and a nice sense of reverence make this a minor gem. Kids should love it.

THE MUNSTERS' REVENGE

USA, 1981. Dir: Don Weis. With: Fred Gwynne, Al Lewis, Yvonne De Carlo, K.C. Martel, Jo McDonnell, Bob Hastings. Universal. Colour.

Terrible made-for-TV movie that revives the characters fifteen years after the regular series finished. The Frankenstein Monster-like Herman (Gwynne) and vampiric Grampa (Lewis) have to prove their innocence when the villainous Dr Dustin Diablo (an over-the-top Sid Caesar) uses robot doubles of the pair to go on a crime spree. Gwynne and Lewis don't look like they've aged at all and they do their best to carry the movie. But Weis' lacklustre direction, an insipid supporting cast (particularly Hastings' aggravating Phantom of the Opera) and the awful dubbed laughter make this reunion a sad mistake. Amongst the waxwork robots is the Creature from the Black Lagoon and another wearing a Tor Johnson mask.

MYSTERY! FRANKENSTEIN — LEGEND OF TERROR

(Orig: KAIKI FURANKENSHUTAIN)
Japan, 1981. Dir: Yugo Serizawa. Voices: Nachi Nozawa, Mami Koyama, Hosei Komatsu, Kei Tomiyama, Ichiroh Nagai, Minori Matsushima. Toei/Terebi (TV) Asahi. Colour.

Feature-length cartoon made for TV and based on Mary Shelley's novel and the Marvel Comics series. Disfigured by a lightning bolt, the Monster (Komatsu) saves the daughter of Dr Victor Frankenstein (Nozawa) from a bear before committing suicide along with its creator. The original title translates as *Mysterious Frankenstein*.
Remake: FRANKENSTEIN (qv; 1984, UK)

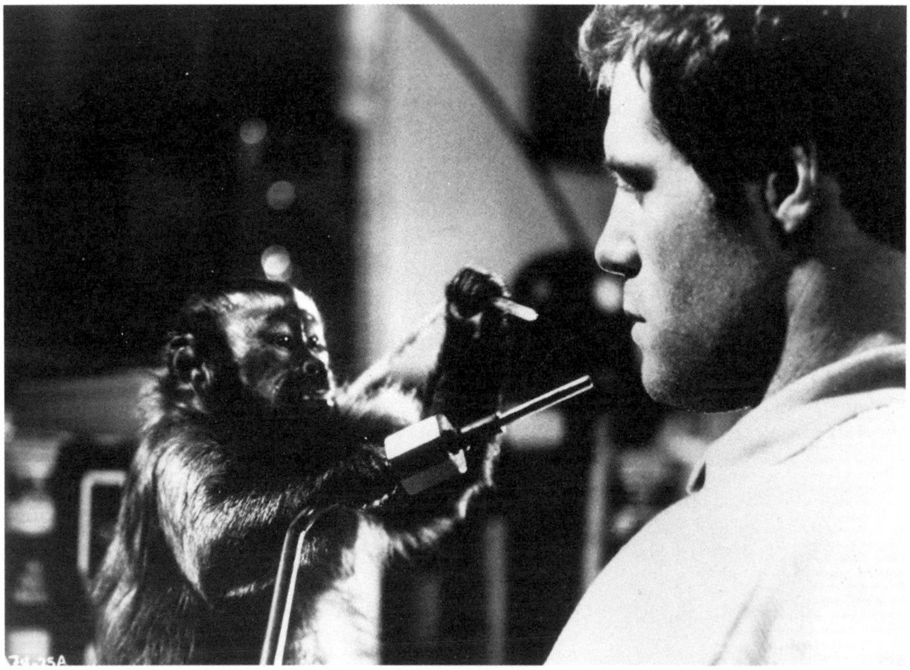

NIGHTMARES

USA, 1983. Dir: Joseph Sargent. With: Cristina Raines, Joe Lambie, Emilio Estevez, Mariclare Costello, Lance Henriksen, Tony Plana. Universal/Mirisch-Beaton. Colour.

Unimaginative quartet of tales originally intended for TV. The first story, 'Terror in Topanga', is a routine stalk 'n' slash thriller about an escaped murderer and features the 1931 *Frankenstein* on television.

OTSTUPNIK

USSR/West Germany/Austria, 1987. Dir: Valery Rubinchik. With: Grigorij Gladij, Nikolaj Eriomenko, Larisa Belogurova, Valentina Shendrikova. Colour.

A scientist clones himself but destroys his creation when the military tries to create an army of such creatures. In the end he creates four clones of the President.

OUR HITLER

West Germany, 1980. Dir: Hans-Jurgen Syberberg. With: Heinz Schubert, Peter Kern, Hellmut Lange, Rainer von Artenfels, Martin Sperr. Colour.

Originally shown on German TV in four parts, this seven hour dramatization of Hitler's rise to power apparently includes scenes of Hitler as Frankenstein. Distributed in cinemas by Francis Ford Coppola.

PROGRAMMED TO KILL

(aka RETALIATOR)
USA, 1987. Dir: Allan Holzman. With: Robert Ginty, Sandahl Bergman, Louise Caire Clark, James Booth, Alex Courtney, Paul W. Walker. Colour.

Low budget science fiction thriller in which wounded terrorist Bergman undergoes brain surgery and is turned into an android assassin by government scientists.

Above left: *Haunted Summer.*
Below left: *Monkey Shines.*
Opposite: *The Monster Squad.*

RE-ANIMATOR

USA, 1985. Dir: Stuart Gordon. With: Bruce Abbott, Barbara Crampton, David Gale, Robert Sampson, Jeffrey Combs, Carolyn Purdy-Gordon. Empire Pictures. Colour.

Based very loosely on H.P. Lovecraft's 1921-22 episodic novella 'Herbert West: Reanimator', this outrageous low budget horror comedy features medical student West (a nicely sardonic performance by Combs) inventing a glowing liquid which can bring the dead back to life — with horrific results. But the real villain is Dr Hill (Gale), a megalomaniac whose still-living decapitated head unleashes an army of walking corpses in the gory, over-the-top climax. Despite some lapses in logic, Gordon directs with a nice sense of fun. The film was released unrated in America because of the violence, and fifty seconds (including a particularly gross sequence involving Hill's head and heroine Crampton) were cut in Britain.

Sequel: BRIDE OF RE-ANIMATOR (qv; 1989)

PROTOTYPE

USA, 1983. Dir: David Greene. With: Christopher Plummer, David Morse, Frances Sternhagen, James Sutorius, Stephen Elliott, Arthur Hill. Richard Levinson-William Link Productions.

Although credited as an updating of *Frankenstein*, this tedious TV movie is in fact about humanoid robot Michael (Morse), created by Plummer's slightly crazy Dr Carl Forrester. The scientist kidnaps his creation when the Pentagon shows interest in its military capabilities. After watching the 1931 *Frankenstein* on television and reading Mary Shelley's novel, the creature destroys itself.

RAIDERS OF THE LIVING DEAD

USA, 1985. Dir: Samuel M. Sherman (and Brett Piper). With: Scott Schwartz, Robert Deveau, Donna Asali, Bob Allen, Bob Sacchetti, Zita Johann. Independent-International. Colour.

Investigating a terrorist incident at a nuclear power plant, a journalist uncovers a plot by a mad scientist to reanimate a skull-faced army of the dead. Veteran actress Johann (*The Mummy* [1932]) turns up in one scene as an aged librarian. This was originally started in 1983 by Piper under the title *Graveyard* and completed by writer/producer Sherman.

LE RAVISSEMENT DE FRANK N. STEIN

Switzerland, 1982. Dir: Georges Schwizgebel.

Nine minute cartoon about 'the creation of life'.

THE REVENGE OF THE STEPFORD WIVES

USA, 1980. Dir: Robert Fuest. With: Julie Kavner, Arthur Hill, Sharon Gless, Audra Lindley, Mason Adams, Don Johnson. Scherick Productions. Colour.

First TV movie sequel to *The Stepford Wives* (1974). Ten years after the original, reporter Gless discovers the chemical secret of the perfect New England housewives. A disappointment from the director of the *Dr Phibes* movies and featuring a cast better known for their various TV series.

Sequel: THE STEPFORD CHILDREN (qv; 1987).

Above: Miami Horror.
Below: Silent Rage.

THE ROCKY PORNO VIDEO SHOW

USA, 1986. Dir: Loretta Stirling. With: Mistress Tantala (Ray), Bionca, Kristara Barrington, Tom Byron, Karen Summer, Marc Wallice. 4-Play. Colour.

What starts out as a wedding night for a young couple becomes a guided tour of sexual perversions and wanton desires in this hardcore pastiche of the cult classic.

ROWING WITH THE WIND

(Orig: REMANDO AL VIENTO) Spain, 1988. Dir: Gonzalo Suárez. With: Lizzy McInnery, Valentina Pelka, Elizabeth Hurley, Hugh Grant. Colour.

Yet another retelling of the meeting in June 1816 between Mary Shelley, Percy Shelley, Lord Byron and Dr Polidori at the Villa Diodati, and the events which led up to Mary writing *Frankenstein.* This was apparently a big hit in Spain.

SCOOBY-DOO AND THE RELUCTANT WEREWOLF

USA, 1988. Dir: Ray Patterson. Voices: Don Messick, Casey Kasem, Hamilton Camp, Jim Cummings, Joanie Gerber, Ed Gilbert. Hanna-Barbera Productions/ Worldvision Enterprises. Colour

Made-for-TV animated feature based on the *Scooby-Doo* series. A green-faced Dracula turns Scooby's friend Shaggy into a werewolf so that he can take part in the Transylvania monster road race. Also includes the Frankenstein Monster, the Mummy, Dr Jekyll and Mr Snyde, and Genghis Kong.

SILENT RAGE

USA, 1982. Dir: Michael Miller. With: Chuck Norris, Ron Silver, Steven Keats, Toni Kalem, William Finley, Brian Libby. Columbia/ Anthony B. Unger/Topick Productions. Colour.

Martial arts expert Norris plays a small town Texas sheriff who battles a scientifically created superman (Libby) in this entertaining action thriller.

SLAPSTICK (OF ANOTHER KIND)

USA, 1982 (1984). Dir: Steven Paul. With: Jerry Lewis, Madeline Kahn, Marty Feldman, Jim Backus, John Abbott, Pat Morita. Steven Paul Productions/Entertainment Releasing. Colour.

Directed by twenty-four year-old Paul and scripted by Kurt Vonnegut Jr, based on his own novel. Veteran Abbott (*The Vampire's Ghost* [1945], etc) portrays Dr Frankenstein, who delivers two monstrous babies, Wilbur and Eliza Swain (Lewis and Kahn, who also play the twins' parents). Although they appear to be morons to outsiders, when together the brother and sister are, in fact, alien geniuses capable of solving the world's problems. With Samuel Fuller, Merv Griffin and the voice of Orson Welles.

THE STEPFORD CHILDREN

USA, 1987. Dir: Alan J. Levi. With: Barbara Eden, Don Murray, Tammy Lauran, Pat Corley, Ken Swofford, Richard Anderson. Taft Entertainment/Edgar J. Scherick. Colour.

Second TV movie sequel to *The Stepford Wives* (1974). This time the menacing Stepford Men's Club is creating well-behaved duplicates of the community's rowdy teenagers. The puppet effects of the half-formed replacements are not very

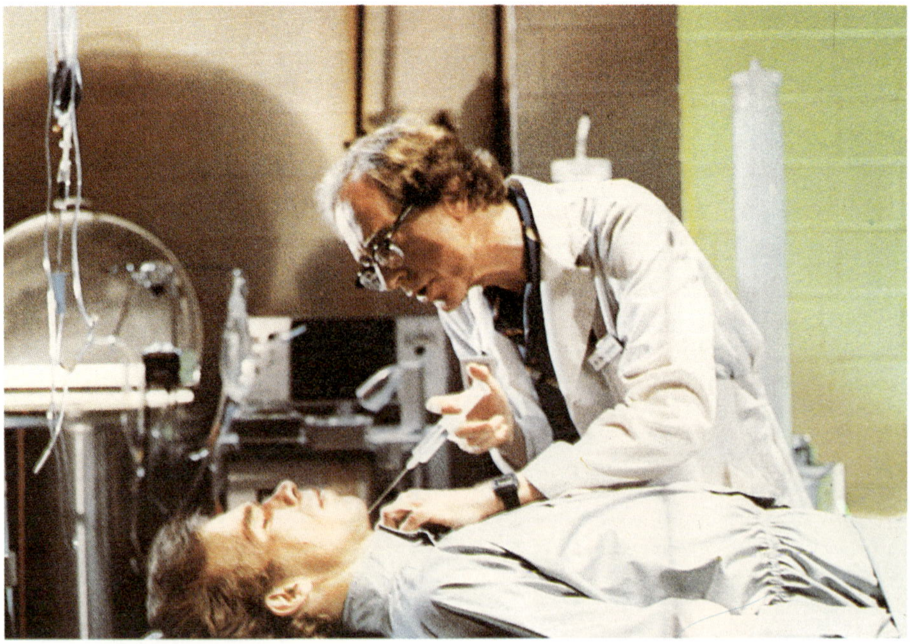

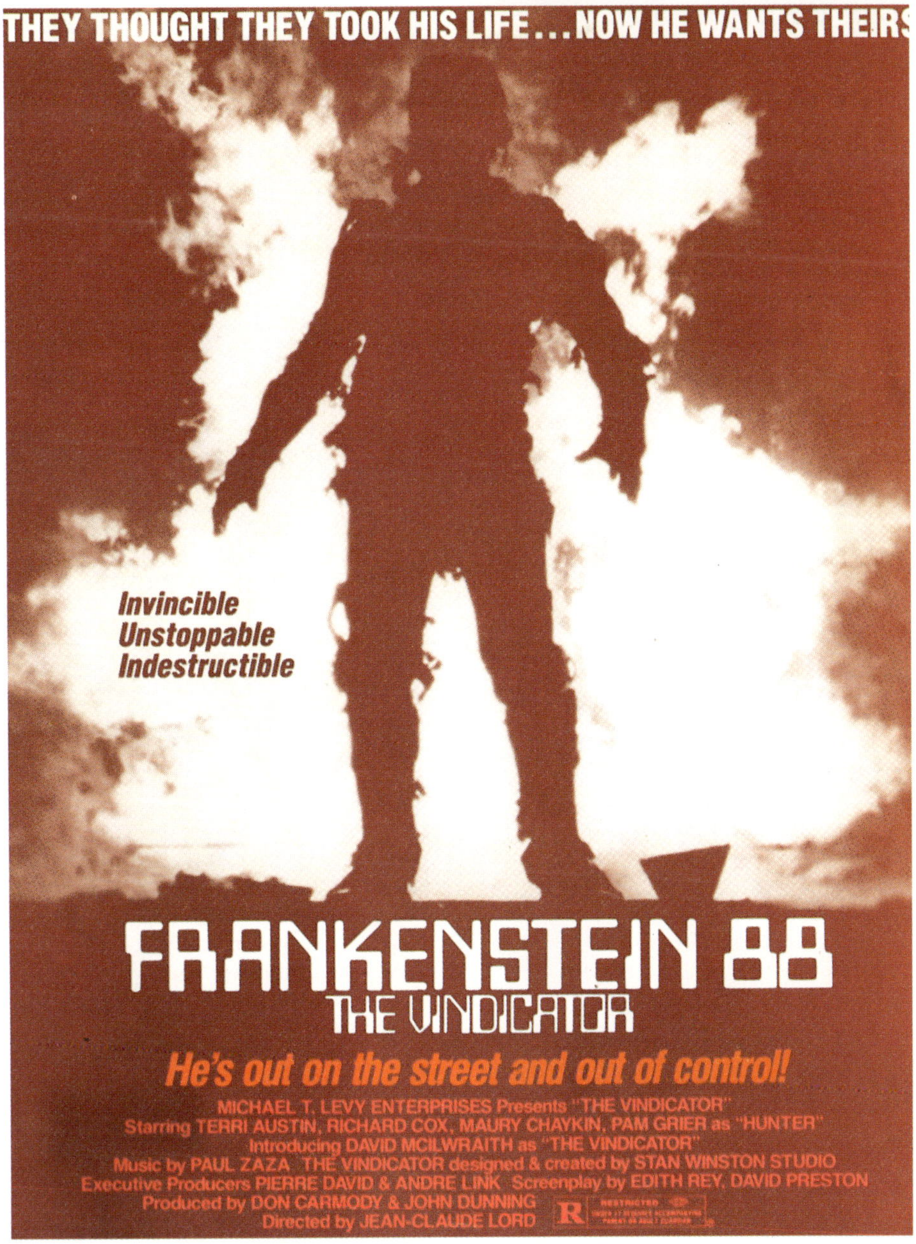

***Right:** The Vindicator.*

convincing and the 'rebellious' teen behaviour appears seriously dated. With James Coco in one of his last roles. Creator Ira Levin doesn't even get a credit.

THINGS

USA, circa 1980s. Dir: Andrew Jordan. With: Barry Gillis, Amber Lynn, Doug Bunston, Bruce Roach. Interamerican Entertainment Corporation. Colour.

When a scientist creates a monster through his experiments with artificial insemination, the deformed creature returns seeking revenge. Low budget, direct-to-video chills.

THRESHOLD

Canada, 1981 (1983). Dir: Richard Pearce. With: Donald Sutherland, Mare Winningham, Jeff Goldblum, John Marley, Sharon Ackerman, Michael Lerner. Paragon/Twentieth Century-Fox. Colour.

Fact-based drama in which Sutherland's dedicated surgeon defies the authorities and transplants a mechanical heart invented by Goldblum into dying patient Winningham. Boris Karloff was doing the same thing for Columbia, much more entertainingly, forty years earlier.

TOMORROW'S CHILD

(Orig: GENESIS)

USA, 1982. Dir: Joseph Sargent. With: Stephanie Zimbalist, William Atherton, Bruce Davison, Ed Flanders, Susan Oliver, Arthur Hill. ABC-TV. Colour.

Made-for-TV movie in which a menacing group of scientists form the Genesis Project, an experiment to grow a foetus completely outside the human body.

TRAILERS ON TAPE: HAMMER HORROR THE CLASSIC SERIES "MONSTERS"

USA, 1987. San Francisco Rush Video. Colour/B&W.

Compilation video of classic Hammer trailers, including all the studio's Frankenstein entries (with Peter Cushing in specially-filmed sequences promoting *The Revenge of Frankenstein* [1958]), plus the Quatermass, Mummy and Dracula series, *The Hound of the Baskervilles* (1959), *The Curse of the Werewolf* (1961), *The Gorgon* (1964), etc. Kate Bush sings 'Hammer Horror'.

TRANSYLVANIA 6-5000

USA/Yugoslavia, 1985. Dir: Rudy De Luca. With: Jeff Goldblum, Ed Begley Jr, Joseph Bologna, Carol Kane, John Byner, Pat Harrington Jr. New World Pictures. Colour.

Goldblum and Begley Jr play two reporters for a sleazy tabloid newspaper sent to Transylvania to get a scoop on the monsters. It turns out that Frankenstein's creature (Peter Buntic) is just an accident victim, the mummy (Ksenija Prohska) has had plastic surgery, the wolfman has a hair condition and the seductive vampire (Geena Davis) wants more attention. Unfunny comedy which steals its title from (a much better) 1963 Bugs Bunny cartoon.

ULTIMATE LOVER

USA, 1986. Dir: Thomas Paine. With: Tracey Adams, Nina Hartley, Amber Lynn, Eric Edwards, Ron Jeremy. Colour.

Hardcore comedy in which Dr Shelly Franklin (Adams) and Dr Mary Stein (Hartley), two women who are going through some rough times in their love lives, decide to clone Ron Jeremy's penis and attach it to Eric Edwards' body. When their well-endowed creation becomes insatiable, he escapes and roams the streets looking for partners.

THE VINDICATOR

(Orig: FRANKENSTEIN 88)
Canada, 1984 (1986). Dir: Jean-Claude Lord. With: Terri Austin, Richard Cox, Maury Chaykin, Pam Grier, David McIlwraith, Denis Simpson. Michael T. Levy Enterprises. Colour.

At the high-tech laboratories of the Aerospace Research Corp (ARC), ruthless scientist Alex Whyte (Cox) murders colleague Carl Lehman (McIlwraith) and transplants his brain and mutilated body into an indestructible spacesuit (created by the Stan Winston Studio). The monster escapes and goes on a murderous rampage, pursued by Hunter (Grier), a tough female samurai.

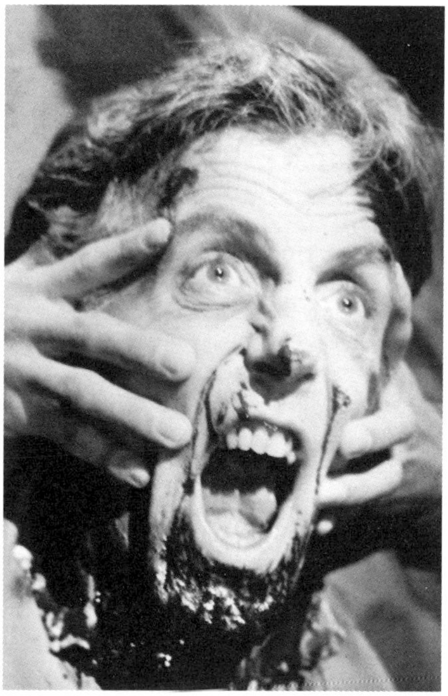

WARLORDS

USA, 1989. Dir: Fred Olen Ray. With: David Carradine, Dawn Wildsmith, Sid Haig, Ross Hagen, Fox Harris, Robert Quarry. Vidmark. Colour.

Low budget, post-apocalyptic science fiction adventure in which Carradine plays the clone of a legendary hero battling Haig's mad scientist. With Brinke Stevens, Michelle Bauer and Victoria Sellers (the daughter of Peter Sellers and Britt Ekland), making her début as a desert nomad.

Above and left: *Re-Animator.*
Below: *Slapstick (of Another Kind).*

WAXWORK

USA, 1988. Dir: Anthony Hickox. With: Zach Galligan, Deborah Foreman, Michelle Johnson, Dana Ashbrook, Miles O'Keefe, John Rhys-Davies. Vestron. Colour.

Six teens take a midnight tour of David Warner's mysterious wax museum and are drawn into the exhibits to confront a werewolf, the mummy, the Marquis De Sade and ex-Tarzan Miles O'Keefe (with long blond hair and designer stubble) as Count Dracula. The ludicrous Keystone Cops-type climax has a wheelchair-bound Patrick Macnee leading an attack on all the above monsters, plus the Golem, Mr Hyde, the Phantom of the Opera, etc. The special effects by Bob Keen's Image Animation (*Hellraiser* [1987], etc) are the best thing in this shoddy horror comedy.
Sequel: WAXWORK II: LOST IN TIME (qv; 1991)

WEIRD FANTASY

USA, circa 1980s. Dir: John Parker and Terry Knight. With: Tracey Adams, Niki Randall, Bambi Allen, Francois Papillon, Steve Drake. The LA Video Corporation. Colour.

Hardcore spoof of *Weird Science* (1985) in which teenage whiz kids Sondra and Julie use a computer to create the perfect man, but end up accidentally creating the perfect woman.

WEIRD SCIENCE

USA, 1985. Dir: John Hughes. With: Anthony Michael Hall, Ilan Mitchell-Smith, Kelly LeBrock, Bill Paxton, Suzanne Snyder, Robert Downey. Universal. Colour.

This has nothing to do with the EC Comics title it borrowed. Instead, it's an often unpleasant fantasy comedy in which a pair of teen nerds (Hall and Mitchell-Smith) create Lisa (LeBrock, looking like a teenage boy's wet dream) when their computer overloads. After taking a quick shower together, the trio set out to pay back all those people who made the boys' lives hell. The results are unfunny and often quite nasty. With a yuckie monster and *colourised* clips from the 1931 *Frankenstein.*

WHO IS AFRAID OF DRACULA

(Orig: FRACCHIA CONTRO DRACULA/FRACCHIA VS DRACULA) Italy, 1985. Dir: Neri Parenti. With: Paolo Villaggio, Gigi Reder, Edmund Purdom, Ania Pieroni, Isabella Fearrare (Ferrari). Faso Film/Titanus/Maura International. Colour.

Horror spoof in which star and co-writer Villaggio recreates his comic character Fantozzi as Fracchia, an unsuccessful estate agent who tries to sell a cheap Transylvanian castle to a myopic client (Reder). Purdom plays a Lugosi-like Dracula and Pieroni turns up as his undead sister, Countess Oniria. The knockabout climax also throws in the Frankenstein Monster and a group of zombies.

WHO IS JULIA?

USA, 1986. Dir: Walter Grauman. With: Mare Winningham, Jameson Parker, Jeffrey DeMunn, Jonathan Banks, Bert Remsen, Mason Adams. Colour.

Made-for-TV movie about a woman who has a brain transplant. Based on the novel by Barbara S. Harris.

ZOMBIE HIGH

USA, 1987 (1988). Dir: Ron Link. With: Virginia Madsen, Richard Cox, Kay E. Kuter, James Wilder, Sherilyn Fenn, Paul Feig. Priest Hill/Vestron. Colour.

Thematically closer to *The Stepford Wives* (1974) than the zombie movies of George Romero. Madsen arrives at an exclusive high school and discovers that her classmates are being turned into 'perfect' pupils by the teachers — members of a secret society who have survived for over a century by operating on the brains of their victims. Director Link's use of the clichéd material is fun and entertaining and, despite the almost mandatory heavy metal soundtrack, this is a surprisingly stylish little thriller.

Above right: *Transylvania 6-500.*

Below right: *Zombie High.*

the

*T*he decade began with Frank Henenlotter's comedy **Frankenhooker (1990)**, and looked set to continue along similar lines with the TV movie **Frankenstein: The College Years (1991)** and **Waxwork II: Lost in Time (1991)**, in which time-travelling teens encountered Martin Kemp's Baron and his creature.

Frankenstein Unbound.

Frankenstein (1992).

Another time traveller met not only Frankenstein and his creation, but also **their** *creator, Mary Shelley, in Roger Corman's enjoyable* **Frankenstein Unbound (1990)**. *Randy Quaid made a sympathetic Monster in another TV movie of* **Frankenstein (1992)**, *but it still wasn't quite the definitive adaptation.*

Despite a mixed critical response, Francis Ford Coppola's overblown version of **Bram Stoker's Dracula (1992)** *eventually went into profit around the world. Like Universal before him, Coppola next turned to* **Mary Shelley's Frankenstein (1994)**, *which was billed as 'a passionate and romantic love story of epic proportions in which man's desire to know the unknowable sweeps him into a living nightmare.' The film also promised to 'return to the spirit of Mary Shelley's Gothic spine-chiller' (echoing a similar, if misleading, claim for Coppola's Dracula movie), and co-writer Frank Darabont added: "I believe my script is the most faithful adaptation to date. I refer back to the book quite a lot and say, 'Now, what did Shelley have in mind, what was her intention...'"*

Principal photography began at Britain's Shepperton Studios on 21 October 1993. It was shot on seven sound-

1990s

stages and on massive exterior sets, the biggest ever constructed at the studio.

Coppola chose Kenneth Branagh to both direct and star as Victor Frankenstein, with Robert De Niro encased in Daniel Parker's full-body prosthetic suit as the Creature (more than a hundred of these were created, the individual hairs sewn on by dedicated film students). In this version of the story, electric eels were used to give the Creature life during the creation sequence. "When he's 'born' you'll see a full body prosthetic," revealed Darabont. "It captures this regal Gothicism, it's just so deformed looking, because the proportions are not quite right – one arm is bigger than the other arm, one leg is bigger than another leg. Part of his face has been replaced and the skin there is a different colour, and one eyeball is a different colour than the other eyeball. One hand is slightly bigger than another. There's a subtle, misshapen quality to it..."

As Elizabeth, Victor's love interest, Branagh resisted TriStar's calls to use a big-name Hollywood star and instead he cast British actress Helena Bonham-Carter in the role. "Elizabeth is an orphan who has been taken in by Victor's parents and raised almost as their daughter," said Branagh. "She is an innocent and whoever ends up playing her has to have the ability to convey this."

Branagh also insisted that the film be shot entirely in Britain, as he explained: "That way I can make the film as I see it and not have every suit in the studio sharing all their views with me. At the moment the whole thing's highly exciting but a bit brown trousering! One thing's for certain, if this is a bloody disaster, they won't be offering me any more $60,000,000 movies!"

What was also certain was that despite the box-office performance of **Mary Shelley's Frankenstein**, *Robert De Niro's interpretation of the Monster as a creature of intelligence and emotion would not be the last to stalk across the screen...*

THE ADDAMS FAMILY

USA, 1991. Dir: Barry Sonnenfeld. With: Anjelica Huston, Raul Julia, Christopher Lloyd, Elizabeth Wilson, Christina Ricci, Judith Malina. Paramount. Colour.

Enjoyable big budget feature based on Charles Addams' wonderfully macabre cartoons, which also inspired the popular TV series (1964-1966). As the vampiric Morticia Addams, Anjelica Huston stars in the role she was born to play. The minor story involves the return of Uncle Fester (Lloyd), who could be an impostor after the Addams Family fortune. Ignore the plot and just sit back and enjoy the constant barrage of black humour. With Carel Struycken as the Frankenstein Monster-like butler Lurch.

Sequel: ADDAMS FAMILY VALUES (qv; 1993)

ADDAMS FAMILY VALUES

USA, 1993. Dir: Barry Sonnenfeld. With: Anjelica Huston, Raul Julia, Christopher Lloyd, Joan Cusack, Christina Ricci, Carol Kane. Paramount. Colour.

The original director and stars are reunited for this delightful sequel to *The Addams Family* (1991), once again based on the bizarre cartoons by Charles Addams. When the vampiric Morticia (Huston) gives birth to moustachioed baby Pubert Pendragon Addams III, the macabre family is joined by a serial killer nanny (Cusack) who has designs on Uncle Fester's (Lloyd) fortune. Ricci steals the film as the deadpan Wednesday when she and Pugsley (Jimmy Workman) are shipped off to the cheery Camp Chippewa summer camp. Carel Struycken recreates his role as Lurch, and director Sonnenfeld has a cameo as the father of Wednesday's weedy boyfriend (David Krumholtz).

THE AMBULANCE

USA, 1990 (1991). Dir: Larry Cohen. With: Eric Roberts, James Earl Jones, Megan Gallagher, Richard Bright, Janine Turner, Eric Braeden. Esparza-Katz Productions. Colour.

One of writer/director Cohen's more coherent films features Roberts as a quirky artist for Marvel Comics on the trail of a sinister vintage ambulance that disappears with its emergency patients in New York. It all turns out to be a plot by mad doctor Braeden to kidnap patients with diabetes for unethical medical research. With good support from Jones as an oddball cop, veteran Red Buttons as an old-time reporter, and cameos by Laurene Landon, Stan Lee and comics artist Eugene Colan.

ARCADE

USA, 1993. Dir: Albert Pyun. With: Megan Ward, Peter Billingsley, John DeLancie, Sharon Farrell, Seth Green, Norbert Weisser. Full Moon Entertainment. Colour.

DeLancie's sinister salesman uses teenagers to test a prototype virtual reality game which is controlled by an organic microchip incorporating the brain cells from an abused young boy. When players start loosing their minds, Alex (Ward) and her friend Nick (Billingsley) enter the electronic world (cheap video effects created by Digital Fantasy) and become part of the deadly game to save their friends' souls. Another direct-to-video release from executive producer Charles Band, who also came up with the original idea.

BLOOD SALVAGE

USA, 1990. Dir: Tucker Johnston. With: Danny Nelson, Lori Birdsong, Ray Walston, John Saxon, Christopher Hesler, Ralph Pruitt. Magnum. Colour.

Low budget black comedy about a family of crazed rednecks who kidnap still-living accident victims and sell their organs for spare part surgery. One of the captives is Elvis! With a cameo by boxing champion Evander Holyfield, who helped finance the film.

THE CLONING OF JOANNA MAY

UK, 1991. Dir: Philip Saville. With: Patricia Hodge, Brian Cox, Billie Whitelaw, Siri Neal. Granada Television. Colour.

Mini-series based on the Fay Weldon novel. In a near-future Britain, Joanna May (Hodge) and her husband Carl (Cox) play murderous sexual games with each other. When she finally leaves him, the ruthless industrialist creates a number of clones from her stolen DNA.

EDISON'S FRANKENSTEIN

USA, 1990. Dir: Robert David. B&W.

Short film which uses stills to reconstruct Edison's 1910 *Frankenstein.*

EDWARD PENISHANDS

USA, 1991. Dir: Paul Norman. With: Sikki Nixx, Jeanna Fine, Alexandria Quinn, Ashley Nicole, Jamie Lee, Dominique Simone. Video Team. Colour.

Clever hardcore parody of Tim Burton's 1990 movie. A saleslady of marital aids (Quinn) discovers artificial man Edward (Nixx in make-up closely resembling Johnny Depp's original), the possessor of the titular appendages. She takes him home, where he falls in love with her daughter (Fine).

Sequel: EDWARD PENISHANDS PART 2 (qv; 1991)

EDWARD PENISHANDS PART 3

USA, 1991. Dir: Paul Norman. With: Sikki Nixx, Fred Lincoln, Monique

EDWARD SCISSORHANDS

USA, 1990. Dir: Tim Burton. With: Johnny Depp, Winona Ryder, Dianne Wiest, Anthony Michael Hall, Vincent Price, Alan Arkin. Twentieth Century Fox. Colour.

Delightful fantasy starring Depp as an artificial man with scissorhands created by a kindly inventor (Vincent Price in his last role, he died in 1993). Following his creator's untimely death, Edward is rescued from his Gothic hiding place by the Avon lady (Wiest) and introduced to suburbia, finding both romance and tragedy. Music by Danny Elfman.

Hall, Teri Diver, Bianca Trump, K.C. Williams. Video Team. Colour.

The second hardcore sequel to the 1991 original. An ageing Edward (Lincoln) reminisces about the sexual exploits of his younger self (again played by Nixx). A compilation of *The Best of Edward Penishands* appeared in 1993.

EDWARD PENISHANDS PART 2

USA, 1991. Dir: Paul Norman. With: Angela Summers, Sikki Nixx, April Rayne, Madison, Jamie Lee, K.C. Williams. Video Team. Colour.

'He's back and he's got something up his sleeves.' Nixx recreates his role as the artificial man with the well-endowed digits in this hardcore sequel.

Sequel: EDWARD PENISHANDS PART 3 (qv; 1991)

FRANKENHOOKER

USA, 1990. Dir: Frank Henenlotter. With: James Lorinz, Patty Mullen, Shirley Stoler, Louise Lasser, Charlotte Helmkamp, Lia Chang. Shapiro Glickenhaus Entertainment. Colour.

Sleazy black comedy from co-writer/director Henenlotter (the *Basket Case* series). When a do-it-yourself mad scientist (Lorinz) accidentally runs his fiancée (Mullen) over with a lawnmower(!), he keeps her head alive and begins to stitch her body back together with parts taken from Times Square hookers. In the end, the sum of the parts take their revenge. The outrageous make-up effects created by Gabe Bartalos add to the fun. With quite a bit of nudity and a cameo by veteran TV horror host John Zacherle as a TV weatherman.

Below: *Edward Scissorhands.*

FRANKENSTEIN

USA, 1990. Dir: Ted Newsom. Robert T. Newsom/Heidelberg Films/Rhino Home Video. B&W/Colour.

Hour-long compilation written and directed by Newsom that includes chronological clips and trailers from all the Universal and Hammer Frankenstein films (including *The Revenge of Frankenstein* [1958] in which Peter Cushing speaks to the audience), plus numerous other movies (from *I Was a Teenage Frankenstein* [1957] to *Young Frankenstein* [1974]), news clips of Boris Karloff as the Monster at a 1941 celebrity baseball match and TV's *Colgate Comedy Hour* (1954) featuring Abbott and Costello. Billed as *Frankenstein A Cinematic Scrapbook* on the 1991 video box by Rhino, who have also released equally fascinating tapes based around Dracula and the Wolf Man.

FRANKENSTEIN

UK/USA/Poland, 1992. Dir: David Wickes. With: Patrick Bergin, John Mills, Randy Quaid, Lambert Wilson, Fiona Gilles, Jacinta Mulcahy. Turner Pictures/David Wickes. Colour.

This overlong, made-for-cable TV movie is not quite the definitive version the producers would have you believe. After creating various animal hybrids in his laboratory, Bergin's boring Professor Victor Frankenstein uses obscure science to birth his fully-grown Monster (a sympathetic Quaid, in effective make-up created by Image Animation's Mark Coulier) in a tank of chemicals containing the 'elements of life'. When the creature is revived by an electrical accident, it shares a symbiotic relationship with its creator. After the aborted birth of a female companion (the film's best sequence), the Monster revenges itself on Frankenstein's family, until the two nemeses finally destroy each other on the Arctic ice. With Mills as the blind hermit and Michael Gothard in one of his last roles (he committed suicide in 1993) as the ship's bosun.

Remake: MARY SHELLEY'S FRANKENSTEIN (qv; 1994)

FRANK ENSTEIN

USA, 1992. Dir: Douglas Richards. Voices: Laura Gabriel, David Nettheim, Lee Perry, Alan Glover. International Family Classics II/ Holric Entertainment Group/INI Entertainment Group. Colour.

Hour-long children's cartoon supposedly based on Mary Shelley's novel. TV news researcher Libby becomes involved with the mad Dr Max Enstein, his dim-witted bionic Monster, Frank, and their attempts to regain a stolen computer disc containing the plans for a water-powered car.

FRANKENSTEIN'S BABY

UK, 1990. Dir: Robert Bierman. With: Nigel Planer, Kate Buffery, Yvonne Bryceland, William Armstrong, Sian Thomas, Gillian Raine. BBC-TV. Colour.

Blackly comic TV movie, written by Emma Tennant. When Paul Hocking (Planer) quarrels with his girlfriend Jane (Buffery) about when they should start a family, Dr Eva Frankenstein (Bryceland) overhears their argument and offers her own, unique solution.

FRANKENSTEIN: THE COLLEGE YEARS

USA, 1991. Dir: Tom Shadyac. With: William Ragsdale, Christopher Daniel Barnes, Larry Miller, Andrea Elson, Voreaux White, Patrick Richwood. FNM Films/Spirit Productions/Twentieth Century Fox. Colour.

Enjoyable made-for-cable TV movie, in which college medical students Mark and Jay (Ragsdale and Barnes) discover the late Professor Lippzigger's experiments with transplant tissue rejection involved Victor von Frankenstein's original Karloffian Monster (Vincent Hammond). When the creature is accidentally revived with electricity, they pass him off as a foreign exchange student named Frank N. Stein and sign him up for the campus football team when an ambitious professor (Miller) starts to suspect the truth. With likeable characters and a lack of nerdiness, this is better than most teen comedies. Includes a TV clip from *Reptilicus* (1962) and the Monster hip-hop dancing.

FRANKENSTEIN UNBOUND

USA/Italy, 1990. Dir: Roger Corman. With: John Hurt, Raul Julia, Bridget Fonda, Catherine Rabett, Jason Patric, Michael Hutchence. Warner Bros./Mount Company. Colour.

In 1985, TriStar announced *Roger Corman's Frankenstein* from a script by Wes Craven. It was never made but, after nearly twenty years, Corman returned to directing with this silly science fiction adventure, based on the novel by Brian W. Aldiss. New Los Angeles scientist Joseph Buchanan (Hurt) messes around with space and time while creating a death ray in 2031 and is sucked through a cloud vortex back to 1817 Switzerland where the mad Dr Frankenstein (Julia, rising above the material) and his ugly but misunderstood Monster (Nick Brimble in make-up created by Nick Dudman) co-exist with their creator, Mary Shelley (Fonda). The film is not helped by the risible dialogue, hammy performances, confusing dream sequences and terribly limp performances by rock star Hutchence as Lord Byron and Patric as Percy Shelley. However, it remains a low budget delight. Welcome back Roger!

KAFKA

USA/France/Czechoslovakia/UK, 1991. Dir: Steven Soderbergh. With: Jeremy Irons, Theresa Russell, Joel Grey, Ian Holm, Jeroen Krabbe, Alec Guinness. Baltimore Pictures/Renn-Pricel. B&W/Colour.

Bizarre fantasy set in 1919 Prague. Insurance clerk Kafka (Irons) investigates the mysterious disappearance of his friend Eduard Raban (Vladimir Gut). In the Escher-like nightmare of the Castle, he discovers the mad Dr Murnau (Holm) conducting his genetic experiments. With Brian Glover, Keith Allen and Robert Flemyng as The Keeper of the Files. From the director/editor of the overrated *Sex, Lies, and Videotape* (1989). Not released in Britain until 1994.

LAST FRANKENSTEIN

Japan, 1991. Dir: Takeshi Kawamura. With: Akira Emoto, Yoshio Harada, Naomasa Musaka. Bandai/BF Film/Rittor Music/Shochhiku. Colour.

Movie début by theatre director Kawamura. A mad scientist, convinced that the only way to save the human race is by rebuilding the human body, comes into conflict with the leader of a religious suicide cult.

LEENA MEETS FRANKENSTEIN

USA, 1993. Dir: Scotty Fox. With: Leena, Randy Spears, Tina Tyler, Brittany O'Connell, Madison, Nicole London. Pinnacle. B&W/Colour.

Hardcore remake of (Abbott and Costello) *Meet Frankenstein* (1948) which changes from black and white to colour for the sex scenes! When their car breaks down, two street-wise babes (Nicole London and Leena) are stranded at a time-share condo with the classic monsters — Dracula (Mike Horner), his vampire wives (Madison and Brittany O'Connell), the Wolfman (Tony Tedeschi) and Frankenstein's creation (Jon Dough). With Spears as an inept Steve van Helsing and London also playing the Bride of Frankenstein. Written and produced by L.S. Talbot(!)

THE LEGEND OF THE FRANKENSTEIN MONSTER

USA, 1993 (1994). Simitar Entertainment. B&W/Colour.

Two-part compilation (*The Creature Is Born/The Creature Lives On*) of stills, excerpts and the usual Universal and Hammer trailers. Slightly more interesting are the trailers for *I Was a Teenage Frankenstein* (1957), *Frankenstein 1970* (1958), *Frankenstein's Daughter* (1958), *Frankenstein Conquers the World* (1964), *Frankenstein Meets the Space-monster* (1965), *Jesse James Meets Frankenstein's Daughter* (1965) and *Lady Fran-*

Above: *Frankenstein (1992).*
Left: *Frankenstein Unbound.*

kenstein (1971), plus clips from *Orlak, El Infierno de Frankenstein* (1960), Hammer's TV *Tales of Frankenstein* (1958) and the creation sequence from the Edison *Frankenstein* (1910). Narrated by Jeffrey Lee.

LA MACHINE

France/Germany, 1994. Dir: François Dupeyron. With: Gerard Depardieu, Nathalie Baye, Didier Bourdon. Hachette Premiere/DD Productions/ Studio Babelsberg. Colour.

Based on the novel by Rene Bettello. Depardieu stars as the evil Dr Marc Lacroix who uses a machine to exchange his mind with a psychopath (Bourdon).

THE MADDAM'S FAMILY

USA, 1992. Dir: Herschel Savage. With: Mike Horner, Ona Zee, Jon Dough, Ron Jeremy, Diedre Holland, Kim Angeli. X-Citement Video. Colour.

Hardcore parody of Charles Addams' bizarre characters. The ending of the Cold War financially ruins Cortez (Horner) when the bottom falls out of the munitions market. However, his wife Horticia (Zee) decides to turn their strange house into a brothel to generate extra cash. With Dough as the Frankenstein Monster-like butler, Crotch.

MARY SHELLEY'S FRANKENSTEIN

UK/USA, 1994. Dir: Kenneth Branagh. With: Robert De Niro, Kenneth Branagh, Helena Bonham-Carter, Aidan Quinn, Tom Hulce, John Cleese. American Zoetrope/ TriStar Pictures. Colour.

As long ago as 1972, Francis Ford Coppola announced that he was planning to direct a so-called 'definitive' version of Mary Shelley's book (he made a similar claim for *Bram Stoker's Dracula* [1992]). He ended up co-producing this big-budget attempt to film the classic novel. Director Branagh stars as Victor Frankenstein, whose experiments with life itself give birth to a creature (De Niro in a body suit designed by Daniel Parker) of intelligence and emotion with the potential for good or evil. The impressive supporting cast also includes Ian Holm, Richard Briers, Robert Hardy and Cherie Lunghi.

NATURAL SELECTION

(UK: DARK REFLECTION)
USA, 1993. Dir: Jack Sholder. With: C. Thomas Howell, Lisa Zane, Miko Hughes, Ethan Phillips, Richard Hamilton, Joanna Miles. Fox West Pictures/World International Network (WIN)/Stillwater Productions. Colour.

Computer programmer Ben Braden (Howell) discovers he is one of a series of clones created by Dr Salazar and tries to stop his evil psychotic duplicate (also Howell) from taking over his family and his life. An entertaining thriller from the director of *The Hidden* (1987), but a shame about the predictable twist ending. Kiefer Sutherland was co-executive producer.

Below: Return from Death.

POPCORN

Canada/Jamaica, 1990 (1991). Dir: Mark Herrier (and Bob Clark and Alan Ormsby). With: Jill Schoelen, Tom Villard, Dee Wallace Stone, Derek Rydall, Ray Walston, Tony Roberts. Studio Three/Movie Partners. Colour.

During a retrospective horror film festival (which includes such parodies as *Attack of the Amazing Electrified Man* [featuring Bruce Glover and Lori Creevay], *The Stench* and the big bug movie *Mosquito*), a group of film students are bumped off by mad slasher Toby (Villard), who is possessed by the spirit of a psycho film director. Ormsby — who was fired after three weeks, but directed most of the fifties

vignettes — contributed the script under the pen name 'Tod Hackett'.

REANIMATOR ACADEMY

1992. With: Steve Westerheit, Connie Speer. Colour.

A college student discovers he can restore life with a reanimation serum. But when a gangster forces him to revive his dead girlfriend, she turns into a decapitating psycho. Low budget direct-to-video chills.

RETURN FROM DEATH

Italy, 1993. Dir: David Hills (Aristide Massaccesi). With: Donal O'Brien, Cinthia Monreale. Filmirage Productions/Eureka Film International. Colour.

Filmed under the title *Frankenstein 2000*. In a coma after suffering a violent assault and rape, Georgia (Monreale) uses her telekinetic powers to revive her murdered friend Ric (O'Brien) with an electric cable to act as the instrument of her revenge. Director Massaccesi is better known under his other pseudonym Joe D'Amato.

SEX SCIENTIST

USA, 1993. With: Pearl Madison, Carl Jammer, Nasty Natasha, Buffy Ho, Don Fernando, Tony Martino. Fat Dog Productions. Colour.

Hardcore comedy in which Dr Spankingtime and his assistant create the most beautiful and sensual nymphomaniac in the world. They then conduct a lengthy series of sexual tests to determine their creation's levels of erotic pleasure and sexual performance.

***Above right:** Kafka.*
***Below:** Waxwork II: Lost in Time.*

UNIVERSAL SOLDIER

USA, 1992. Dir: Roland Emmerich. With: Jean-Claude Van Damme, Dolph Lundgren, Ally Walker, Ed O'Ross, Jerry Orbach, Leon Rippy. Carolco. Colour.

Big budget science fiction adventure in which the corpses of US soldiers killed in Vietnam are revived years later by a secret military unit as unstoppable zombie warriors. However, for two of the bio-mechanical soldiers, old habits die hard. When Van Damme starts to recall his previous life, so psychotic killer Lundgren does as well. Pretty soon the two enemies are tearing up the countryside trying to kill each other while TV reporter Walker is caught in the middle. Despite the simple plot, director Emmerich stages some impressive action sequences and great stunts.

WAXWORK II: LOST IN TIME

(UK: LOST IN TIME)
USA, 1991 (1992). Dir: Anthony Hickox. With: Zach Galligan, Alexander Godunov, Monika Schnarre, Martin Kemp, Sophie Ward, Bruce Campbell. Electric Pictures. Colour.

Great-looking comedy sequel to *Waxwork* (1988), in which the surviving severed hand from the first film frames Sarah (Schnarre) for a murder it commits. To prove her innocence, Mark (Galligan) takes her through the looking-glass time doors into various alternate worlds where Good fights Evil using characters and situations from horror films and fiction. These include clever pastiches of *Frankenstein* (with Martin Kemp as the Baron), *The Haunting* (1963; in black and white), *Alien* (1979) and an original story inspired by Edgar Allan Poe. During their adventures, the time-travelling teens also meet Nosferatu, Mr Hyde, Jack the Ripper, Godzilla, the zombies from *Dawn of the Dead* (1979) and such guest stars as Juliet Mills, David Carradine, John Ireland (his last role), Joe Baker, Patrick Macnee (as a raven!), Maxwell Caulfield, Drew Barrymore and director Hickox. Special effects by Bob Keen's Image Animation.

Appendix 1:

Frankensteins on tv

This is a selected guide to some of the more interesting television appearances of Frankenstein-type scientists and monsters over the years. It doesn't pretend to be complete, but once you've seen all the movies listed in this book, you can start tracking down some of the following...

ABBOTT AND COSTELLO: *MONSTER MUDDLED*

USA, 1966. Voices: Bud Abbott, Stan Irwin. Hanna-Barbera. Colour.

Five minute cartoon in which policemen Bud and Lou attend a costume party and meet the real Frankenstein Monster and other creatures.

THE ABC COMEDY HOUR: *THE KOPYKATS*

UK/USA, 1972. ABC-TV. Colour.

Various episodes of this hour-long musical comedy show featured Tony Curtis as Count Dracula meeting Frank Gorshin, playing both Frankenstein and his Monster.

THE ABC SATURDAY SUPERSTAR MOVIE: *MAD, MAD, MAD MONSTERS*

USA, 1972. Dir: Steve Nakagawa. Rankin-Bass/ ABC-TV. Colour.

Hour-long cartoon special. Baron von Frankenstein creates a bride for his Monster. When she is kidnapped by a giant prehistoric ape, the Monster sets out to rescue her. Among the wedding guests are Frankenstein's assistant Igor, the Invisible Man and his invisible wife, the Creature, the Mummy, the Wolf Man, and Count Dracula and his vampiric offspring Boobula. This was a semi-sequel to the same producers' 1966 movie *Mad Monster Party?*.

MINI-MUNSTERS

USA, 1973. Voices: Al Lewis, Richard Long, Bob Diamond. ABC-TV. Colour.

Hour-long cartoon special, with Lewis recreating his role as Grampa and Long as the voice of Herman. A Dracula-type relative sends his two teenagers, the Frankenstein Monster-like Igor and the vampiric Lucretia, to stay with the Munsters. The plot involves a hearse that runs on music, thereby eliminating the pollution caused by exhaust fumes.

Sequel: THE MUNSTERS TODAY (qv; 1988-91)

PORKY PIG AND DAFFY DUCK MEET THE GROOVIE GOOLIES

USA, 1972. Voices: Mel Blanc. Filmation/Warner Bros/ABC-TV. Colour.

Hour-long cartoon special in which Frankie, Cousin Drac and Wolfie from *The Groovie Goolies* TV series save a number of classic Warner Bros characters from a Phantom of the Opera-type villain. During the climax, the monsters appear in live-action.

THE ADDAMS FAMILY

USA, 1964-66. With: Carolyn Jones, John Astin, Jackie Coogan, Ted Cassidy, Blossom Rock, Lisa Loring, Ken Weatherwax. Filmways/ABC-TV. B&W.

Based on Charles Addams' macabre *New Yorker* cartoons. The oddball family includes the vampiric Morticia (Jones), her husband Gomez (Astin), Uncle Fester (Coogan), the Frankenstein Monster-like butler Lurch (Cassidy), Grandmama (Rock), the diabolical children Wednesday (Loring) and Pugsley (Weatherwax), and Thing (who of course plays itself).

Sequel: THE ADDAMS FAMILY (qv; 1973)

THE ADDAMS FAMILY

USA/UK, 1973. Voices: Jackie Coogan, Ted Cassidy, Janet Waldo, Lennie Weinrib, Cindy Henderson, Jodie Foster. Hanna-Barbera/NBC-TV. Colour.

Almost-forgotten children's series, which ran for sixteen half-hour episodes. Based on the look of Charles Addams' cartoons (animated in Britain by Halas & Batchelor), each week the oddball family travelled in their haunted trailer to a different American city. Only Coogan and Cassidy (as the Frankenstein Monster-like Lurch) returned from the original TV series. Pugsley was voiced by a young Jodie Foster.

Sequel: THE ADDAMS FAMILY (qv; 1992)

THE ADDAMS FAMILY

USA, 1992. Dir: Robert Alvarez, Don Lusk and Carl Urbano. Voices: John Astin, Dick Beals, Ruth Buzzi, Carol Channing, Jim Cummings, Debi Derryberry. Hanna-Barbera Productions/ Fil-Cartoons. Colour.

Half-hour cartoon series which retains the style of Charles Addams' original illustrations. Astin recreates his role as Gomez from the original TV series.

THE ALL-NEW POPEYE HOUR: *POPEYE MEETS THE BLUTOSTEIN MONSTER*

USA, 1978. Dir: Alex Lovy. Voices: Jack Mercer, Marilyn Schreffer, Allan Melvin, Daws Butler. Hanna-Barbera Productions/CBS-TV. Colour.

Seven minute cartoon. When Olive (Schreffer) is kidnapped by the Blutostein monster (Melvin), Popeye (Mercer) rescues her from the castle of its creator, Viktor (Butler).

THE TERRIFYING TRANSYLVANIAN TREK

USA, 1978. Dir: Alex Lovy. Voices: Jack Mercer, Marilyn Schreffer, Allan Melvin, Daws Butler. Hanna-Barbera Productions/CBS-TV. Colour.

Eleven minute cartoon in which Popeye and Olive meet Dracula (Melvin), Vampetta (Schreffer) and the Frankenstein Monster (Melvin) while searching for treasure in the Count's castle.

ANIMANIACS: *PHRANKEN-RUNT*

USA/Japan, 1993. Voices: Rob Paulsen, Jess Harnell, Tress MacNeille, Frank Welker, Sherri Stoner, Chuck Vennera. Warner Bros Animation/Amblin Entertainment. Colour.

Musical cartoon series, set around the Warner Bros studio in Hollywood. Rita the cat has to stop mad scientist the Bride of Phrankenstein from transferring the brain of Runt the dog into her monster canine. Executive produced by Steven Spielberg.

Above: Frankenstein (1968).

ARSENIC AND OLD LACE

USA, 1969. With: Fred Gwynne, Bob Crane, Sue Lyon, Jack Gilford, Helen Hayes, Lillian Gish, David Wayne. ABC-TV. Colour.

Updated version of Joseph Kesserling's play, shot on video. The great cast includes Hayes and Gish as Abby and Martha, and Gwynne as Jonathan Brewster with a stitched together, Frankenstein Monster-like face created by Dick Smith.

ASTRO BOY: *COLOSSO*

(Orig: TETSUWAN ATOM: *FRANKEN*)
Japan, 1963. Mush Productions.

Half-hour cartoon series based on the popular Japanese comic book. A giant robot named Franken (Colosso in the American version) malfunctions and is used by a criminal to rob banks until defeated by Astro Boy. Apparently, there was also a live-action series based on the same character which featured the Frankenstein Monster.

ATTACK OF THE KILLER TOMATOES: *FRANKENSTEM*

USA, 1990. Dir: Beth Gunn. Voices: John Astin, Chris Guzek, Kath Souci, Neil Ross, Thom Bray, Cam Clark. Fox Children's Network/Four Square Productions/Akom Productions/ Marvel Productions. Colour.

Half-hour children's cartoon, based on the film series, about giant mutant tomatoes which can change into human form and want to rule the world. Astin recreates his movie role as the evil Dr Putrid T. Gangreen.

THE AVENGERS: *NEVER, NEVER SAY DIE*

UK, 1967. Dir: Robert Day. With: Patrick Macnee, Diana Rigg, Christopher Lee, Jeremy Young, Patricia English, David Kernan. Associated British Corporation Television Films. Colour.

When the corpse of a hit-and-run victim gets up and walks out on John Steed (Macnee) and Emma Peel (Rigg), their investigations lead to a top-secret project where robot duplicates created by Professor Frank N. Stone (Lee) are replacing humans.

THE POSITIVE-NEGATIVE MAN

UK, 1968. Dir: Robert Day. With: Patrick Macnee, Diana Rigg, Ray McAnally, Michael Latimer, Caroline Blakiston, Sandor Eles. Associated British Corporation Television Films. Colour.

When Steed and Mrs Peel learn that a number of electrocuted scientists had been working on the abandoned Project 90, they track a glowing killer to a shocking conclusion.

BEST OF BROADWAY: *ARSENIC AND OLD LACE*

USA, 1955. With: Helen Hayes, Billie Burke, Peter Lorre, Boris Karloff. CBS-TV. B&W.

Early TV version of Joseph Kesserling's play. Karloff recreates his Broadway stage success as psychopath Jonathan Brewster.

Remake: HALLMARK HALL OF FAME: *ARSENIC AND OLD LACE* (qv; 1962)

CAROL BURNETT SHOW

USA, 1972. With: Carol Burnett, Vincent Price, Harvey Korman, Vicki Lawrence. CBS-TV. Colour.

Hour-long comedy series that includes 'House of Terror', in which Dr Frankenstein (Price) plans to use the parts of his new bride (Burnett) to restore his mother's youth. His artificially-created hunchbacked assistant Igor (Korman) falls in love with the woman and refuses to help complete the experiment.

THE COLGATE COMEDY HOUR: *ABBOTT AND COSTELLO*

USA, 1951. With: Bud Abbott, Lou Costello, Sidney Fields, Lon Chaney. NBC-TV. B&W.

Chaney Jr recreates his role as the Frankenstein Monster in a sketch featuring the comedy duo looking for treasure in a haunted house (incorporating routines from [Abbott and Costello] *Meet Frankenstein* [1948]), and dances during a musical number at the end of the show.

ABBOTT AND COSTELLO

(aka ABBOTT AND COSTELLO MEET THE CREATURE/MEET THE MONSTERS)
USA, 1953. With: Bud Abbott, Lou Costello, Glenn Strangle (Strange), Ricou Browning. NBC-TV. B&W.

Bud and Lou visit the Universal property department (complete with dummies of Dracula, a gorilla and Mr Hyde), where Lou recreates some of the best comedy routines from (Abbott and Costello) *Meet Frankenstein* (1948) and encounters the Invisible Man, the Creature from the Black Lagoon (Browning) and Frankenstein's Monster (Strange, whose name was apparently misspelled on the end credits).

DANNY KAYE SHOW

USA, 1966. With: Danny Kaye, Vincent Price. CBS-TV. Colour.

Comedy sketch in which Price's Dr Frankenstein creates a Karloff-like Monster played by Kaye.

DARK SHADOWS

USA, 1966-71. With: Jonathan Frid, Joan Bennett, Alexandra Moltke, Grayson Hall, Lara Parker. Dan Curtis Productions/ABC-TV. Colour.

Five-days-a-week, half-hour video soap opera that clocked up an incredible 1,225 episodes and two movie spin-offs during its five year run. During the 1967-68 season, Robert Rodan joined the cast as Adam, created from corpses by Dr Eric Lang (Addison Powell) and brought to life by Dr Julia Hoffman (Hall) and 175 year-old vampire Barnabas Collins (Frid), who shares a psychic link with the creature. A mate was also created for Adam, cleverly named Eve (Marie Wallace).

Remake: DARK SHADOWS (1990)

DOCTOR WHO: *THE BRAIN OF MORBIUS*

UK, 1975. Dir: Christopher Barry. With: Tom Baker, Elisabeth Sladen, Philip Madoc, Colin Fay, Cynthia Grenville, Gilly Brown. BBC-TV. Colour.

In this four part story, the Doctor (Baker) and his companion Sarah Jane Smith (Sladen) discover the TARDIS has been diverted to a planet where mad scientist Solon (Madoc) and his misshapen assistant (Fay) have created a patchwork body out of alien parts. The crowning achievement will be the Doctor's head, which will house the brain of a renegade Time Lord.

JOURNEY INTO TERROR

UK, 1965. Dir: Richard Martin. With: William Hartnell, William Russell, Jacqueline Hill, Maureen O'Brien, John Maxim, Malcolm Rogers. BBC-TV. B&W.

The Daleks pursue the TARDIS across time and space in a series of linked episodes entitled 'The Chase'. In the fourth episode, the Doctor (Hartnell) and his companions land in a 'haunted' Gothic castle where they are

Below: The Man from U.N.C.L.E.: The Deadly Games Affair.

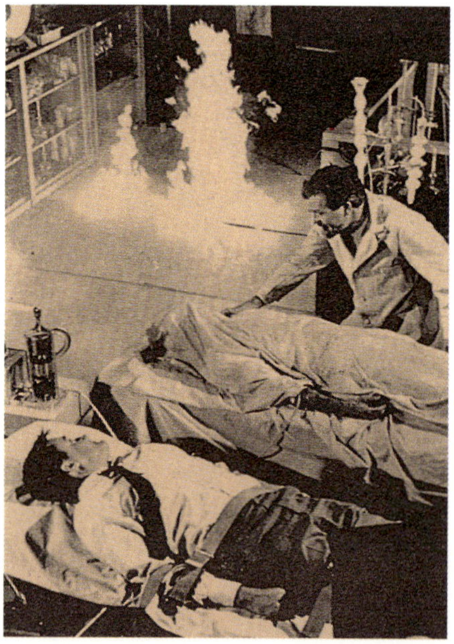

menaced by a Karloff-like Frankenstein Monster (Maxim) and Count Dracula (Rogers), who turn out to be robots in a futuristic amusement park, Frankenstein's House of Horrors.

THE DRACK PACK

(UK: THE DRAK PACK)
USA, 1980. Dir: Chris Cuddington and Steve Lumley. Voices: Jerry Dexter, Bill Callaway, Hans Conried, Chuck McCann, Julie McWhirter, Don Messick. Hanna-Barbera/CBS-TV. Colour.
Half-hour cartoon series in which Frankie Frankenstein, Drack Jr and Howler, the teenage sons of famous monsters, become heroes and foil Dr Dred and his Organisation of Generally Rotten Endeavours (OGRE), whose members include Mummy Man, Toad, Fly and Vampira.

DREAM ON: *THE SON ALSO RISES*

USA, 1992. Dir: Betty Thomas. With: Brian Benben, Chris Demetral, Denny Dillon, Wendie Malick, Dorien Wilson, Bryn Erin. MTE/Home Box Office/Kevin Bright/St. Clare Entertainment. Colour.
Adult comedy/fantasy series, co-executive produced by John Landis. Martin (Benben) is disturbed when he discovers that his thirteen year-old son Jeremy has some condoms hidden in his room. With numerous clips from *Frankenstein* (1931) and *Bride of Frankenstein* (1935).

ENGELBERT HUMPERDINCK

USA, 1970. With: Engelbert Humperdinck, Jerry Lewis. ABC-TV. Colour.
Hour-long musical comedy show. In one sketch, Dr Frankenstein (Lewis) creates a monster (singer Humperdinck) which behaves like Jerry Lewis.

EVERYMAN: *THE TRUE STORY OF FRANKENSTEIN*

UK, 1986. Dir: Daniel Wolf. BBC-TV. Colour.
Documentary presented as a 'dramatised collage' examining the Frankenstein story.

Below: *The Munsters.*

FAMOUS ADVENTURES OF MR. MAGOO: *DOCTOR FRANKENSTEIN*

USA, 1965. Dir: Abe Levitow. Voices: Jim Backus. UPA. Colour.
Half-hour cartoon in which Frankenstein's Monster escapes and plans to create an army of monsters until a repentant Mr Magoo/Dr Frankenstein blows up the laboratory. This was later included in the compilation feature film *Mr. Magoo, Man of Mystery* (1967).

FANTASY ISLAND: *THE LADY AND THE MONSTER/THE LAST COWBOY*

USA, 1981. Dir: Don Chaffey. With: Ricardo Montalban, Herve Villechaize, Wendy Schaal, Lynda Day George, William Smith, Dick Bakalyan. Spelling-Goldberg Productions/ Columbia/ABC-TV. Colour.
Long-running series in which visitors spend $50,000 to live out their wildest fantasies on the secluded island of the mysterious Mr Roarke (Montalban) and the diminutive Tatoo (Villechaize). In this Halloween episode, Dr Carla Frankenstein (George) visits her disgraced ancestor's castle where she discovers his gentle Monster (Smith).

THE FLINTSTONE COMEDY HOUR: *THE FRANKENSTONES*

USA, 1980. Dir: Gordon Hunt. Voices: Charles Nelson Reilly, Ruta Lee, Paul Reubens, Zelda Rubenstein, Frank Welker, Henry Corden. Hanna-Barbera Productions/NBC-TV. Colour.
Fifteen minute segment of the cartoon series featuring the Flintstone's new neighbours, the Frankenstones, who consist of father Frank (Reilly), his wife Hidea (Lee), son Freaky (Reubens), daughter Atrocia (Rubenstein) and dog Rockjaw (Welker). The characters also appeared in *The Flintstones Comedy Show.*

THE FLINTSTONES

USA, 1966. Dir: William Hanna and Joseph Barbera. Voices: Alan Reed, Mel Blanc, Jean Vanderpyl, Gerry Johnson, Don Messick, Harvey Korman. Hanna-Barbera Productions/ABC-TV. Colour.
In this episode of the popular half-hour cartoon series, mad Dr Len Frankenstone (looking like TV's Ben Casey) transfer's Fred Flintstone's personality into Dino, his pet dinosaur.

THE FLINTSTONES MEET ROCKULA AND FRANKENSTONE

USA, 1980. Dir: Ray Patterson and Chris Cuddington. Voices: Henry Corden, Jean Vanderpyl, Mel Blanc, Gay Autterson, Ted Cassidy, Casey Kasem. Hanna-Barbera Productions/NBC-TV. Colour.
Hour-long cartoon special in which modern Stone Age families the Flintstones and Rubbles win a trip to Count Rockula's castle in Rocksylvania. There they discover the Count's Frankenstone Monster (Cassidy), which is revived by lightning.

THE FLINTSTONES' NEW NEIGHBORS

USA, 1980. Dir: Carl Urbano. Voices: Henry Corden, Jean Vanderpyl, Mel Blanc, Gay Autterson, Jim McGeorge, Julie McWhirter. Hanna-Barbera Productions/NBC-TV. Colour.
Half-hour cartoon special in which Fred Flintstone's new neighbours are the Frankenstones, a family of friendly monsters consisting of father Frank, 'Bride' Olivia, teenage daughter Hidea and young son Stubby.
Sequel: THE FLINTSTONE COMEDY HOUR: *THE FRANKENSTONES* (qv; 1980)

FRANKENSTEIN

West Germany, 1965. Dir: Julian Beck and Judith Malina. With: Julian Beck, The Living Theatre Company.
Film record of the Berlin performance of *Frankenstein* by The Living Theatre Company. Co-directed by Beck (*Poltergeist II The Other Side* [1986]), who also stars as Dr Frankenstein.
Remake: FRANKENSTEIN (qv; 1968)

FRANKENSTEIN

UK, 1968. With: Ian Holm, Sarah Badel. Thames Television. Colour.
Hour-long drama, written by Robert Muller and loosely based on Mary Shelley's novel. When the bandaged Monster's face is revealed, it has the features of its creator (Holm).
Remake: FRANKENSTEIN UNE HISTOIRE D'AMOUR (qv; 1974)

FRANKENSTEIN JR. AND THE IMPOSSIBLES

USA, 1966. Dir: William Hanna and Joseph Barbera. Voices: Dick Beals, Ted Cassidy, John Stephenson. Hanna-Barbera Productions/ CBS-TV. Colour.
Half-hour cartoon show which includes an eight minute Frankenstein Jr episode. Young Buzz (Beals) and his father, Dr Conroy (Stephenson), create a giant crime-fighting robot called Frankenstein Jr (Cassidy), controlled by Buzz's radar ring. Frankenstein Jr cartoons later appeared in *Space Ghost and Frankenstein Jr* (circa 1970s) and the syndicated series *Hanna-Barbera's World of Super Adventures.*

FRANKENSTEIN'S AUNTIE

Czechoslovakia/West Germany, 1986. Dir: Juraj Jakubisko. With: Viveca Lindfors, Ferdy Mayne, Jacques Herlin, Flavio Bucci, Gerhard Karzel, Eddie Constantine. Beta Film/Slovensky Film. Colour.
Series in which Lindfors portrays the title character, with Mayne as Count Dracula, Bucci as a werewolf, Herlin as Igor and Karzel as Albert, Frankenstein's sympathetic Monster. In some European countries this was also edited into a ninety minute feature.

FRANKENSTEIN UNE HISTOIRE D'AMOUR

France, 1974. Dir: Bob Thenault. With: Gerard Benard, Karin Petersen, François Lugagne, Gerard Boncaron, Nicolas Silberg, Jean Lepage.
French adaptation of Mary Shelley's novel, in which Benard portrays Frankenstein and the Monster's features are never revealed.

GET SMART: *SHOCK IT TO ME*

USA, 1969. Dir: Jay Sandrich. With: Don Adams, Barbara Feldon, Edward Platt, Tom Poston, Sid Haig, Milton Parsons. Talent Associates/Norton Simon/NBC-TV. Colour.
In this episode of the half-hour sci-spy spoof, KAOS mad scientist Dr Eric Zharko (Poston) revives dead agents with

his stolen electrical apparatus and plans to put Maxwell Smart (Adams) and Agent 99 (Feldon) into suspended animation. With Haig as Bruce the hunchback and horror veteran Parsons as Mr Obler, the morgue attendant.

THE WAX MAN

USA, 1967 (1968). Dir: James Komack. With: Don Adams, Barbara Feldon, Edward Platt, Richard Devon, Robert Ridgely, Robert Lussier. Talent Associates/Norton Simon/NBC-TV. Colour.

Devon plays a KAOS agent and the sinister owner of a wax museum, who sends apparently living figures of the Frankenstein Monster and Dracula after Maxwell Smart (Adams) and Agent 99 (Feldon).

THE GHOST BREAKERS

USA, 1975. Dir: Norman Abbott. With: Forrest Tucker, Larry Storch, Bob Burns, Bernie Kopell, Bill Engesser. Sid and Marty Krofft Productions/CBS-TV. Colour.

Half-hour comedy series, shot on video. In one episode, Kong and Spencer (Tucker and Storch) encounter the ghosts of Dr Frankenstein (Kopell) and his Monster (Engesser), who are searching for the world's most gullible brain. Naturally, they decide Spencer's is perfect to transplant into the Monster.

THE GIRL FROM U.N.C.L.E.: *THE CARPATHIAN CAPER AFFAIR*

USA, 1966 (1967). Dir: Barry Shear. With: Stefanie Powers, Noel Harrison, Leo G. Carroll, Ann Southern, Stan Freberg, Jack Cassidy. Arena/NBC-TV. Colour.

UNCLE agents April Dancer (Powers) and Mark Slate (Harrison) discover a plot by THRUSH agent Mother Magda (Southern) to replace world leaders with clones.

GRAVESDALE HIGH

USA, 1990. Voices: Rick Moranis, Shari Belafonte, Eileen Brennan, Georgia Brown, Tim Curry, Jonathan Winters. NBC Productions. Colour.

Cartoon series about a school for monsters. With modern teen versions of the Frankenstein Monster, Dracula, the Creature from the Black Lagoon, a werewolf, the Mummy, Igor, etc.

THE GROOVIE GOOLIES

USA, 1970. Dir: Hal Sutherland. Voices: Larry Storch, Don Messick, Howard Morris, Jane Webb, Dallas McKenna, John Irwin. Filmation/CBS-TV. Colour.

Hour-long musical cartoon series set in Horrible Hall, with Frankie, Cousin Drac, Wolfie, Mummy, Bella La Ghostly, Hagatha, Batso, Ratzo and Gauntelroy.

Sequel: SABRINA, THE TEENAGE WITCH (qv; 1971)

HALLMARK HALL OF FAME: *ARSENIC AND OLD LACE*

USA, 1962. With: Tony Randall, Dorothy Stickney, Mildred Natwick, Boris Karloff. NBC-TV. B&W.

The second television version of Joseph Kesserling's Broadway hit, with Karloff again recreating his role as Jonathan Brewster.

Remake: ARSENIC AND OLD LACE (qv; 1969)

THE HALLOWEEN THAT ALMOST WASN'T

USA, 1979. Dir: Bruce Bilson. With: Judd Hirsch, Mariette Hartley, Henry Gibson, John Schuck, Jack Riley, Josip Elic. Concepts Unlimited/ABC-TV. Colour.

Emmy Award-winning half-hour special for children. There will be no more Halloween unless the Frankenstein Monster (Schuck), Count Dracula (Hirsch), Wolf Man (Riley), the Mummy (Robert Fitch), the Zombie and Igor (Gibson) can convince the Witch (Hartley) to fly over the moon.

HAPPY DAYS

USA, 1980. Dir: Jerry Paris. With: Henry Winkler, Marion Ross, Anson Williams, Erin Moran, Al Molinaro, Tom Bosley. Paramount/Miller-Milkis-Boyett Productions/Henderson Production Company/ABC-TV. Colour.

Long-running comedy show set in 1950s suburbia. In one episode, after watching *Frankenstein's Doctor* on television, Fonzie (Winkler) dreams he meets a Count Dracula lookalike scientist (Bosley) who transfers his 'coolness' into a monster named Doggie (also Winkler).

THE HARDY BOYS/NANCY DREW MYSTERIES: *THE HARDY BOYS AND NANCY DREW MEET DRACULA*

USA, 1977. Dir: Joseph Pevney. With: Parker Stevenson, Shaun Cassidy, Pamela Sue Martin, Lorne Greene, Paul Williams, Richard Kiel, Lisa Eilbacher. Glen A. Larson Productions/Universal/ABC-TV. Colour.

Two part juvenile mystery set in a nightclub with a horror motif. Kiel (Jaws in *Moonraker* [1979]) plays a bouncer who looks like the Frankenstein Monster.

HENSHIN NINJA ARASHI

Japan, 1981. Colour.

Children's series featuring a patchwork Frankenstein Monster (named 'Franken'), Dracula, Wolf Man, Mummy Man, Sphinx and Witch Gorgon.

HERE'S BOOMER: *CAMITYVILLE'S BOOMER*

USA, 1982. Dir: Larry Stewart. With: Victor Buono, Rick Lohman, Forbesy Russell, Allan Arbus, Richard Moll, Terry Hart. A.C. Lyles Productions/DWP Productions/Paramount/NBC-TV. Colour.

Half-hour series in which a young couple and Boomer the dog take shelter from a thunderstorm in the home of Dr Frankenstein (Buono), where they discover his laboratory and encounter his grey-faced 'Monster' (Moll).

HIGHCLIFF MANOR

USA, 1979. Dir: Nick Havinga. With: Shelley Fabares, Stephen McHattie, Eugenie Ross-Leming, Christian Marlowe, Harriet White Medin. T.A.T. Productions/NBC-TV. Colour.

Four part, half-hour Frankenstein spoof, shot on video. Scientist Frances (Ross-Leming) creates her own Monster lover named Bram (Marlowe) in a basement laboratory.

THE HILARIOUS HOUSE OF FRIGHTENSTEIN

USA, 1974. Dir: Riff Markowitz. With: Vincent Price, Billy Van, Rais Fishka, Professor Julius Sumner Miller, Joe Torby, Guy Big. Colour.

Syndicated musical comedy special hosted by Price, in which Count Frightenstein (Van) is a vampire exiled from Transylvania when he fails to bring his Monster (named Bruce!) to life. This became a repetitive, five-days-a-week, half-hour series from 1974-75 (130 episodes). With Fishka as Igor, the Count's assistant.

HOORAY FOR HOLLYWOOD

USA, 1970. Dir: Grey Lockwood. With: Don Adams, Don Rickles, Charlton Heston. Youngstreet Productions/Stacey Productions/ABC-TV. Colour.

Hour-long special featuring a comedy sketch in which co-producer/co-writer/star Adams (*Get Smart*) plays Dr Frankenstein, who temporarily cures hunchback Egor (Rickles). Narrated by Heston.

JAMES HOUND: *THE MONSTER MASTER*

USA, 1960s. Terrytoons. Colour.

Seven minute cartoon in which secret agent James Hound short-circuits Professor Mad's army of Frankenstein Monsters.

JONATHAN WINTERS SHOW

USA, 1968. With: Jonathan Winters, Boris Karloff. CBS-TV. Colour.

Karloff's last television appearance was in this Halloween comedy special portraying a Frankenstein-like scientist and performing the song 'It Was a Very Good Year'.

KAIBUTSU KUN

Japan, 1968. Studio Zero/Tokyo Movie Shinsha Company. Colour.

Cartoon series based on the popular comic books created by Fujiko Fujio. The Li'l Monster Prince (Kaibutsu Kun) arrives on Earth and lives with Franken (a childlike Frankenstein Monster), Dracula and the Wolf Man. With the help of their neighbour Hiroshi they battle the evil BEMs. Other Japanese cartoon series which feature the Frankenstein Monster include *Lupin III* (in which the Monster battles a master thief) and *Dr. Slump* (featuring various Frankenstein Monsters, including one which is also a werewolf!).

***Left:** The Munsters.*

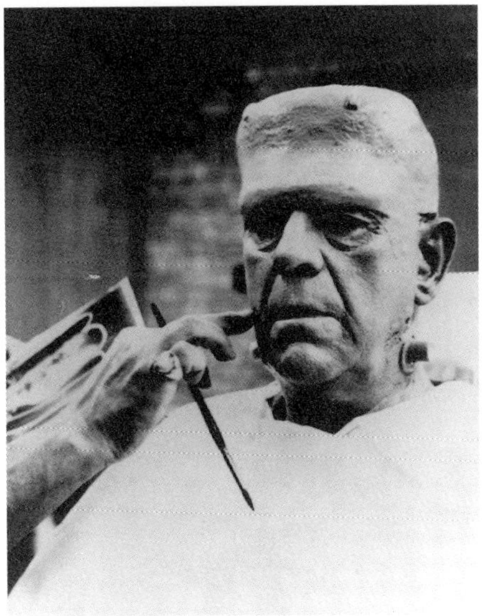

This page: *Behind-the-scenes, Route 66: Lizard's Leg and Owlet's Wing. (FJA).*

LAND OF THE GIANTS: *THE CLONES*

USA, 1969. Dir: Nathan Juran. With: Gary Conway, Deanna Lund, Don Matheson, Kurt Kasnar. Irwin Allen Productions/Twentieth Century-Fox/ABC-TV. Colour.

As an experiment, a giant scientist (William Schallert) creates clones of miniature space travellers Valerie (Lund) and Barry (Stefan Arngrim).

LAUREL & HARDY: *MONSTER BASH*

USA, 1966. Dir: Joseph Barbera and William Hanna. Voices: Larry Harmon, Jim Mac George, Hal Smith, Don Messick, Doug Young, Paul Frees. Wolper Productions/Larry Harmon Pictures/Hanna-Barbera Productions. Colour.

Five minute cartoon in which Stan (Harmon) and Ollie (Mac George) attend a party where they meet the Frankenstein Monster and other creatures.

MADAME'S PLACE

USA, 1982. Dir: Paul Miller. With: Wayland Flowers, Susan Tolsky, Johnny Haymer, Judy Landers, Bill Kirchenbauer, Carl Balantine. Brad Lachman Productions/Madame, Inc/ Paramount. Colour.

Half-hour syndicated adult comedy series which combines puppets with live actors. In this episode, after an encounter with vampire Baron Von Leer (Kirchenbauer), Madame (voiced by Flowers) goes off with Dr Steiner who, with the help of his assistant Igor, transforms her into the Bride of Frankenstein.

THE MAN FROM U.N.C.L.E.: *THE DEADLY GAMES AFFAIR*

USA, 1964. Dir: Alvin Ganzer. With: Robert Vaughn, David McCallum, Leo G. Carroll, Alexander Scourby, Burt Brinckerhoff, Janine Gray. Arena/NBC-TV. Colour.

UNCLE agents Napoleon Solo (Vaughn) and Illya Kuryakin (McCallum) discover that ex-Nazi scientist Professor Amadeus (Scourby) is continuing his experiments to revive the dead using the body of Adolf Hitler.

MATINEE THEATER: *FRANKENSTEIN*

USA, 1957. With: Primo Carnera, John Conte. NBC-TV. Colour.

Hour-long drama, loosely based on Mary Shelley's novel. Frankenstein is blinded during his experiment, but the Monster (former world heavyweight boxing champion Carnera) visits his creator in hospital and demands a mate before falling from a castle parapet to his apparent death. Hosted by Conte.

Remake: FRANKENSTEIN (qv; 1965)

MILTON THE MONSTER

USA, 1966. Hal Seegar Productions. Colour.

Half-hour cartoon series (also featuring Fearless Fly) containing six minute segments starring the kindly Milton, accidentally created by the evil Professor Weirdo and Count Kook in their Horror Hill laboratory.

THE MONKEES: *I WAS A TEENAGE MONSTER*

USA, 1966. Dir: Sidney Miller. With: David Jones, Micky Dolenz, Michael Nesmith, Peter Tork, John Hoyt, Byron Foulger. Raybert Productions/Columbia/NBC-TV. Colour.

In this episode of the popular musical, half-hour comedy series, the mad Dr Mendoza (veteran Hoyt) creates Franky Frankenstein (Richard Kiel), an android which looks like the Monster. Mendoza plans to transfer all the group's musical abilities into his creation. With electrical effects created by Ken Strickfaden.

THE MONSTROUS MONKEE MASH

USA, 1967. Dir: James Frawley. With: David Jones, Micky Dolenz, Michael Nesmith, Peter Tork, Ron Masak, Arlene Martel. Raybert Productions/Columbia/NBC-TV. Colour.

In this episode, Count Dracula (Masak) and his vampiric daughter Lorelei (Martel) want to turn Davy into one of the undead. Also includes a Frankenstein-like monster (Dick Karp), a werewolf (David Pearl) and a mummy (Bruce Barbour).

MONSTER FORCE

USA, 1994. MCA Television/Universal Cartoon Studios. Colour.

Cartoon series which includes super-scientific versions of the Frankenstein Monster and the Wolf Man.

MONSTER SQUAD

USA, 1976. Dir: Jim Sheldon, Wes Kenney, Herman Hoffman and William P. D'Angelo. With: Fred Gandy, Mike Lane, Buck Kartalian, Henry Polic II. D'Angelo Productions/NBC-TV. Colour.

Short-lived (thirteen episodes) half-hour series in which the monsters — Frankenstein (Lane), Bruce the Wolfman (Kartalian, the star of *Please Don't Eat My Mother!* [1972]) and Count Dracula (Polic II) — pose as wax dummies in a museum by day and are revived by Walt (Gandy) at night to battle outlandish criminals! The guest cast includes Alice Ghostley, Billy Curtis, Marty Allen, Edward Andrews, Sid Haig, Jonathan Harris, Julie Newmar, Arthur Mallet, Geoffrey Lewis, Avery Schreiber and Vito Scotti.

THE MORECAMBE & WISE SHOW

UK, 1980. Dir: John Ammonds. With: Eric Morecambe, Ernie Wise, Ian Carmichael, Ann

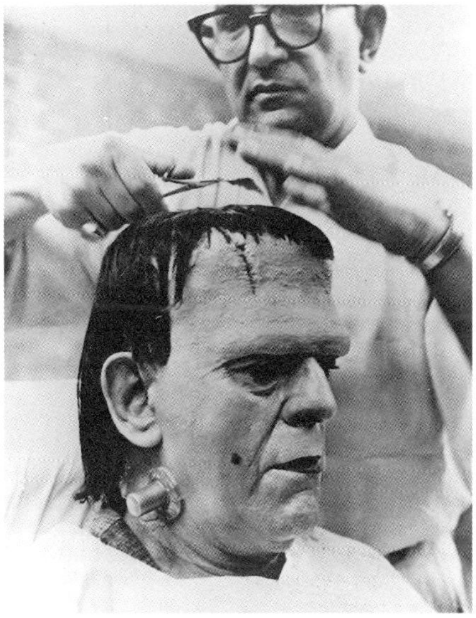

Hamilton. BBC-TV. Colour.

This episode of the comedy series includes a sketch in which Baron Frankenstein (Carmichael), with the aid of Igor (Morecambe), creates a Monster (Wise). For many years, Peter Cushing was a semi-regular on the comedy duo's Christmas specials in a long-running joke about being paid.

MORK & MINDY: MINDY, MINDY, MINDY

USA, 1981. Dir: Howard Storm. With: Robin Williams, Pam Dawber, Conrad Janis, Tom Poston, Jay Thomas, Gina Hecht. Paramount/ Henderson Production Company/Miller-Milkis Productions. Colour.

Half-hour sitcom in which crazy alien Mork (Williams) becomes lonely while his girlfriend Mindy (Dawber) is away on a trip. He asks the Orkan Elder (Vidal I. Peterson) to clone her, with predictably disastrous results.

THE MUNSTERS

USA, 1964-66. With: Fred Gwynne, Yvonne De Carlo, Al Lewis, Butch Patrick, Beverly Owen, Pat Priest. Kayro-Vue Productions/Universal/ CBS-TV. B&W.

CBS's answer to ABC's slightly better *The Addams Family* features another group of friendly monsters: the Frankenstein Monster-like Herman (Gwynne, who could wear the Karloff-style make-up because Universal studios owned the copyright), the vampiric Lily (De Carlo), Grampa (Lewis, who is revealed to be Count Dracula himself), wolf boy Eddie (Patrick) and the 'horribly' normal Marilyn (played by Owen and, later, Priest). John Carradine originally turned down the role of Herman, but did appear in several episodes as Mr Gateman, the owner of the mortuary where Herman worked. A fifteen minute pilot film, 'My Fair Munster' (1964; Dir: Norman Abbott), with Joan Marshall as Phoebe (instead of Lily) and Happy Derman as Eddie, was never telecast. The series ran for seventy half-hour episodes and spawned two movies.

Sequel: THE ABC SATURDAY SUPERSTAR MOVIE: *MINI-MUNSTERS* (qv; 1973)

THE MUNSTERS TODAY

USA, 1988-91. With: John Shuck, Lee Meriwether, Howard Morton, Hilary Van Dyke, Jason Marsden. MCA-TV. Colour.

Ill-conceived attempt to revive the popular 1960s series with an all-new cast. Shuck plays the Frankenstein

Monster-like Herman in this shot-on-video disaster. Incredibly, it survived for seventy-two episodes — two more than the original series!

NBC STARSHIP RESCUE

USA, 1973. With: Bo Svenson. NBC-TV. Colour.
Half-hour special that previews NBC's Saturday morning shows for kids, with a live-action framing sequence involving alien invaders opposed by a heroic Frankenstein Monster (Svenson, who played the creature the same year in Dan Curtis' *Frankenstein*).

THE NEW AVENGERS: *THE EAGLE'S NEST*

UK/France, 1978. Dir: Desmond Davis. With: Patrick Macnee, Gareth Hunt, Joanna Lumley, Peter Cushing, Derek Farr, Sydney Bromley. Avengers Enterprises/TV Productions/I.D.T.V. Colour.
John Steed (Macnee), Purdy (Lumley) and Mike Gambit (Hunt) uncover a plot by Nazi leader Von Claus (Cushing) to start a Fourth Reich on a remote island by restoring the body of Adolf Hitler to life.

THE NEW FRED AND BARNEY SHOW: *FRED AND BARNEY MEET THE FRANKENSTONES*

USA, 1979. Voices: Henry Corden, Jean Vanderpyl, Mel Blanc, Gay Autterson. Hanna-Barbera Productions/NBC-TV. Colour.
Pilot episode for *The Frankenstones* series, in which Fred Flintstone (Corden) and Barney Rubble (Blanc) meet the weird family of Frank, Hidea, Freaky and Atrocia. This cartoon was later included in the series *Fred and Barney Meet the Thing* and *Fred and Barney Meet the Shmoo*.
Sequel: THE FLINTSTONE COMEDY HOUR: *THE FRANKENSTONES* (qv; 1980)

OBAKE NO SAMBA, MON MON MONSTER

Japan, 1980. Dir: Yukito Aizawa. With: Hitoshi Omeae, Minoru Sado, Takeshi Sasano, Midori Fukuhara, Jiro Sakagami. Watanabe Kikaku/ Tokyo Hoso 12. Colour.
Half-hour musical sitcom series featuring Dracula (Sado), the Wolf Man (Sasano) and the Frankenstein Monster (Omeae), who live in a fake haunted house attraction with the witch Tabasa (Fukuhara) and ghost Baku (Sakagami). Whenever the Monster drinks wine he turns gay!

ONCE UPON A TIME: *FRANKENSTEIN*

UK, 1973. Dir: Gerry Hill. With: John Stride, Geoffrey Bayldon, John Stratton, David Ryall, Derrick O'Connor, Ted Carroll. Granada Television. Colour.
Clever sequel to Mary Shelley's novel, written by John Stevenson. The Monster was last seen clinging to an ice floe, but what happened to his creator, Baron Frankenstein (Bayldon)? As *The Phoenix* moves further north into the ice packs of the Arctic, the crew want to turn back. But the ship's master, Robert Walton (Stride), has his own secret reasons to press forward...

THE OUTER LIMITS: *THE BRAIN OF COLONEL BARHAM*

USA, 1964 (1965). Dir: Charles Haas. With: Grant Williams, Elizabeth Perry, Anthony Eisley, Douglas Kennedy, Paul Lukather, Martin Kosleck. Daystar Productions/Villa di Stefano Productions/United Artists/ABC-TV. B&W.
A dying astronaut (Eisley) has his brain removed and connected to a computer designed to control an unmanned space probe to Mars. The evil super-mind begins to grow, developing telepathic powers and the ability to discharge electrical bolts. In the end, the brain is shot to death.

OUT OF THE UNKNOWN: *FRANKENSTEIN MARK II*

UK, 1966. With: Rachel Roberts, David Laughton, Bernard Archard, Wolfe Morris. BBC-TV. B&W
Set in a futuristic space research establishment. Anna Preston (Roberts) discovers that her missing husband has been used in a bizarre experiment.

POPEYE: *MUELLER'S MAD MONSTER*

USA. Dir: Paul Fennel. King Features. Colour.
Five minute cartoon in which Olive Oyle is kidnapped by Mueller's Frankenstein Monster. Popeye saves her by knocking it apart and rebuilding it to resemble Elvis Presley.

RED SKELTON HOUR

USA, 1968. With: Red Skelton, Boris Karloff, Vincent Price. CBS-TV. Colour.
Hour-long musical comedy show starring comedian Skelton. In this episode, scientist Dr Nelson (Karloff) and his son (Price!) create a miniature Frankenstein Monster and a perfect woman.

ROALD DAHL'S TALES OF THE UNEXPECTED: *WILLIAM AND MARY*

UK, 1979. Dir: Donald McWhinnie. With: Marius Goring, Elaine Stritch, Roald Dahl. Anglia Television. Colour.
Half-hour episode of the anthology series hosted by writer Dahl. After years of abuse by her domineering husband William, Mary (Stritch) discovers he has cheated death through convincing an eminent neurosurgeon (Goring) to keep his brain and one of his eyes alive by connecting them to a machine. She insists on taking the brain home with her, where she begins her revenge...

ROD SERLING'S NIGHT GALLERY: *JUNIOR*

USA, 1971. Dir: Theodore J. Flicker. With: Wally Cox, Barbara Flicker, Bill Svanoe, Rod Serling. Universal/NBC-TV. Colour.
Half-hour anthology series introduced by Rod Serling. In this vignette, a man gets out of bed to get a glass of water for 'Junior', who turns out to be the Universal Frankenstein Monster (Svanoe).

ROUTE 66: *LIZARD'S LEG AND OWLET'S WING*

USA, 1962. Dir: Robert Gist. With: Martin Milner, George Maharis, Peter Lorre, Lon Chaney, Martita Hunt, Boris Karloff. Lancer Productions/Screen Gems/ABC-TV. B&W.
Classic Hallowe'en episode of the hour-long series, scripted by Sterling Silliphant, in which Tod (Milner) and Buzz (Maharis) get jobs at Chicago's O'Hare Inn and become involved with a competition between horror stars Karloff (as the Frankenstein Monster), Chaney Jr (as the Hunchback, Mummy and Wolf Man) and a sinister Lorre to prove that the old-style scares are still effective. Jack Pierce's original make-ups were disappointingly recreated by Ben Lane.

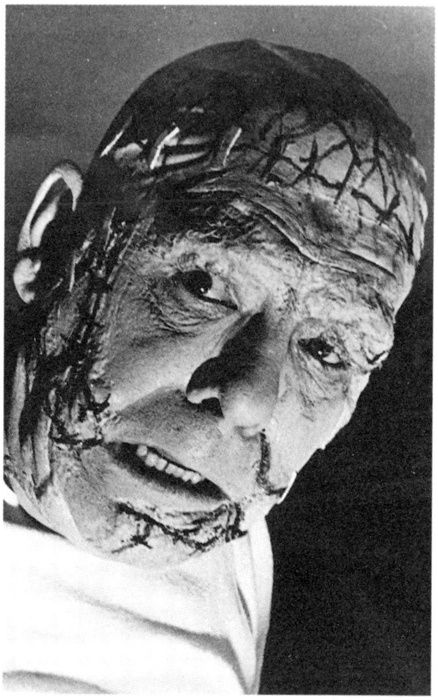

Above: Tales of Tomorrow: Frankenstein.(FJA).

SABRINA, THE TEENAGE WITCH

USA, 1971. Filmation/CBS-TV. Colour.
Half-hour animated series, based on the *Archie* comic book. Includes Frankie and the rest of the monsters from *The Groovie Goolies* (1970) in supporting roles.
Sequel: THE ABC SATURDAY SUPERSTAR MOVIE: *PORKY PIG AND DAFFY DUCK MEET THE GROOVIE GOOLIES* (qv; 1972)

SCOOBY-DOO: *A GAGGLE OF GALLOPING GHOSTS*

USA, 1969. Dir: Ted Nichols. Voices: Don Messick, Casey Kasem, Frank Welker, Heather North, Nichole Jaffe. Hanna-Barbera Productions/CBS-TV. Colour.
Popular half-hour cartoon series. Searching for lost jewels in the Franken castle, a criminal actor disguises himself as the Frankenstein Monster, Dracula and a werewolf to scare people away.

STAR TREK: *SPOCK'S BRAIN*

USA, 1968. Dir: Marc Daniels. With: William Shatner, Leonard Nimoy, DeForest Kelley, Marj Ousay, James Doohan, Walter Koenig. Norway Productions/Paramount/NBC-TV. Colour.
A beautiful woman (Ousay) materialises on board the *Enterprise* and steals Mr Spock's (Nimoy) brain. She plans to use it to control an underground civilisation of dumb blondes in one of the more mindless episodes of the popular space opera.

STRUCK BY LIGHTNING

USA, 1979. With: Jack Elam, Jeffrey Kramer, Millie Slavin, Bill Erwin, Jeff Cotler, Richard

Stahl. The Fellows-Keegan Company/ Paramount/NBC-TV. Colour.
Short-lived (three episodes!), half-hour comedy sitcom series featuring veteran Elam as Frank, the ageing Monster, and Kramer as Ted Stein/Frankenstein. Several other episodes were apparently shot but never telecast.

THE SUPERFRIENDS: *THE MONSTER OF DR. DROID*

USA, cicra 1970s. Hanna-Barbera Productions/ ABC-TV. Colour.
In this episode of the half-hour cartoon series, Superman, Wonder Woman, Batman and Robin battle a Frankenstein-like monster created in the laboratory of Dr Droid (a caricature of Boris Karloff).

THE SUPERFRIENDS MEET FRANKENSTEIN

USA, 1979. Hanna-Barbera Productions/ABC-TV. Colour.
Dr Frankenstein revives his ancestor's Monster, which captures Batman and steals the superpowers from Superman and Wonder Woman until it is defeated by Robin with Kryptonite.

SUPERNATURAL: *NIGHT OF THE MARIONETTES*

UK, 1977. Dir: Alan Cooke. With: Gordon Jackson, Kathleen Byron, Vladek Sheybal, Andre Van Gyseghem, Pauline Moran, Sydney Bromley. BBC-TV. Colour.
Short-lived (eight episodes), hour-long series set in Victorian times. Each guest star has to recount a tale of the supernatural to gain entrance into the Club of the Damned. Writer Howard Lawrence (Jackson) and his family stay at an inn in the Swiss Alps and witness a bizarre entertainment featuring life-size puppets. These turn out to be living creatures created from corpse parts by mysterious innkeeper Hubert (Sheybal), a descendant of Frankenstein. Lawrence learns that a century before, Mary Shelley and her companions stayed at the same inn. Scripted by Robert Muller.

***Below:** Thriller: The Incredible Doktor Markesan.*

SUR LES TRACES DE FRANKENSTEIN

France, 1968.
While researching Mary Shelley in Geneva, a young student fears that she is being followed by the Frankenstein Monster.

TALES OF FRANKENSTEIN

USA, 1958. Dir: Curt Siodmak. With: Anton Diffring, Helen Westcott, Don Megowan, Ludwig Stossel, Richard Bull, Raymond Greenleaf. Hammer Films/Screen Gems. B&W.
Half-hour pilot episode for an unsold series, scripted by Catherine (C.L. Moore) and Henry Kuttner and filmed under the title 'The Face in the Tombstone Mirror'. When a woman pleads with Baron Frankenstein (Diffring), he transplants the brain of her dead husband into the Karloff-like Monster (Megowan) he has created. Based on a story by associate producer/director Siodmak, this was finally shown as part of *Target*, a syndicated anthology series. A second episode, 'Frankenstein Meets Dr Varno', written by Jerome Bixby, was announced but never made.

TALES OF TOMORROW: *FRANKENSTEIN*

USA, 1952. With: Lon Chaney, John Newland, Mary Alice Moore. George F. Foley Productions/ ABC-TV. B&W.
Half-hour drama based on Mary Shelley's novel. Dr Victor Frankenstein (Newland) brings his bald-headed Monster to life (Chaney Jr, who was apparently so drunk he went through the entire live transmission believing it was a rehearsal!). When the creature goes berserk, it stumbles around the painted castle sets, falls through a window and strangles the housekeeper before being electrocuted. Chaney's scarred make-up was effectively created by Vincent Kehoe.
Remake: MATINEE THEATER: *FRANKENSTEIN* (qv; 1957)

THE TEX WILLIAMS SHOW

USA, circa 1951. With: Tex Williams, Glenn Strange. NBC-TV. B&W.
Strange recreates his role as the Frankenstein Monster during the singer's musical/comedy show.

THRILLER: *THE INCREDIBLE DOKTOR MARKESAN*

(UK: BORIS KARLOFF PRESENTS)
USA, 1961 (1962). Dir: Robert Florey. With: Boris Karloff, Dick York, Carolyn Kearney, Richard Hale, Henry Hunter. Hubbell Robinson Productions/Universal/NBC-TV. B&W.
Based on the short story by August Derleth and Mark Schorer. Host Karloff also stars as deceased scientist Doktor Konrad Markesan who has discovered a method of bringing the dead back to life to exact a terrible revenge. Director Florey was originally set to helm *Frankenstein* (1931).

THE TOMORROW PEOPLE: *CASTLE OF FEAR*

UK, 1978. Dir: Vic Hughes. With: Nicholas Young, Hazel Adare, Mike Holloway, Misako Koba, Nigel Rhodes. Thames Television. Colour.
Two part story in which the Homo Superior teens search for the Loch Ness monster, dream of a headless highlander and meet Frankenstein's creation.

THE TWILIGHT ZONE: *FATHER AND SON GAME*

USA, 1988. Dir: Randy Bradshaw. With: Ed Marinaro, Eugene Robert Glazer, Patricia Phillips, George Touliatos, Richard Monette, Mark Melymick. CBS Entertainment Productions/Persistence of Vision. Colour.
Set in the future, a seventy-nine year-old tycoon (Marinaro) decides he wants to live forever, so he has his brain transplanted into an artificial body. But his son (Glazer) cannot accept his 'new' father and plans to take control of the family business.

WAYNE AND SHUSTER TAKE AN AFFECTIONATE LOOK AT THE MONSTERS

Canada, 1966.
Special featuring clips from most of the Universal Frankenstein series.

WEIRD SCIENCE

USA, 1994. With: John Mallory Asher, Michael Manasseri, Vanessa Angel. Universal. Colour.
Half-hour series, based on the 1985 movie, in which two teenage nerds use their computer to create Lisa (Angel), their perfect woman.

THE WILD, WILD WEST: *THE NIGHT OF THE BIG BLAST*

USA, 1966. With: Robert Conrad, Ross Martin, Ida Lupino. CBS-TV. Colour.
Sci-spy western series set in the 1870s. Dr Faustina (Lupino) creates monster versions of special government agents James T. West (Conrad) and Artemus Gordon (Martin) from corpses brought to life with electricity.

THE NIGHT OF THE UNDEAD

USA, 1965. With: Robert Conrad, Ross Martin, Hurd Hatfield. CBS-TV. Colour.
In the swamps of the deep South, Jim West (Conrad) battles scientific zombies created by Hatfield's mad scientist.

WITCH'S NIGHT OUT

USA, 1979. Dir: John Leach. Voices: Gilda Radner, Bob Lurch, Don Leach, Naomi Leach, Tony Molesworth, Gerry Salsbero. Leach/ Rankin Productions/NBC-TV.
Half-hour cartoon special in which has-been witch Godmother (Radner) transforms two children on Hallowe'en into a werewolf and a ghost, and their babysitter Bazooie (Salsbero) into Frankenstein's Monster.

THE X FILES: *EVE*

Canada/USA, 1993. Dir: Fred Gerber. With: David Duchovny, Gillian Anderson, Harriet Harris, Erika Krievins, Sabrina Krievins, Jerry Hardin. Twentieth Century Fox/Ten Thirteen Productions. Colour.
In this episode of the hour-long series, FBI agents Fox Mulder (Duchovny) and Dana Scully (Anderson) investigate two exsanguinated murder victims and uncover a conspiracy involving a group of genetically-created children who have developed into super-intelligent psychopaths.

Appendix 2:

Index of Film Reviews

Index

Bibliography

I am indebted to the authors and editors of the following books and magazines which were consulted in the compilation of this work:

Adult Entertainment Guide
Adult Video News
The Aurum Film Encyclopedia: Horror (Aurum Press, 1993) edited by Phil Hardy
The Aurum Film Encyclopedia: Science Fiction (Aurum Press, 1991) edited by Phil Hardy
Cinefantastique
Il Cinema dei Licantropi (Fanucci Editore, 1987) by Riccardo Esposito
Cliffhanger: A Pictorial History of the Motion Picture Serial (A&W Publishers, 1977) by Alan G. Barbour
Epi-Log Special No 3
Famous Monsters of Filmland
Fantastic Television (Titan Books, 1987) by Gary Gerani with Paul H. Schulman
The Films of Boris Karloff (The Citadel Press, 1974) by Richard Bojarski and Kenneth Beals
Forgotten Horrors: Early Talkie Chillers from Poverty Row (A.S. Barnes & Co, 1979) by George E. Turner and Michael H. Price
Frankenstein (Flare Books/Avon, 1974) edited by Richard J. Anobile
The Frankenscience Monster (Ace Books, 1969) presented by Forrest J Ackerman
The Frankenstein Catalog (McFarland & Company, 1984) by Donald F. Glut
The Frankenstein File (New English Library, 1977) edited by Peter Haining
Gore Creatures No 23, January 1975
Halliwell's Filmgoer's Companion 10th Edition (HarperCollins, 1993) edited by John Walker
Halls of Horror
Hoffman's Guide to SF, Horror and Fantasy Movies 1991-92 (Corgi Books, 1991)
Horror Man: The Life of Boris Karloff (Leslie Frewin Publishers, 1972) by Peter Underwood
The House of Hammer
The House of Horror: The Complete Story of Hammer Films (Lorrimer, 1981) edited by Allen Eyles, Robert Adkinson and Nicholas Fry
The Illustrated Frankenstein (Westbridge Books, 1980) by John Stoker
It's Alive! The Classic Cinema Saga of Frankenstein (A.S. Barnes & Company/The Tantivy Press, 1981) by Gregory William Mank
Karloff the Man, the Monster, the Movies (Curtis Books, 1973) by Dennis Gifford
Leonard Maltin's TV Movies and Video Guide 1993 (Signet/New American Library, 1992)
Mad Movies
Monster! International
Monthly Film Bulletin
Obsession — The Films of Jess Franco (Graf Haufan and Frank Trebbin, 1993) by Lucas Balbo, Peter Blumenstock, Christian Kessler and Tim Lucas
Picture Show No 682, 28 May 1932
Psychotronic
The Psychotronic Encyclopedia of Film (Ballantine Books, 1983) by Michael Weldon
A Reference Guide to American Science Fiction Films Volume 1 (T.I.S. Publications, 1981) by A.W. Strickland and Forrest J Ackerman
Reference Guide to Fantastic Films (Chelsea-Lee Books, 1972, 1973, 1974; three volumes) compiled by Walt Lee
Shock Xpress 1 (Titan Books, 1991) edited by Stefan Jaworzyn
Universal Horrors: The Studio's Classic Films, 1931-1946 (McFarland & Company, 1990) by Michael Brunas, John Brunas and Tom Weaver
Videohound's Golden Movie Retriever (Visible Ink, 1993)
Video Watchdog
The Video Watchdog Book (Video Watchdog, 1992) by Tim Lucas
The Warner Brothers Cartoons (The Scarecrow Press, 1981) by Will Friedwald and Jerry Beck

and Calvin T. Beck's *Castle of Frankenstein*, for inspiring the review index this series of guides is based on.

Opposite and below: *Behind-the-scenes, Bride of Frankenstein.*

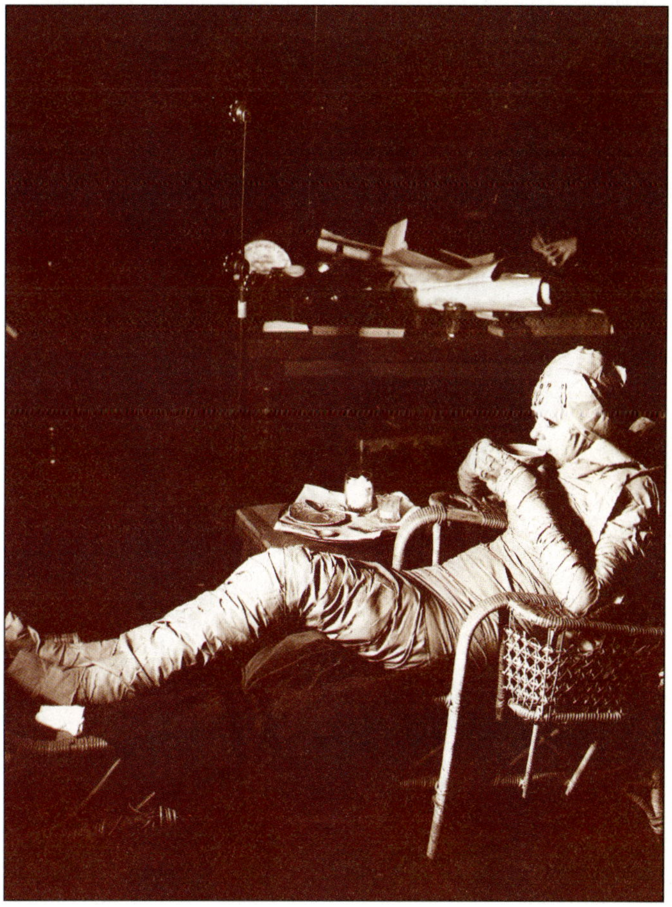

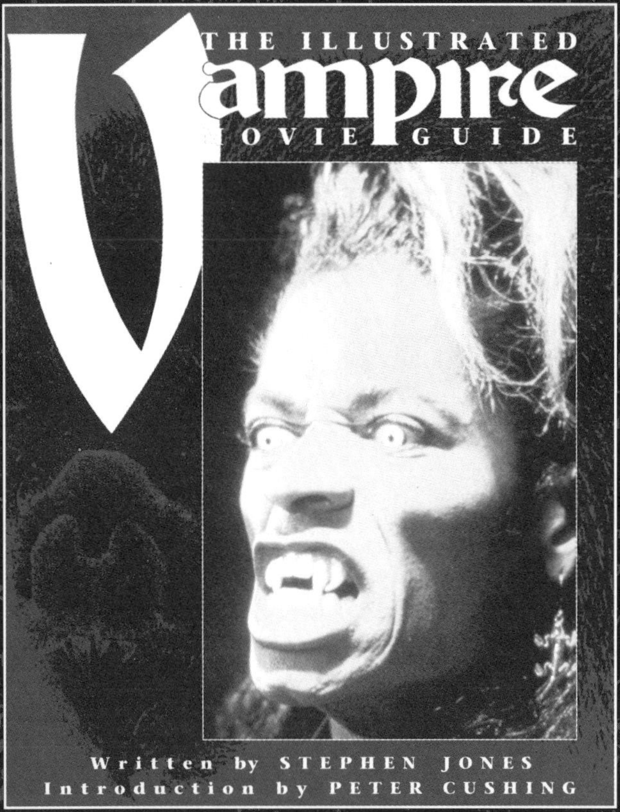
THE ILLUSTRATED
Vampire
MOVIE GUIDE
Written by STEPHEN JONES
Introduction by PETER CUSHING

THE ILLUSTRATED
MOVIE GUIDE
Written by STEPHEN JONES
Introduction by RAY HARRYHAUSEN

THE
HELLRAISER
CHRONICLES
INTRODUCED BY CLIVE BARKER
EDITED BY STEPHEN JONES

SHOCK
XPRESS
THE ESSENTIAL GUIDE TO EXPLOITATION CINEMA
Edited by STEFAN JAWORZYN
For Adults Only